COLUMBIA CRITICAL

Herman Melville

Moby-Dick

EDITED BY NICK SELBY

Series editor: Richard Beynon

COLUMBIA UNIVERSITY PRESS ◣◢ NEW YORK

Columbia University Press
Publishers Since 1893
New York   Chichester, West Sussex
Editor's text copyright © 1998 Nick Selby
All rights reserved

First published in the Icon Critical Guides series in 1998
by Icon Books Ltd.

Library of Congress Cataloging-in-Publication Data

Herman Melville, Moby-Dick / edited by Nick Selby.
        p.   cm. — (Columbia critical guides)
      Includes bibliographical references and index.
      ISBN 0–231–11538–5 (cloth : alk. paper). —
    ISBN 0–231–11539–3 (pbk. : alk. paper)
      1. Melville, Herman, 1819–1891.   Moby Dick.   2. Sea
    stories, American—History and criticism.   3. Whaling in
    literature.   4. Whales in literature.   I. Selby, Nick.   II. Series.
    PS2384.M62H47   1999
    813'.3—dc21   98–39507

Printed in the United States of America

c 10 9 8 7 6 5 4 3 2 1
p 10 9 8 7 6 5 4 3 2 1

Contents

To Maggie

'But far beneath this wondrous world upon the surface, another and still stranger world met our eyes as we gazed over the side. For, suspended in those watery vaults, floated the forms of the nursing mothers of the whales, and those that by their enormous girth seemed shortly to become mothers.'

Moby-Dick, Chapter 87, 'The Grand Armada.'

Introduction

THE NARRATIVE of *Moby-Dick* (1851) opens, famously, with an act of naming. 'Call me Ishmael' is a bold statement of self-definition, and it is an invitation to the reader's imaginative and interpretive faculties. From the outset, then, *Moby-Dick* makes us aware that acts of naming and of defining are complex and problematic. They are, necessarily, reciprocal: to define himself, Ishmael needs a readership. To a large extent, just what *Moby-Dick* is has been defined by its readers and critics. Indeed, the critical history of *Moby-Dick* that is sketched by this Guide can be seen to be a series of attempts to define the book, to name it and thus to place it within an understood tradition.

Such an attempt to name and define *Moby-Dick* is made all the more pressing because it is an American book. And, at the time of *Moby-Dick*'s first publication, there was little critical consensus as to what might constitute an American book, let alone an American literary tradition. It was generally agreed that American 'writing' was inferior to the 'literature' of England, and that any literary qualities it did display were but poor imitations of its European precursors. Writing in 1840, in his massively influential book *Democracy in America,* Alexis de Tocqueville notes that 'the Americans have not yet, properly speaking, got any literature'. He continues his observations about America's literary characteristics by stating 'Only the journalists strike me as truly American.'[1] It is hardly surprising, given the snobbish attitude of which de Tocqueville's comment is typical, that American authors were felt not to warrant serious attention.

But with *Moby-Dick*, the possibilities for American literature seemed a little different. Melville's masterpiece seemed to signal a changed attitude, it showed American literature coming into its own. Here was a book that defined itself, and that named its own terms of analysis. Surprisingly, perhaps, it was de Tocqueville who had set out what those terms might be. He had argued that America would soon be able to carry forth into its literature the promise of its democratic politics. His prediction of American literature's defining characteristics, made more than a decade before *Moby-Dick*, is shrewd. And, if we discount his assertion that American books are more typically 'short works' than 'long' ones, when measured against this definition, *Moby-Dick* seems to be *the* archetypical American book, it answers his call pretty accurately:

■ By and large the literature of a democracy will never exhibit the order, regularity, skill, and art characteristic of aristocratic literature; formal qualities will be neglected or actually despised. The style will often be strange, incorrect, overburdened, and loose, and almost always strong and bold. Writers will be more anxious to work quickly than to perfect details. Short works will be commoner than long books, wit than erudition, imagination than depth. There will be a rude and untutored vigour of thought with great variety and singular fecundity. Authors will strive to astonish more than to please, and to stir passions rather than to charm taste.[2] □

Throughout this book, we shall see that criticism of *Moby-Dick* has gone hand-in-hand with such attempts to define what American literature might be. By extension, then, the struggle to define *Moby-Dick* witnesses America's own struggles, as a new nation, to name and define the terms of its own culture. *Moby-Dick* is therefore a vital document, so to speak, in an American declaration of cultural independence. All the essays in this Critical Guide show how a reading of *Moby-Dick* has been used to plot the co-ordinates in a reading of America. *Moby-Dick* has thus been seen as *the* key text in the growth, development and reassessment of American Studies. The arguments that are rehearsed over Melville's text are ones that tell of wider debates in American culture and ideology in general. In 1851, then, Melville provided America with a language to examine its liberal democracy and its emerging capitalism, a means to define how its different voices and identities compete within a united text, and how its struggles for power mark its growing identity within world politics. Up to the present day, criticism of *Moby-Dick* is still assessing this language, still engaging with the book as a means of engaging with America.

It was Melville himself who set out many of the terms by which subsequent criticism would engage with *Moby-Dick*. This he did in his review essay 'Hawthorne and His Mosses' (1850) which was written whilst he was at work on *Moby-Dick*. In this essay, he reviews a book of short stories, *Mosses from an Old Manse*, by Nathaniel Hawthorne. Melville had just recently made the acquaintance of Hawthorne. As neighbours living on a rural estate near Pittsfield, Massachusetts, the two were to become firm friends. 'Hawthorne and His Mosses' is important not simply for the enthusiastic account it gives of Hawthorne's work, but also because it delineates many of Melville's attitudes towards American literature, attitudes that are relevant to a reading of *Moby-Dick*. The extracts from 'Hawthorne and His Mosses' which follow trace some of these attitudes, especially Melville's idea of American literary genius, his sense of the relationship of the American writer to Shakespeare, and the importance of democracy to American literature.

Melville's essay recognises that Hawthorne's genius is marked by his ability to tell profound truths, despite his apparent lightness of style. Whilst this is an effect of Hawthorne's use of symbol and metaphor – especially in the contrast between darkness and light – it is also the consequence of his Americanness, which displays a Puritanic sense of doom and original sin:

■ All over him, Hawthorne's melancholy rests like an Indian Summer, which though bathing the whole country in one softness, still reveals the distinctive hue of every towering hill, and each far-winding vale.

But it is the least part of genius that attracts admiration. Where Hawthorne is known, he seems to be deemed a pleasant writer, with a pleasant style, – a sequestered, harmless man, from whom any deep and weighty thing would hardly be anticipated: – a man who means no meanings. But there is no man, in whom humor and love, like mountain peaks, soar to such a rapt height, as to receive the irradiations of the upper skies; – there is no man in whom humor and love are developed in that high form called genius; no such man can exist without also possessing, as the indispensable complement of these, a great, deep intellect, which drops down into the universe like a plummet.

. . . For spite of all the Indian-summer sunlight on the hither side of Hawthorne's soul, the other side – like the dark half of the physical sphere – is shrouded in a blackness, ten times black. But this darkness but gives more effect to the ever-moving dawn, that forever advances through it, and circumnavigates his world. Whether Hawthorne has simply availed himself of this mystical blackness as a means to the wondrous effects he makes it to produce in his lights and shades; or whether there really lurks in him, perhaps unknown to himself, a touch of Puritanic gloom, – this, I cannot altogether tell. Certain it is, however, that this great power of blackness in him derives its force from its appeals to that Calvinistic sense of Innate Depravity and Original Sin, from whose visitations, in some shape or other, no deeply thinking mind is always and wholly free. For, in certain moods, no man can weigh this world, without throwing in something, something like Original Sin, to strike the uneven balance. At all events, perhaps no writer has ever wielded this terrific thought with greater terror than this same harmless Hawthorne. Still more: this black conceit pervades him, through and through. You may be witched by his sunlight, – transported by the bright gildings in the skies he builds over you; – but there is the blackness of darkness beyond; and even his bright gildings but fringe, and play upon the edges of thunder-clouds. – In one word, the world is mistaken in this

Nathaniel Hawthorne. He himself must often have smiled at its absurd misconception of him. He is immeasurably deeper than the plummet of the mere critic. For it is not the brain that can test such a man; it is only the heart. You cannot come to know greatness by inspecting it; there is no glimpse to be caught of it, except by intuition; you need not ring it, you but touch it, and you find it is gold.[3] □

In the next paragraph Melville continues by comparing Hawthorne, in his plummeting of such dark depths, with Shakespeare. The very force of this comparison, and the strength of Melville's language, testify to the great pressure in mid-nineteenth-century American literature to discover a literary genius of its own. Such a comparison also sets the terms by which critics have read *Moby-Dick*. As we shall see throughout this Guide, many subsequent analyses of *Moby-Dick* return to this following passage from 'Hawthorne and His Mosses' to explain the depths of (American) genius that Melville's novel sounds:

■ Now it is that blackness in Hawthorne, of which I have spoken, that so fixes and fascinates me. It may be, nevertheless, that it is too largely developed in him. Perhaps he does not give us a ray of his light for every shade of his dark. But however this may be, this blackness it is that furnishes the infinite obscure of his background, – that background, against which Shakespeare plays his grandest conceits, the things that have made for Shakespeare his loftiest, but most circumscribed renown, as the profoundest of thinkers. . . . But it is those deep far-away things in him; those occasional flashings-forth of the intuitive Truth in him; those short, quick probings at the very axis of reality; – these are the things that make Shakespeare, Shakespeare. Through the mouths of the dark characters of Hamlet, Timon, Lear, and Iago, he craftily says, or sometimes insinuates the things, which we feel to be so terrifically true, that it were all but madness for any good man, in his own proper character, to utter, or even hint of them. Tormented into desperation, Lear the frantic King tears off the mask, and speaks the sane madness of vital truth.[4] □

Here, in Melville's characterisation of Shakespeare, are heard the growing, embryonic cadences of Ahab, whose rhetoric, like Hawthorne's blackness, also 'fixes and fascinates' Melville. The probing 'at the very axis of reality' which Melville describes here, not only partakes of an Ahab-like rhetoric but also describes its powerful effect, and thus provides a key to understanding *Moby-Dick*. We see this especially in the final image of Lear tearing off the mask to expose the 'madness of vital truth'. Such an image is echoed by Melville in 'The Quarter-Deck' chapter of *Moby-Dick* where Ahab rages against his first mate Starbuck, and against his arch-adversary Moby Dick. Because this one scene, out of the whole of *Moby-Dick*, has received by far the most critical attention, and is referred to repeatedly in the critical essays that make up this book, it is quoted below. It 'tasks' and 'heaps' readers of *Moby-Dick*, not least because it seems to promise a revelation of 'vital truth' comparable to that which Melville's 'Mosses' essay describes in *King Lear*.

■ 'All visible objects, man, are but as pasteboard masks. But in each event – in the living act, the undoubted deed – there, some unknown but still reasoning thing puts forth the mouldings of its features from behind the unreasoning mask. If man will strike, strike through the mask! How can the prisoner reach outside except by thrusting through the wall? To me, the white whale is that wall, shoved near to me. Sometimes I think there's naught beyond. But 'tis enough. He tasks me; he heaps me; I see in him outrageous strength, with an inscrutable malice sinewing it. That inscrutable thing is chiefly what I hate; and be the white whale agent, or be the white whale principal, I will wreak that hate upon him.'[5] □

On returning to the 'Hawthorne and His Mosses' essay we see Melville's argument about Shakespeare developing into one about literary tradition and America's place within it. What becomes clear in the following extract is Melville's belief that the defining characteristic of America's literature is its embracing of democratic principles. Indeed, the very notion of a literary tradition of over-venerated writers is, suggests Melville, inimical to such principles. American writing, he argues, must display a 'republican progressiveness', and part of its newness must be to explore the 'superabundance of material' that is part of the American experience. In short, Melville argues for a home-grown American literature, not one of deference towards England. 'Hawthorne and His Mosses' sets the terms, then, in which *Moby-Dick* is a declaration of independence from an English literary tradition:

■ Some may start to read of Shakespeare and Hawthorne on the same page. They may say, that if an illustration were needed, a lesser light might have sufficed to elucidate this Hawthorne, this small man of yesterday. But I am not, willingly, one of those who, as touching Shakespeare at least . . . to teach all noble-souled aspirants that there is no hope for them, pronounce Shakespeare absolutely unapproachable. But Shakespeare has been approached. There are minds that have gone as far as Shakespeare into the universe. And hardly a mortal man, who, at some time or other, has not felt as great thoughts in him as any you will find in Hamlet. . . . This absolute and unconditional adoration of Shakespeare has grown to be a part of our Anglo Saxon superstitions. . . . Intolerance has come to exist in this matter. You must believe in Shakespeare's unapproachability, or quit the country. But what sort of belief is this for an American, a man who is bound to carry republican progressiveness into Literature, as well as into Life? Believe me, my friends, that Shakespeares are this day being born on the banks of the Ohio. And the day will come, when you shall say who reads a book by an Englishman that is a modern? The great mistake seems to be, that even with those Americans who look forward to the coming of a great literary genius among us, they somehow fancy he will come in the costume of Queen Elizabeth's day, – be a writer of dramas founded upon old English history, or the tales of Boccaccio. Whereas great geniuses are parts of the times; they themselves are the times; and possess a correspondent coloring.

. . . This, too, I mean, that if Shakespeare has not been equalled, he is sure to be surpassed, and surpassed by an American born now or yet to be born. For it will never do for us who in most other things out-do as well as out-brag the world, it will not do for us to fold our hands and say, In the highest department advance there is none. Nor will it do to say, that the world is getting grey and grizzled now, and has lost that fresh charm which she wore of old, and by virtue of which the great poets of past times made themselves what we esteem them to be. Not so. The world is as young today, as when it was created; and this Vermont morning dew is as wet to my feet, as Eden's dew to Adam's. Nor has nature been all over ransacked by our progenitors, so that no new charms and mysteries remain for this latter generation to find. Far from it. The trillionth part has not yet been said; and all that has been said, but multiplies the avenues to what remains to be said. It is not so much paucity, as superabundance of material that seems to incapacitate modern authors.

. . . Let America then prize and cherish her writers; yea, let her glorify them. They are not so many in number, as to exhaust her goodwill. . . . Let America first praise mediocrity even, in her own children, before she praises (for everywhere, merit demands acknowledgement from every one) the best excellence in the children of any other land. Let her own authors, I say, have the priority of appreciation. I was much pleased with a hot-headed Carolina cousin of mine, who once said, – 'If there were no other American to stand by, in Literature, – why, then, I would stand by Pop Emmons and his 'Fredoniad,' and till a better epic came along, swear it was not very far behind the *Iliad*.' Take away the words, and in spirit he was sound.

. . . And we want no American Goldsmiths; nay we want no American Miltons. It were the vilest thing you could say of a true American author, that he were an American Tompkins. Call him an American, and have done; for you can not say a nobler thing of him. –

But it is not meant that all American writers should studiously cleave to nationality in their writings; only this, no American writer should write like an Englishman, or a Frenchman; let him write like a man, for then he will be sure to write like an American.

. . . Let us away with this Bostonian leaven of literary flunkeyism towards England. If either must play the flunkey in this thing, let England do it, not us. And the time is not far off when circumstances may force her to it. While we are rapidly preparing for that political supremacy among the nations, which prophetically awaits us at the close of the present century; in a literary point of view, we are deplorably unprepared for it; and we seem studious to remain so. Hitherto, reasons might have existed why this should be; but no good reason exists now. And all that is requisite to amendment in this matter, is simply this: that, while freely acknowledging all excellence, everywhere, we should refrain from unduly lauding foreign writers and, at the same time, duly recognize the meritorious writers that are our own; – those writers, who breathe that unshackled, democratic spirit of Christianity in all things which now takes the practical lead in this world, though at the same time led by ourselves – us Americans. Let us boldly contemn all imitation, though it comes to us graceful and fragrant as the morning; and foster all originality, though, at first, it be crabbed and ugly as our own pine knots. And if any of our authors fail, or seem to fail, then, in the words of my enthusiastic Carolina cousin, let us clap him on the shoulder, and back him against Europe for his second round. The truth is, that in our point of view, this matter of a national literature has come to such a pass with us, that in some sense we must turn bullies, else the day is lost, or superiority so far beyond us, that we can hardly say it will ever be ours.[6] □

In tracing the inextricable links between America's literary and political aspirations, 'Hawthorne and His Mosses' is a crucial document in the naming and definition of an American literary consciousness. If 'Hawthorne and His Mosses' represents Melville's call for a truly American book, then *Moby-Dick*, with its reliance upon the facts and the myths of whaling – America's most important industry at the time – and with its exploitation of a language of democracy, is his fullest reply to that call. 'Hawthorne and His Mosses', then, sets the agenda for *Moby-Dick* criticism.

When *Moby-Dick* was first published on 18 October 1851, in London (under the title *The Whale*), and in New York on 14 November 1851, Melville was already a celebrated American writer. The sensual descriptions of life amongst South Sea islanders in his first two books *Typee* (1846) and *Omoo* (1847) had brought Melville great fame, and a certain degree of notoriety. As a young man, a sailor turned author of romantic sea-faring fictions, he was a literary sex-symbol. But Melville's fame was short-lived. The same impetuosity of character and financial insecurity that had sent him, in the first place, on the sea voyages upon which his first books were based, were to haunt him throughout his whole life.

Herman Melville was born on 1 August 1819 in New York to an aristocratic family, the son of Maria Gansevoort and Allan Melville (originally Melvill). The family of four girls and four boys, however, suffered greatly from Allan Melville's business failures. The financial insecurity that meant Herman's childhood came to be characterised by hasty house moves to avoid creditors, only grew more intense on the death of Allan Melville, bankrupt, when Herman was aged only twelve.

On the death of his father, the young Melville tried a number of jobs. He worked as a bank-clerk, a cabin-boy on a merchant ship bound for Liverpool, and an elementary school teacher. In January 1841 he set sail aboard the whaleship *Acushnet*, and so *Moby-Dick*'s long gestation was begun. Melville deserted the *Acushnet* in the Marquesas, and made his way to Tahiti and Honolulu. His experiences on these islands were to provide the inspiration for his first two books. He returned to Boston in 1844 on board the frigate *United States*. Married, in August 1847, to Elizabeth Shaw – the daughter of Lemuel Shaw, the chief justice of Massachusetts – Melville settled to writing as a means of making a living for himself and his young family. But the success of *Typee* and *Omoo* was soon eclipsed by the critical and popular failure of his next book *Mardi* (1849). This ambitious and complex book, the first indication of Melville's literary experimentalism, was not what the public wanted. Though America had, at the time, the largest expanding literary market-place, and a remarkably literate population, the public wanted adventure fiction, sensationalist novels, and gothic-style horrors. With the pressing need for money driving his writing, then, Melville wrote, over the spring and summer of 1849, two more novels that derived from his adventures as a sailor. *Redburn* (1849), based on his experiences as a cabin-boy, and *White-Jacket* (1850), which deals with the reformist theme of naval flogging, came as a relief to his critics and readers. At last, they felt, Melville had returned to his best writing. His reputation enjoyed an all too brief revival. Nothing prepared his readers for the curious, experimental amalgam of fact and fantasy, adventure story and moral fable that was *Moby-Dick* when it appeared in 1851.

Moby-Dick sealed Melville's fate as a writer. The themes that he was exploring in it were ones in which the reading public had no interest. The serious philosophical and moral concerns that Melville had plotted in his 'Hawthorne and His Mosses' piece, and which *Moby-Dick* articulates, were misunderstood by his readers and taken as tokens of impending insanity. The complexity and literary tricks of his next novel, *Pierre, or the Ambiguities* (1852) confirmed these feelings in his readers.

Melville turned from writing and spent his latter years as a deputy inspector in the New York Custom House. He died on 28 September 1891 leaving the manuscript of a novella, *Billy Budd, Sailor*, unfinished and undiscovered until 1924. Only in the twentieth century has Melville's status as one of America's greatest writers been finally established. And only now is *Moby-Dick* fully appreciated as the literary apotheosis of antebellum America.

This Critical Guide can be seen to chart this movement in the appreciation of *Moby-Dick* from literary curiosity to masterpiece of American expression. In so doing, it also charts the changing understandings – from 1851 up to the present day – of what America and its culture might mean. A pattern that emerges from all the essays in this book is the way in which criticism of *Moby-Dick* has always seen *Moby-Dick* as a text which exposes the ways in which American ideology can be seen to operate. Perhaps this is the lasting lesson of both *Moby-Dick* and its criticism: Melville's masterpiece is an act of cultural self-definition, a naming of America's possibilities.

It should not be forgotten, though, that *Moby-Dick* does not start with the act of naming 'Call me Ishmael'. It starts with etymological fragments of the word 'whale', and extracts from past writings about whales. These are supplied by a 'Late Consumptive Usher' and a 'Sub-Sub-Librarian' respectively. As a reader of *Moby-Dick* the temptation is to feel oneself being cast in these roles, and for the editor of a collection of critical extracts about *Moby-Dick* this temptation is even greater. In its ability to make a new text out of old extracts, *Moby-Dick* sounds a resonantly American note. Hopefully the new combination of old texts in this Critical Guide will inspire the continuing process of re-reading and reassessment of *Moby-Dick*. It is this process which is, indeed, *Moby-Dick*'s deepest characteristic. It is encapsulated in the baffled madness of Pip that speaks wisdom as he considers the various different ways in which the members of the *Pequod*'s crew 'read' the doubloon which Ahab has nailed to the ship's main mast. In Melville's strangely poetic, strangely symbolic way, Pip's words sum up the community of readings that make up *Moby-Dick* scholarship, and signify the idea of 'unity in diversity' which lies at the heart of American ideology:

■ 'I look, you look, he looks: we look, ye look, they look.' □

A Note on the Text

Throughout the editorial narrative the title of Melville's novel is given in the form *Moby-Dick*, and the name of the white whale itself as Moby Dick. This convention is not necessarily followed by all the essays in this book. Each extract reproduces the usage of its original. The title of Melville's book, and the name of the white whale, appear variously in the critical extracts, therefore, with or without a hyphen, and sometimes in italics, sometimes not. In all cases, though, the context makes clear to what the author is referring.

CHAPTER ONE

Early Reviews

ONE OF the earliest critical assessments of *Moby-Dick* is by Melville himself, in a letter to Nathaniel Hawthorne which he wrote shortly after the publication of his novel. He writes in the letter as someone who has completed a long and difficult task, and though his actual description of the book itself is brief, the letter sets up the terms in which the book is to be read. *Moby-Dick* is morally and aesthetically ambiguous, a mystery whose deeper meanings must be unlocked before it can be fully 'understood':

■ A sense of unspeakable security is in me this moment, on account of your having understood the book. I have written a wicked book, and feel spotless as the lamb. Ineffable socialities are in me. I would sit down and dine with you and all the gods in old Rome's pantheon. It is a strange feeling – no hopefulness in it, no despair. Content – that is it; and irresponsibility; but without licentious inclination. I speak now of my profoundest sense of being, not of an incidental feeling.[1] □

Initial reactions to *Moby-Dick*, as seen in the extracts that follow, were ones of bafflement and wonder, ones that struggled to understand the sorts of ambiguities hinted at in Melville's letter. Whether condemning it as a wicked book displaying no hopefulness, or praising it as one which produces a spotless feeling 'without licentious inclination', early reviewers often made extravagant claims for the text's ability to speak at a profound level. Because they felt *Moby-Dick* concealed some deep secret, they sought the key to the text in its very ambiguity, and in their consequent inability to categorise it as simply an adventure yarn, or a moral fable, an existential allegory, or a more-or-less scientific treatise on whaling. Such critical bafflement is indicative of the inherently conservative notions of novelistic form, style and content within – and against – which Melville was working in mid-nineteenth-century America. It also shows the extent to which *Moby-Dick* was seen as something completely new and unprecedented in literature. Both praised and condemned for its inventiveness, *Moby-Dick* was seen either as the work of a genius or the incoherent rantings of a madman. Melville himself was troubled by the apparently inextricable link between genius and madness that his book exposed. Towards the end of the same letter quoted from above, he writes:

■ My dear Hawthorne, the atmospheric skepticisms steal into me now, and make me doubtful of my sanity in writing you thus. But, believe me, I am not mad, most noble Festus! But truth is ever incoherent, and when the big hearts strike together, the concussion is a little stunning.[2] □

The worries that Melville articulates here, uncannily anticipate the terms within which *Moby-Dick* was received by its first reviewers. On the one hand, it was hailed as a stunning masterpiece, with its apparent incoherence taken as a sign of its struggle to deliver some universal truth. But on the other hand, its stylistic and formal incoherence was read as a morally dangerous incoherence, certainly blasphemous, and most probably insane. In either case, though, the critical ground upon which such assessments rest is very often a confession, on the part of the reviewer, of perplexity in the face of mystery. Indeed, from the time of its first publication up to the present day, this can be seen as one of the keynotes in the critical reception of *Moby-Dick*.

Melville's own sense of perplexity with the book he was writing is revealed further in the following extracts from letters he wrote during the composition of *Moby-Dick*. These extracts serve to emphasise the increasing strangeness with which Melville viewed his novel as it was progressing, and chart its development from a seemingly straightforward narrative of a whaling voyage to the multifaceted, mystic-allegory that readers were faced with when it was eventually published. The sense in these letters that it is a text troubled by dualities – whether the documentary of a whaling voyage or allegorical fantasy; truth or fiction; good or evil; sane or insane – is one that is repeated in the extracts from early reviews of the novel that then make up the rest of this chapter.

On 1 May 1850 Melville wrote to his friend Richard Henry Dana, Jr., the author of a famous autobiographical seafaring adventure *Two Years Before the Mast* (1840). This letter contains the first recorded reference by Melville to *Moby-Dick*, and seems to indicate that the idea for Melville to write an account of his experiences aboard the whaleship *Acushnet* came from Dana. This would not be surprising: Dana had earlier encouraged Melville to write of his experiences aboard the frigate *United States*, the starting point for *White-Jacket* which had been published in March 1850.[3] In its style and imagery the letter displays the pressure to which Melville was already subjecting his language in his efforts to get to 'the truth of the thing' about whaling:

■ About the 'whaling voyage' – I am half way in the work, & am very glad that your suggestion so jumps with mine. It will be a strange sort of a book, tho', I fear; blubber is blubber you know; tho' you may get oil out of it, the poetry runs as hard as sap from a frozen maple tree; – & to cook the thing up, one must needs throw in a little fancy, which from the nature of the thing, must be ungainly as the gambols of the whales themselves. Yet I mean to give the truth of the thing, spite of this.[4] □

Even at this early stage in the writing of *Moby-Dick* Melville senses that any attempt to write of his whaling experiences will be accompanied by a struggle with doubleness. But this is a doubleness that cuts deeper than an author's battle with recalcitrant materials. The turning of 'blubber' into 'poetry' is envisioned here not simply as a problem of form, or aesthetic propriety, but as a problem of getting to the 'truth', to 'the nature of the thing'. This 'truth' acknowledges both the beauty and the ungainliness of its subject, it recognises that fact and fancy are mutually dependent, and that any attempt to give a detailed account of the realities of whaling life will, to some degree, involve Melville in a voyage after universal Truth. Melville writes in 'Hawthorne and His Mosses' that 'you must have plenty of sea-room to tell the Truth in'. In his letter to Dana, written only three months earlier, he has already realised that whaling will provide him with just such 'sea-room': this will be no ordinary 'whaling voyage', Melville warns. No wonder, then, that he anticipates the feelings of *Moby-Dick*'s early reviewers when, still only half written, he declares it to be a 'strange sort of a book'.

Along with this early recognition of the ambiguous strangeness of his novel, Melville's letter to Dana also anticipates some of the curious imagery and rhetoric with which *Moby-Dick* attempts to articulate the 'Truth'. Again, this arises out of an apprehension of doubleness. This is especially true in the letter's opening paragraph, where Melville's friendship with Dana is perceived as a bond that unites them across a whole series of complex dualities, all of which reflect – or perhaps, deflect – Melville's anxieties as a writer. In imagery that startlingly prefigures Ishmael's description of his friendship with Queequeg in chapter 72, 'The Monkey-Rope', Melville describes here 'a sort of Siamese link of affectionate sympathy' between himself and Dana, one that he had felt on first reading Dana's *Two Years Before the Mast* just after his first sea voyage.[5] This image of mutual understanding effectively short-circuits the images of divisive duality out of which the rest of the passage is constructed, and which seem to trouble Melville throughout the letter.

Melville notes that Dana's praise of 'any thing I have written about the sea' is of more importance to him 'than acres & square miles of the superficial shallow praise of the publishing critics' because it is based in Dana's knowledge and understanding of the struggle to accommodate 'plenty of sea-room' in one's writing. Melville asserts, then, that both he and Dana understand, far better than 'superficial . . . critics', how assumed polar opposites such as fact and fantasy become merged in sea tales. So, whilst Melville's image of a 'Siamese link' is an elaborate means for him to dispel any sense of inferiority to the older writer of sea yarns, one moreover that seems to close the gaps between truth and fiction, older and younger writers, self and other, it is dependent upon an assertion of a different set of dualities: those between writer and critic, and, as we shall see, between writing for artistic satisfaction and writing for money.

The degree to which Melville seems troubled by the demands of the literary marketplace is encapsulated in the curiously convoluted syntax of the next section of this letter:

■ In fact, My Dear Dana, did I not write these books of mine [*Redburn* and *White-Jacket*] almost entirely for 'lucre' – by the job, as a woodsawyer saws wood – I almost think, I should hereafter – in the case of a sea book – get my M.S.S. neatly and legibly copied by a scrivener – send you that one copy – & deem such a procedure the best publication.[6] □

The anxieties that are here displayed are recognisably those of America's emerging literary culture of the mid-nineteenth century. Popular literary tastes of the time, fuelled by an unprecedented expansion of publishing, and helped by the introduction of the cylinder press in 1847, called for novels of high adventure and sensationalism to match the fantastic, often grotesquely lurid (and supposedly 'true') accounts of trials, debaucheries and depravities with which the popular market was saturated in the form of penny newspapers, reformist pamphlets, dime novels, and pornographic fables.[7] Melville was only too aware of the volatility of such a market. Consequently, he worried deeply that the popularity he had gained from his early fiction, adventure fiction in the mould of Dana's, was unstable and would eventually disappear. That Melville is prepared – albeit reluctantly – to 'throw in a little fancy' in his writing of *Moby-Dick* to ensure his continued popularity is an indication of the commercial pressures under which he felt himself to be working. Yet his letter also clearly indicates the unease he felt in writing for money or, as he has it, 'almost entirely for "lucre"'. Two ironies can be seen to be in operation here, both of which stem from the initial critical response to *Moby-Dick*, and both of which are traced throughout the history of critical debate over the book. They are grounded in the tensions that Melville's letter articulates, between artistic integrity and the need for cash, between the demands of a popular mass culture and those of an elite literary culture. But these are the very tensions and dualities out of which antebellum America was struggling to shape itself.

The first irony is the fact that although *Moby-Dick* received a reasonably positive response from its first reviewers (with some notable exceptions, which follow later in this chapter) it was pretty much ignored by the popular readership, and was a commercial flop that was only resurrected as a masterpiece of American literature in the second decade of this century. This leads to the second irony: according to the 'standard' critical versions, *Moby-Dick*'s lack of commercial success is attributable to the fact that it is a masterpiece, the product of a 'high' or an 'elite' literary culture, a text that demonstrates the arrival of American culture at levels of maturity and sophistication nearly comparable with those of the old mother-country England. But *Moby-Dick* – in its sensationalism, melodrama, and scurrilousness – is steeped in the popular culture of its time, just as much as in the 'high' literary culture of Shakespeare and Greek tragedy. Indeed, its very representativeness as an American text lies in the heterogeneity that marks it off as the product of a culture, a mere decade away from civil war, intensely aware of the ambiguity, doubleness, and tensions lying underneath its superficial claims of unity.

The image of Siamese connection between Dana and Melville is a case in point. Whilst deriving from American popular culture of the 1840s it is used by Melville as a means to express a concept of selfhood that seems more at home in the 'high' literary culture of America at that time. The image itself clearly derives from the two 'original' 'Siamese Twins' Chang and Eng who were touring America at the time as part of 22   23ness it is also an echo of Emerson's image of an 'iron string' to which 'every heart vibrates' and which asserts 'the connection of events' in his essay 'Self-Reliance'.[9] Melville's use of imagery from both 'popular' and 'high' culture shows him, here, to be testing his linguistic resources, to be experimenting with a language appropriate to the task at hand in *Moby-Dick*. Though such language must be able to vibrate to the tensions within a Transcendentalist doctrine of self-reliance, it must also be one alive to the realities of everyday experience in antebellum America.

It is interesting in this respect, then, that in both this letter to Dana, and in the 'Monkey-Rope' chapter of *Moby-Dick* the figure of a 'Siamese connection' is superseded by a figure which derives from the world of burgeoning capitalism. As we have seen, Melville continues in his letter by decrying the extent to which 'lucre' gets in the way of a real connection, writer-to-writer, between himself and Dana. The implication is that what he deems to be the means of 'best publication' has, necessarily, been displaced by the imposition of marketplace ethics, by the need to make a living. Perhaps, he implies, what really unites himself and Dana is less any metaphysical notion of the interconnectedness of human experience in the quest to get at the 'truth of the thing', and more a sense of the joint struggle to survive in the literary marketplace.

The turn around from romantic idealism to cynical realism is rapid and acute here, but it does seem that in it Melville is testing the terms within which the irony of Ishmael's discourse will operate in *Moby-Dick*. In fact, such irony pervades even *Moby-Dick*'s opening chapter where, with unabashed ease, Ishmael romantically speculates on the unity of human experience that is encapsulated by the myth of Narcissus, which is, he says, 'the key to it all' (5). But this is only a bare page before a hard-headed cynicism leads him to claim that his reason for going to sea as a sailor is because it involves 'being paid' (6). This ironic pattern is repeated in the 'Monkey-Rope' chapter, and indicates the pervasiveness of the language and imagery of the marketplace. Initially Ishmael notes that he and Queequeg are joined together, twinned, by 'an elongated Siamese ligature [that] united us' (320). Ishmael interprets this figure metaphysically, seeing it as indicative of the ties that bind man to man within an idea of Humanity, but even as he does so, the figure changes, and becomes one of commercial interdependence. Selfhood, now, for Ishmael seems dependent less on moral or social bonds, than on the stability of the stock market: 'I seemed distinctly to perceive that my own individuality was now merged in a joint stock company of two' (320). Such examples signal deep-seated anxieties about a culture in which commercial relationships were seen increasingly to be replacing personal ones. And though such anxieties mark Melville's own struggles to engage both the popular and the literary cultures of his day, the greatest irony about the early critical reception of *Moby-Dick* is that, even where this engagement was recognised, the novel's success or failure was measured either as populist adventure fiction or as high literature, and never both at once. In the extracts from early reviews that follow it will be seen that the most important critical appraisals of the book struggled to articulate their sense of its complex ambiguities, tensions and ironies.

That the book's moral ambiguity both fascinated and worried Melville is clear from the closing sentences of another of his letters to Hawthorne. This one, dated 29 June 1851, is the last of the known letters he wrote to Hawthorne whilst finishing *Moby-Dick*, or as he refers to it here, the *Whale*. His disclosure here of what he calls the 'book's motto' (albeit 'the secret one') is a useful measure against which to evaluate the aesthetic and moral judgements made of the book by its first reviewers:

■ Shall I send you a fin of the *Whale* by way of a specimen mouthful?

The tail is not yet cooked – though the hell-fire in which the whole book is broiled might not unreasonably have cooked it all ere this. This is the book's motto (the secret one), – Ego non baptiso te in nomine – but make out the rest yourself.[10] □

The full version of this motto appears in chapter 113 of *Moby-Dick*, 'The Forge'. As Ahab baptises the harpoon destined for Moby Dick in the mingled pagan bloods of Tashtego, Queequeg and Daggoo he cries deliriously '"Ego non baptizo te in nomine patris, sed in nomine diaboli!"' (489), which translates as 'I baptise you, not in the name of the father, but in the name of the devil'.

A common feature of *Moby-Dick*'s early reviews is their remarking upon the curious doubleness of the book, on its defiance of easy categorisation, its generic ambiguity. Clearly puzzled by this, reviewers very often sought to explain such ambiguity as Melville's attempt to convey a sense of a wider ambiguity at the heart of our apprehension of the world itself. In short, right from the start, *Moby-Dick* was read as an allegorical fable that attempts to tell us of our place in the universe. Whether judged successful or not in this aim, is largely a matter of the reviewer's own moral temper and sense of artistic propriety. For George Ripley, reviewing *Moby-Dick* in *Harper's New Monthly Magazine* (December 1851), Melville's new work was a resounding success, which

■ in point of richness and variety of incident, originality of conception, and splendour of description, surpasses any of the former productions of this highly successful author.[11] □

He continues by equating the multifaceted nature of the book with its depths of moral analysis. *Moby-Dick*, Ripley argues, is morally sound. It amply demonstrates the skill of its author in weaving together his heterogeneous materials, and in so doing illustrates 'the mystery of human life'. He argues that from a relatively simple story of revenge and 'frantic passion' Melville has constructed a profound work.

■ On this slight framework, the author has constructed a romance, a tragedy, and a natural history, not without numerous gratuitous suggestions on psychology, ethics and theology. Beneath the whole story, the subtle, imaginative reader may perhaps find a pregnant allegory, intended to illustrate the mystery of human life. Certain it is that the rapid, pointed hints which are often thrown out, with the keenness and velocity of a harpoon, penetrate deep into the heart of things, showing that the genius of the author for moral analysis is scarcely surpassed by his wizard power of description.[12] □

The following anonymous review from the London *Spectator* (25 October 1851) tells a different story. Leaving aside the fact that the reviewer here had read the shorter, expurgated version of the book entitled *The Whale* that had been published in England a fortnight before *Moby-Dick* was published in America, it is interesting that what provided Ripley with evidence of Melville's 'consummate skill', namely the book's transgression of literary genres, is the very ground upon which the *Spectator's* reviewer condemns it for literary impropriety. Displaying more than a hint of literary snobbishness, such condemnation is typical of the attitudes of English critics at the time towards the cultural efforts of their 'provincial' American cousins.

■ This sea novel is a singular medley of naval observation, magazine article writing, satiric reflection upon the conventionalisms of civilized life and rhapsody run mad. So far as the nautical parts are appropriate and unmixed, the portraiture is truthful and interesting. Some of the satire, especially in the early parts, is biting and reckless. The chapter-spinning is various in character; now powerful from the vigorous and fertile fancy of the author, now little more than empty though sounding phrases. The rhapsody belongs to wordmongering where ideas are the staple; where it takes the shape of narrative or dramatic fiction, it is phantasmal – an attempted description of what is impossible in nature and without probability in art; it repels the reader instead of attracting him.

. . . It is a canon with some critics that nothing should be introduced into a novel which it is physically impossible for the writer to have known: thus, he must not describe the conversation of miners in a pit if they *all* perish. Mr. Melville hardly steers clear of this rule, and he continually violates another, by beginning in the autobiographical form and changing ad libitum into the narrative. His catastrophe overrides all rule: not only is Ahab, with his boat's-crew, destroyed in his last desperate attack upon the white whale, but the Pequod herself sinks with all on board into the depths of the illimitable ocean. Such is the go-ahead method.[13] □

What is here taken to be Melville's betrayal of all the rules of narrative, and ascribed to the 'go-ahead method', is actually due to a printing error. Inexplicably, the English edition of *The Whale* was published with the *'Epilogue'* missing.[14] Ignorant, therefore, of Ishmael's survival of the *Pequod's* destruction, many English reviewers were content to condemn the novel for what they felt to be its odd narrative form. A commonplace of many English reviews was to see such oddness as a mark of the author's deranged sensibilities. Analyses of the treatment of Ahab's madness, the author's 'attempts [at] delineating the wild imaginings of

monomania', as the *Spectator*'s reviewer has it,[15] thus become insinuations of Melville's own madness.

A crowning example of this tendency is the review of *The Whale*
which appeared in the London *Athenaeum* of 25 October 1851. Copies of
this review reached American readers on the eve of the American publication of *Moby-Dick*. Because the *Athenaeum* was as highly respected a
journal in Boston and New York literary circles as it was in London,
the unrelieved severity of this review proved fatal to the commercial
success of Melville's novel. From the following extracts it is not difficult
to see why.

■ This is an ill-compounded mixture of romance and matter-of-fact.
The idea of a connected and collected story has obviously visited
and abandoned its writer again and again in the course of composition. The style of his tale is in places disfigured by mad (rather than
bad) English; and its catastrophe is hastily, weakly, and obscurely
managed.

. . . Frantic though such an invention seems to be, it might possibly
have been accepted as the motive and purpose of an *extravaganza* had
its author been consistent with himself. Nay, in such a terrible cause –
when Krakens and Typhoons and the wonders of Mid-Ocean, &c &c.
were the topics and toys to be arranged and manoeuvred – we might
have stretched a point in admission of electrical verbs and adjectives
as hoarse as the hurricane. There is a time for everything in imaginative literature; – and, according to its order, a place – for rant as well as
for reserve; but the rant must be good, honest, shameless rant, without
flaw or misgiving. . . . Ravings and scraps of useful knowledge flung
together salad-wise make a dish in which there may be much surprise,
but in which there is little savour. . . . Our author must be henceforth
numbered in the company of the incorrigibles who occasionally tanta-
lize us with indications of genius, while they constantly summon us to
endure monstrosities, carelessnesses, and other such harassing mani-
festations of bad taste as daring or disordered ingenuity can devise.

Mr. Melville has to thank himself only if his horrors and his heroics
are flung aside by the general reader, as so much trash belonging to
the worst school of Bedlam literature, – since he seems not so much
unable to learn as disdainful of learning the craft of an artist.[16] □

This review anticipates, and is representative of, subsequent critical
arguments about *Moby-Dick* in several important ways. Its starting point,
the book's seeming ill-composition and its apparent lack of consistency,
remains highly troublesome to critics and general readers alike. When
faced with the book the tendency is, still, to throw one's hands up in
despair and exclaim 'but what is this – how am I meant to read it?'

Another common problem that this review makes clear, though unintentionally, is the ease with which the motives and rhetoric of characters are mistaken for those of Melville himself. If the *Athenaeum*'s reviewer finds it difficult to accept 'rant' that is not 'good, honest, shameless rant, without flaw or misgiving', this is because Ahab's rhetoric (or even Ishmael's) is here being mistaken for that of Melville. Much critical debate on *Moby-Dick*'s narrative methods has been generated out of precisely this slippage between author and character, with the focus of attention having gradually shifted away from the role of Ahab and onto that of Ishmael. But perhaps the most notable ways in which this review prefigures later critical appraisals are its tone and style. In an attempt to describe Melville's own wild imaginings, it verges on hysterical rant and wild metaphors itself. But, like so much writing about *Moby-Dick*, this is itself testimony to Melville's linguistic energies and infectious originality. *Moby-Dick* has inspired some weird and wonderful imagery as critics have struggled to pin down just what is so powerfully admirable or detestable in it.

Whether the wicked or spotless book of Melville's letter to Hawthorne, one of overt or secret meanings that struggles to reconcile good and evil, poetry and blubber, art and commerce, popular and literary cultures, from the very outset *Moby-Dick* has been seen as a work of high drama and peculiarly heterogeneous tastes. It is perhaps because of this that the imagery of food and cooking which Melville used in describing his book to Hawthorne ('Should I send you a fin of the *Whale* by way of a specimen mouthful?') occurs again and again in early reviews of the book. In their attempts to categorise this strange literary dish, the book's first reviewers fell upon elaborate metaphors of stews, soups and salad-dressings to express their sense of the curious mixture of flavours they encountered in it. Such imagery discloses, perhaps, another secret pattern of significance for a book cooked up in a culture of burgeoning consumerism.

The following extracts from Evert Duyckinck's review of *Moby-Dick* for the New York *Literary World* (22 November 1851) give an intelligent and perceptive overview of the novel. Its description of the book as 'an intellectual chowder' – or fish-stew – is in keeping with the curious (and often culinary) metaphors used by many of *Moby-Dick*'s first reviewers. But here, the metaphor is apt: strange as chowder may seem, it is a homely New England dish. The review is important not only because it is by a close friend of Melville's, who was also a publisher's reader, but also because it highlights the main problems on which other reviewers of the book focused. Duyckinck's drawing of attention to the book's ambiguous doubleness: is it a romance, or a factual narrative, he asks; his sense of the weirdness of its composition; and the way in which his confirmation of the book's 'strong powers' leads to a rather begrudging affirmation of the book's importance; all delineate the terms within which *Moby-Dick* was first read:

■ A difficulty in the estimate of this, in common with one or two other of Mr. Melville's books, occurs from the double character under which they present themselves. In one light they are romantic fictions, in another statements of absolute fact. When to this is added that the romance is made a vehicle of opinion and satire through a more or less opaque allegorical veil . . . the critical difficulty is considerably thickened. It becomes quite impossible to submit such books to a distinct classification as fact, fiction, or essay. . . . Under these combined influences of personal observation, actual fidelity to local truthfulness in description, a taste for reading and sentiment, a fondness for fanciful analogies, near and remote, a rash daring in speculation, reckless at times of taste and propriety, again refined and eloquent, this volume of Moby Dick may be pronounced a most remarkable sea-dish – an intellectual chowder of romance, philosophy, natural history, fine writing, good feeling, bad sayings – but over which, in spite of all uncertainties, and in spite of the author himself, predominates his keen perceptive faculties, exhibited in vivid narration.

There are evidently two if not three books in Moby Dick rolled into one. Book No. I. we could describe as a thorough exhaustive account admirably given of the great Sperm Whale. The information is minute, brilliantly illustrated, as it should be – the whale himself so generously illuminating the midnight page on which his memoirs are written – has its level passages, its humorous touches, its quaint suggestion, its incident usually picturesque and occasionally sublime. All this is given in the most delightful manner in 'The Whale.' Book No. 2 is the romance of Captain Ahab, Queequeg, Tashtego, Pip & Co., who are more or less spiritual personages talking and acting differently from the general business run of the conversation on the decks of whalers. They are for the most part very serious people, and seem to be concerned a great deal about the problem of the universe. They are striking characters withal, of the romantic spiritual cast of German drama; realities of some kinds at bottom, but veiled in all sorts of poetical incidents and expressions. As a bit of German melodrama, with Captain Ahab for the Faust of the quarter-deck, and Queequeg with the crew, for Walpurgis night revellers in the forecastle, it has its strong points, though here the limits as to space and treatment of the stage would improve it. Moby Dick in this view becomes a sort of fishy moralist, a leviathan metaphysician . . . After pursuing him in this melancholic company over a few hundred squares of latitude and longitude, we begin to have some faint idea of the association of whaling and lamentation, and why blubber is popularly synonymous with tears.

The intense Captain Ahab is too long drawn out; something more of *him* might, we think, be left to the reader's imagination. The value of this kind of writing can only be through the personal consciousness of the reader, what he brings to the book; and all this is sufficiently evoked by a dramatic trait or suggestion. If we had as much of Hamlet or Macbeth as Mr. Melville gives us of Ahab, we should be tired even of their sublime company. Yet Captain Ahab is a striking conception, firmly planted on the wild deck of the Pequod – a dark disturbed soul arraying itself with every ingenuity of material resources for a conflict at once natural and supernatural in his eye, with the most dangerous extant physical monster of the earth, embodying, in strongly drawn lines of mental association, the vaster moral evil of the world. The pursuit of the White Whale thus interweaves with the literal perils of the fishery – a problem of fate and destiny – to the tragic solution of which Ahab hurries on, amidst the wild stage scenery of the ocean. To this end the motley crew, the air, the sky, the sea, its inhabitants are idealized throughout. It is a noble and praiseworthy conception; and though our sympathies may not always accord with the train of thought, we would caution the reader against a light or hasty condemnation of this part of the work.

Book III., appropriating perhaps a fourth of the volume, is a vein of moralizing, half essay, half rhapsody, in which much refinement and subtlety, and no little poetical feeling, are mingled with quaint conceit and extravagant daring speculation. This is to be taken as in some sense dramatic; the narrator throughout among the personages of the Pequod being one Ishmael, whose wit may be allowed to be against everything on land, as his hand is against everything at sea. This piratical running down of creeds and opinions, the conceited indifferentism of Emerson, or the run-a-muck style of Carlyle is, we will not say dangerous in such cases, for there are various forces at work to meet the powerful onslaught, but it is out of place and uncomfortable. We do not like to see what, under any view, must be to the world the most sacred associations of life violated and defaced.

. . . So much for the consistency of Ishmael – who, if it is the author's object to exhibit the painful contradictions of this self-dependent, self-torturing agency of a mind driven hither and thither as a flame in a whirlwind, is, in a degree, a successful embodiment of opinions, without securing from us, however, much admiration for the result.

With this we make an end of what we have been reluctantly compelled to object to in this volume. With far greater pleasure, we acknowledge the acuteness of observation, the freshness of perception, . . . the weird influences of his ocean scenes, the salient imagination which connects them with the past and distant, the world of books and the life of experience – certain prevalent traits of manly sentiment. These are strong powers with which Mr. Melville wrestles in this book. It would be a great glory to subdue them to the highest uses of fiction. It is still a great honor, among the crowd of successful mediocrities which throng our publishers' counters, and know nothing of divine impulses, to be in the company of these nobler spirits on any terms.[17] □

The troubled attention which is given here to defining just what sort of book *Moby-Dick* is, is typical of its early reviews. Whilst most reviewers – whether hostile or favourable – were willing to see the book as a sort of cosmic drama, with Ahab as its tragic protagonist, Duyckinck is atypical in giving more than scant attention to the character of Ishmael, and in seriously questioning his role as narrator. Indeed, for Duyckinck to see Ishmael as the seat of moral ambiguity in the book, sounds a remarkably modern note. He goes against the grain of virtually all critical appraisals of the book that appeared before the Second World War, and which see Ahab as the moral linchpin who is either praised for his dramatically rebellious rhetoric, or condemned for his blasphemies.

Further instances of the strange use of food imagery to describe the book are to be found in another couple of reviews, clearly influenced by that of the *Athenaeum* which was quoted earlier. In a dismissive vein remarkably similar to that of the *Athenaeum*, the New York *Albion* of 22 November 1851 describes *Moby-Dick* as an uncontrolled hotch-potch culled from 'authors innumerable'. The reviewer continues, in a metaphor clearly meant to go one better than the *Athenaeum*'s dish 'flung together salad-wise', by stating that 'We do not like the innovation. It is having oil, mustard, vinegar, and pepper served up as a dish, in place of being scientifically administered sauce-wise.'[18] And, whilst the influence of the *Athenaeum* is evident in the reference to Melville's 'heroics and horrors' in the review of *Moby-Dick* in *Bell's New Weekly Messenger* (2 November 1851), its culinary metaphor allows for a positive, if reticent, evaluation of the book:

■ There are people who delight in mulligatawny. They love curry at its warmest point. Ginger can not be too hot in the mouth for them. Such people, we should think, constitute the admirers of Herman Melville. He spices up his narrative with uncommon courage, and works up a story amazingly. If you love heroics and horrors he is your man. Sit down with him on a winter's eve, and you'll find yourself calling for candles before the night sets in. If you desire your hair to stand on end in a natural Brutus, or your teeth to chatter in unnatural discord, listen to what this man of strange lands and strange waters has to tell, and your wishes will be fulfilled. You will have supper for a very long night's digestion.[19] □

Inevitably, such struggles to describe the digestibility – or otherwise – of *Moby-Dick* have led reviewers and critics, again and again, to ask whether it is a work of genius or of madness. Again it is the *Athenaeum* review which seems to have set this ball rolling with its description of Melville's work as one belonging to 'the worst school of Bedlam literature'. Anonymous support of this view is given by *The Southern Quarterly Review* (January 1852) which notes that

■ [Ahab's] ravings, and the ravings of some of the tributary characters, and the ravings of Mr. Melville himself, meant for eloquent declamation, are such as would justify a writ *de lunatico* against all the parties.[20] □

Another witness for the prosecution is William Harrison Ainsworth, writing in the July 1853 edition of the London *New Monthly Magazine*:

■ The style is maniacal – mad as a March hare – mowing, gibbering, screaming, like an incurable Bedlamite, reckless of keeper or straight-waistcoat.[21] □

Equally vociferous, however, are the claims made for Melville's unparalleled genius. 'In whatever light it may be viewed', writes William Butler in the Washington *National Intelligencer* (16 December 1851),

■ no one can deny it [*Moby-Dick*] to be the production of a man of genius . . . [who has] a strange power to reach the sinuosities of a thought . . . he touches with his lead and line depths of pathos that few can fathom, and by a single word can set a whole chime of sweet or wild emotions into a pealing concert.[22] □

The case is put quite simply by the reviewer for *Bentley's Miscellany*, who notes that there is no room for 'contest or dispute about the matter', but that 'Herman Melville is a man of the truest and most original genius'.[23]

With the critical battle-lines thus drawn between madness and genius, and the general indifference of the reading public, *Moby-Dick* fell rapidly into an obscurity that was not helped by the universally damning reviews of his next book *Pierre; or The Ambiguities* that started appearing in August 1852. Pretty much sinking, like the *Pequod*, without a trace, *Moby-Dick* received virtually no serious critical attention, until after the First World War. A brief flurry of reappraisals of Melville's work immediately following his death in September 1891 just about kept the book on the (albeit 'underground') literary scene. But it was not until the post-war period, when the 'Melville Revival' was under way and was reviving the book's critical fortunes, that the world seemed ready to tackle

Melville's masterpiece. One of the few people to write about *Moby-Dick* during the 1880–90 period was the English critic Henry S. Salt. His two essays, from which the following extracts are taken, are crucially important in the history of *Moby-Dick* criticism because they signal the sort of change around in attitude toward Melville's genius and artistry that was necessary, nearly twenty years later, to the 'Melville Revival'. In this first essay, written in 1889, two years before Melville's death, Salt is already developing the anxieties about the book's irregularity of composition, and the question of Melville's genius, that were so problematic to its early reviewers, into the grounds for reading it as a mythical epic of the human condition.

■ The book is a curious compound of real information about whales in general and fantastic references to this sperm-whale in particular . . . which is studied . . . in a metaphysical and ideal aspect. . . . Wild as the story is, there is a certain dramatic vigour in the 'quenchless feud' between Ahab and Moby Dick which at once arrests the reader's attention, and this interest is well maintained to the close, the final hunting-scene being a perfect nightmare of protracted sensational description.

. . . [Melville's] literary power . . . is also unmistakable, his descriptions being at one time rapid, concentrated, and vigorous, according to the nature of his subject, at another time dreamy, suggestive and picturesque. . . . The death of the white whale in *Moby Dick* rises to a sort of epic grandeur and intensity.[24] □

Salt's later piece on *Moby-Dick*, written in 1891, some six months after Melville's death, anticipates, in its eulogising tone, some of the rhapsodic excesses of the 'Melville Revival'. More importantly, though, the attention it gives to reading the book seriously, as a mystic puzzle of 'esoteric significance', alongside its attempt to see the book as somehow typical of American literature, goes a long way towards reconfiguring the aesthetic criteria within which it would be read by subsequent critics.

■ It is in 'The Whale' that we see Melville casting to the winds all conventional restrictions, and rioting in the prodigality of his imaginative vigour. It is in 'The Whale' that we find the fullest recognition of that magical influence of the sea – the 'image of the ungraspable phantom of life' – which from first to last was the most vital inspiration of his restless and indomitable genius. . . . Ostensibly nothing more than a wild story of a strange voyage of vengeance, a 'quenchless feud' between a fierce old sea-captain and a particular white sperm-whale of renowned strength and audacity, the book, which abounds with real facts concerning the details of the whale-fishery, has a mystic esoteric significance which lifts it into a wholly different category. In the character of Captain Ahab, who 'looked like a man cut away from the stake when the fire has overrunningly wasted all the limbs without consuming them,' we see a lurid personification of the self-destructive spirit of Hatred and Revenge, while Moby Dick, the white whale, 'swam before him as the monomaniac incarnation of all those malicious agencies which some deep men feel eating in them.' . . . 'The Whale,' faulty as it is in many respects, owing to the turgid mannerisms of Melville's transcendental mood, is nevertheless the supreme production of a master mind – let no one presume to pass judgement on American literature unless he has read, and re-read, and wonderingly pondered, the three mighty volumes of 'The Whale.'[25] □

CHAPTER TWO

The 'Melville Revival'

THE CENTENARY of Melville's birth in 1919 brought to the surface an interest in his work that had largely been confined to 'progressive' literary circles up to the turn of the century, but which had gradually been growing over the first decade of the century. Whilst many different factors are at play in this 'Melville Revival', the mere fact of a resurgence of interest in Melville, and most especially in *Moby-Dick*, at this time, speaks of a sense among critics and readers that the world had eventually caught up with Melville's book. This is apparent in the extracts that follow, all of which treat *Moby-Dick* as a serious and important precursor of modernism. In fact, many of the techniques and practices of *Moby-Dick* that had bemused, and in some cases outraged, its early reviewers are ones that have come to be seen as the mainstays of modernist aesthetics. *Moby-Dick* mixes literary styles and genres. Its narrator is unreliable, and it employs 'stream-of-consciousness' passages. It displays irreverence and seriousness in equal amounts, whilst its wordplay shows a fascination with language itself as a literary resource. And *Moby-Dick* pushes localised events toward universalised meanings by a use of mythical and allegorical patterning. All these devices would be at home in the work of modernist writers such as Joyce, Eliot, Pound, Lawrence and Woolf, among others, whose work was starting to achieve literary currency in the first decades of this century.

But it would be wrong to think of *Moby-Dick* as simply a proto-modernist novel whose time had come at last with the Melville centenary. To do so would be to ignore the extent to which it is the product of America in the immediate run-up to the Civil War. It would also seriously misrepresent the 'Melville Revival'. Rather than suddenly bursting onto the literary scene as if from nowhere, *Moby-Dick*'s arrival had been carefully prepared for in the conversations, letters and essays of a handful of writers and critics: Robert Buchanan, Henry Salt (extracts from whose essays closed the previous chapter) and other members of his literary circle such as George Bernard Shaw and William Morris,

J.M. Barrie, whose Captain Hook is modelled on Captain Ahab, and the English poet and sailor, John Masefield.[1] In 1907 Joseph Conrad was invited, by Oxford University Press, to write the introduction to their 'World Classics' edition of *Moby-Dick*. This invitation demonstrates that *Moby-Dick*'s 'classic' status was now accepted. Though Conrad declined the invitation, and gave a negative evaluation of *Moby-Dick*, his description of the book as a 'rhapsody' is in tune with the way it was thought of throughout the 'Melville Revival'.

■ Years ago I looked into *Typee* and *Omoo*, but as I didn't find there what I am looking for when I open a book I did go no further. Lately I had in my hand *Moby Dick*. It struck me as a rather strained rhapsody with whaling for a subject and not a single sincere line in the 3 vols. of it.[2] □

Carl Van Doren's essay on Melville, included in the 1917 edition of the *Cambridge History of American Literature*, was instrumental in reviving the reputation of *Moby-Dick* in America. Whilst rhapsodically claiming the book to be 'one of the greatest of sea romances in the whole literature of the world', Van Doren, like Conrad, also considers the question of the book's sincerity. Unlike Conrad, though, he argues that in *Moby-Dick*, Melville shifted 'his interest from the actual to the abstruse and symbolical'. Melville does not, therefore, commit a disservice to truth, but discovers the 'perilous border' between fact and fiction, and it is 'the peculiar mingling of speculation and experience', Van Doren notes, 'which lends *Moby Dick* its special power'.[3] Important, too, is the emphasis Van Doren places on the uniquely American circumstances out of which such a conflict between truth and imagination arises:

■ The time was propitious for such a book. The golden age of the whalers was drawing to a close, though no decline had yet set in, and the native imagination had been stirred by tales of deeds done on remote oceans by the most heroic Yankees of the age in the arduous calling in which New England, and especially the hard little island of Nantucket, led and taught the world. A small literature of whaling had grown up, chiefly in the records of actual voyages or novels like those of Cooper in which whaling was an incident of the nautical life. But the whalers still lacked any such romantic record as the frontier had. Melville brought to the task a sound knowledge of actual whaling, much curious learning in the literature of the subject, and, above all, an imagination which worked with great power upon the facts of his own experience.[4] □

Moby-Dick, the essay further asserts, struggles to turn conflict – fact versus fiction, good versus evil, the 'forces of nature' versus the 'enmity of man' – into allegory. By focusing on such conflicts, Van Doren's essay neatly summarises the terms within which *Moby-Dick* was read during the 'Melville Revival'.

The following extract is taken from the chapter on *Moby-Dick* in D.H. Lawrence's *Studies in Classic American Literature*. Though published first in 1922, Lawrence had been working on this book since 1915. Despite, maybe because of, Lawrence's extravagantly idiosyncratic and wildly refreshing style as a critic, this book has itself become a classic among critical evaluations of American literature. Throughout his study Lawrence responds to the newness he hears in the old (that is nineteenth-century) American literary classics, and struggles to wrest judgement upon them away from European critical prejudices. 'It is hard to hear a new voice,' he writes, 'as hard as it is to listen to an unknown language. We just don't listen. There is a new voice in the old American classics.'[5] He listens intently to Melville, and to his struggle with language, with truth, and with America. At times mystified by *Moby-Dick*, at others startlingly perceptive toward it, Lawrence gives us a modernist roller-coaster version of the book. In reviving *Moby-Dick* for the modern world, he turns it into a book of the modern world. As a book born out of conflict, it becomes his means to come to terms with the cultural devastation that followed the First World War. And while it is true to say that the post-war world was more willing to hear Melville's dark allegory of evil and madness, it is equally important to note that throughout the history of its critical reception, each new generation of readers has appropriated *Moby-Dick* for its own cultural purposes.

■ *Moby Dick, or the White Whale.*

A hunt. The last great hunt.

For what?

For Moby Dick, the huge white sperm whale: who is old, hoary, monstrous, and swims alone; who is unspeakably terrible in his wrath, having so often been attacked; and snow-white.

Of course he is a symbol.

Of what?

I doubt if even Melville knew exactly. That's the best of it.

He is warm-blooded, he is lovable. He is lonely Leviathan, not a Hobbes sort. Or is he?

But he is warm-blooded, and lovable. The South Sea Islanders, and Polynesians, and Malays, who worship shark, or crocodile, or weave endless frigate-bird distortions, why did they never worship the whale? So big!

Because the whale is not wicked. He doesn't bite. And their gods had to bite.

He's not a dragon. He is Leviathan. He never coils like the Chinese dragon of the sun. He's not a serpent of the waters. He is warm-blooded, a mammal. And hunted, hunted down.

It is a great book.

At first you are put off by the style. It reads like journalism. It seems spurious. You feel Melville is trying to put something over you. It won't do.

And Melville really is a bit sententious: aware of himself, self-conscious, putting something over even himself. But then it's not easy to get into the swing of a piece of deep mysticism when you just set out with a story.

Nobody can be more clownish, more clumsy and sententiously in bad taste, than Herman Melville, even in a great book like Moby Dick. He preaches and holds forth because he's not sure of himself. And he holds forth, often, so amateurishly.

The artist was so *much* greater than the man. The man is a rather tiresome New Englander of the ethical mystical-transcendentalist sort: Emerson, Longfellow, Hawthorne, etc. So unrelieved, the solemn ass even in humour. So hopelessly *au grand serieux* [of great serious-ness], you feel like saying: Good God, what does it matter? If life is a tragedy, or a farce, or a disaster, or anything else, what do I care! Let life be what it likes. Give me a drink, that's what I want just now.

For my part, life is so many things I don't care what it is. It's not my affair to sum it up. Just now it's a cup of tea. This morning it was wormwood and gall. Hand me the sugar.

One wearies of the *grand serieux*. There's something false about it. And that's Melville. Oh, dear, when the solemn ass brays! brays! brays!

But he was a deep, great artist, even if he was rather a sententious man. He was a real American in that he always felt his audience in front of him. But when he ceases to be American, when he forgets all audience, and gives us his sheer apprehension of the world, then he is wonderful, his book commands stillness in the soul, an awe.

In his 'human' self, Melville is almost dead. That is, he hardly reacts to human contacts any more: or only ideally: or just for a moment. His human-emotional self is almost played out. He is abstract, self-analytical and abstracted. And he is more spell-bound by the strange slidings and collidings of Matter than by the things men do. In this he is like Dana.[6] It is the material elements he really has to do with. His drama is with them. He was a futurist long before futurism found paint.[7] The sheer naked slidings of the elements. And the human soul experiencing it all. So often, it is almost over the border: psychiatry. Almost spurious. Yet so great.

It is the old same thing as in all Americans. They keep their old-fashioned ideal frock-coat on, and an old-fashioned silk hat, while they do the most impossible things. There you are: you see Melville hugged in bed by a huge tattooed South Sea Islander, and solemnly offering burnt offering to this savage's little idol, and his ideal frock-coat just hides his shirt-tails and prevents us from seeing his bare posterior as he salaams, while his ethical silk-hat sits correctly over his brow the while. That is so typically American: doing the most impossible things without taking off their spiritual get-up. Their ideals are like armour which has rusted in, and will never more come off. And meanwhile in Melville his bodily knowledge moves naked, a living quick among the stark elements. For with sheer physical, vibrational sensitiveness, like a marvellous wireless-station, he registers the effects of the outer world. And he records also, almost beyond pain or pleasure, the extreme transitions of the isolated, far-driven human soul, the soul which is now alone, without any real human contact.

The first days in New Bedford introduce the only human being who really enters into the book, namely Ishmael, the 'I' of the book. And then the moment's hearts-brother, Queequeg, the tattooed, powerful South Sea harpooner, whom Melville loves as Dana loves 'Hope.' The advent of Ishmael's bedmate is amusing and unforget-table. But later the two swear 'marriage,' in the language of the savages. For Queequeg has opened again the flood-gates of love and human connection in Ishmael.

. . . So they smoke together, and are clasped in each other's arms. The friendship is finally sealed when Ishmael offers sacrifice to Queequeg's little idol, Gogo.[8]

. . . You would think this relation with Queequeg meant something to Ishmael. But no. Queequeg is forgotten like yesterday's newspaper. Human things are only momentary excitements or amuse-ments to the American Ishmael. Ishmael, the hunted. But much more, Ishmael the hunter. What's a Queequeg? What's a wife? The white whale must be hunted down. Queequeg must be just 'KNOWN,' then dropped into oblivion.

And what in the name of fortune is the white whale?

Elsewhere Ishmael says he loved Queequeg's eyes: 'large, deep eyes, fiery black and bold.' No doubt, like Poe, he wanted to get the 'clue' to them. That was all.

The two men go over from New Bedford to Nantucket, and there sign on the Quaker whaling ship, the Pequod. It is all strangely fantastic, phantasmagoric. The voyage of the soul. Yet curiously a real whaling voyage, too. We pass on into the midst of the sea with this strange ship and its incredible crew. The Argonauts were mild lambs in comparison. And Ulysses went defeating the Circes and over-coming the wicked hussies of the isles. But the Pequod's crew is a collection of maniacs fanatically hunting down a lonely, harmless white whale.

As a soul history, it makes one angry. As a sea yarn, it is marvellous: there is always something a bit over the mark, in sea yarns. Should be. Then again the masking up of actual seaman's experience with sonorous mysticism sometimes gets on one's nerves. And again, as a revelation of destiny the book is too deep even for sorrow. Profound beyond feeling.

You are some time before you are allowed to see the captain, Ahab: the mysterious Quaker. Oh, it is a God-fearing Quaker ship.

Ahab, the captain. The captain of the soul.

'I am the master of my fate.
I am the captain of my soul!'

Ahab!

'Oh, captain, my captain, our fearful trip is done.'

The gaunt Ahab, Quaker, mysterious person, only shows himself after some days at sea. There's a secret about him? What?

Oh, he's a portentous person. He stumps about on an ivory stump, made from sea-ivory. Moby Dick, the great white whale, tore off Ahab's leg at the knee, when Ahab was attacking him.

Quite right, too. Should have torn off both his legs, and a bit more besides.

But Ahab doesn't think so. Ahab is now a monomaniac. Moby Dick is his monomania. Moby Dick must DIE, or Ahab can't live any longer. Ahab is atheist by this.[9] □

To this point, despite the histrionics, Lawrence has dealt with *Moby-Dick* in terms (if not means) that are recognisable from its early reviews. But the mixing of bafflement, dramatic tension, plot summary, with fairly equal amounts of praise and damnation, begins to sit uneasily with the attempts to bring the book alongside other American writers. So Lawrence seems to try again. He continues his essay by introducing into the 'score' notes not heard before in Melville criticism. Questions of race, power and social hierarchy, and their bearing upon America and its industry, propel him toward his doomy conclusion.

■ All right.

This *Pequod*, ship of the American soul, has three mates.

1. Starbuck: Quaker, Nantucketer, a good responsible man of reason, forethought, intrepidity, what is called a dependable man. At the bottom, *afraid*.

2. Stubb: 'Fearless as fire, and as mechanical.' Insists on being

reckless and jolly on every occasion. Must be afraid too, really.

3. Flask: Stubborn, obstinate, without imagination. To him 'the wondrous whale was but a species of magnified mouse, or water-rat – '

There you have them: a maniac captain and his three mates, three splendid seamen, admirable whalemen, first class men at their job.

America!

It is rather like Mr. Wilson and his admirable, 'efficient' crew, at the Peace Conference.[10] Except that none of the Pequodders took their wives along.

A maniac captain of the soul, and three eminently practical mates.

America!

Then such a crew. Renegades, castaways, cannibals: Ishmael, Quakers.

America!

Three giant harpooners, to spear the great white whale.

1. Queequeg, the South Sea Islander, all tattooed, big and powerful.

2. Tashtego, the Red Indian of the sea-coast, where the Indian meets the sea.

3. Daggoo, the huge black negro.

There you have them, three savage races, under the American flag, the manic captain, with their great, keen harpoons, ready to spear the *White* whale.

And only after many days at sea does Ahab's own boat crew appear on deck. Strange, silent, secret, black-garbed Malays, fire-worshipping Parsees. These are to man Ahab's boat, when it leaps in pursuit of that whale.

What do you think of the ship *Pequod*, the ship of the soul of an American?

Many races, many peoples, many nations, under the Stars and Stripes. Beaten with many stripes.

Seeing stars sometimes.

And in a mad ship, under a mad captain, in a mad, fanatic's hunt.

For what?

For Moby Dick, the great white whale.

But splendidly handled. Three splendid mates. The whole thing practical, eminently practical in its working. American industry!

And all this practicality in the service of a mad, mad chase.

Melville manages to keep it a real whaling ship, on a real cruise, in spite of all fantastics. A wonderful, wonderful voyage. And a beauty that is so surpassing only because of the author's awful flounderings in mystical waters. He wanted to get metaphysically deep. And he got deeper than metaphysics. It is a surpassingly beautiful book. With an awful meaning. And bad jolts.

. . . The bird of heaven, the eagle, St. John's bird, the Red Indian bird, the American, goes down with the ship, nailed by Tashtego's hammer, the hammer of the American Indian. The eagle of the spirit. Sunk!

> Now small fowls flew screaming over the yet yawning gulf; a sullen white surf beat against its steep sides; then all collapsed; and then the great shroud of the sea rolled on as it rolled five thousand years ago.

So ends one of the strangest and most wonderful books in the world, closing up its mystery and its tortured symbolism. It is an epic of the sea such as no man has equalled; and it is a book of exoteric symbolism of profound significance, and of considerable tiresomeness.

. . . But it is a great book, a very great book, the greatest book of the sea ever written. It moves awe in the soul.

The terrible fatality.

Fatality.

Doom.

Doom! Doom! Doom! Something seems to whisper it in the very dark trees of America. Doom!

Doom of what?

Doom of our white day. We are doomed, doomed. And the doom is in America. The doom of our white day.

Ah, well, if my day is doomed, and I am doomed with my day, it is something greater than I which dooms me, so I accept my doom as a sign of the greatness which is more than I am.

Melville knew. He knew his race was doomed. His white soul, doomed. His great white epoch, doomed. Himself, doomed. The idealist, doomed. The spirit, doomed.

. . . That great horror of ours! It is our civilization rushing from all havens astern.

The last ghastly hunt. The White Whale.

What then is Moby Dick? – He is the deepest blood-being of the white race. He is our deepest blood-nature.

And he is hunted, hunted, hunted by the maniacal fanaticism of our white mental consciousness. We want to hunt him down. To subject him to our will. And in this maniacal conscious hunt of ourselves we get dark races and pale to help us, red, yellow, and black, east and west, Quaker and fire-worshipper, we get them all to help us in this ghastly maniacal hunt which is our doom and our suicide.

The last phallic being of the white man. Hunted into the death of upper consciousness and the ideal will. Our blood-self subjected to our will. Our blood-consciousness sapped by a parasitic mental or ideal consciousness.

Hot-blooded sea-born Moby Dick. Hunted by monomaniacs of the idea.

Oh God, oh God, what next, when the *Pequod* has sunk?

She sank in the war, and we all are flotsam.

Now what next?

Who knows? *Quien sabe? Quien sabe, señor?* ['Who knows? Who knows, sir?']

Neither Spanish, nor Saxon America has any answer.

The *Pequod* went down. And the *Pequod* was the ship of the white American soul. She sank, taking with her Negro and Indian and Polynesian, Asiatic and Quaker and good, businesslike Yankees and Ishmael: she sank all the lot of them.

Boom! As Vachel Lindsay would say.

To use the words of Jesus, IT IS FINISHED.

Consummatum est![11]

But *Moby Dick* was first published in 1851. If the great White Whale sank the ship of the Great White Soul in 1851, what's been happening ever since?

Post mortem effects, presumably.

Because, in the first centuries, Jesus was Cetus, the Whale. And the Christians were the little fishes. Jesus, the Redeemer, was Cetus, Leviathan. And all the Christians all his little fishes.[12] □

Lawrence's quite extraordinary reading of *Moby-Dick* for the modern world is counterbalanced by the measured rationality of E. M. Forster's response to the novel which appears in his famous critical exploration of the art of novel writing, *Aspects of the Novel*, and from which the next extract is taken. First published in 1927, *Aspects of the Novel* originated as a series of lectures given at Trinity College, Cambridge. Whereas Lawrence makes dramatic play out of his ambiguous response to *Moby-Dick*, and thereby ends in a curiously dismissive affirmation of the book's worth, Forster defends the novel by emphasising its troubling ambiguities. There is little doubt in his mind that *Moby-Dick* is a work of the highest importance in world literature. Aware, though, of both the august surroundings in which he was lecturing, and the inherent snobbery of the literary establishment, his careful easing of *Moby-Dick* away from the common critical assumptions made about it – that *Moby-Dick* is a curiously poetic, but nevertheless mundane, whaling yarn – is a masterpiece of understated critical persuasion.

The accounts of *Moby-Dick* given by Lawrence and Forster may differ greatly in tone, but they do share a sense that the book's greatness lies in the mysterious depths sounded by its symbolism. Both admit to not fully understanding what the text is up to, and both suspect that neither did Melville. Such insistence that the truth which underpins the novel is an 'ungraspable' one, lying outside words, is typical of critical responses to the novel at this time, and is a characteristic of many subsequent 'Americanist' readings of it. For Forster, *Moby-Dick* is central to his consideration of Prophecy and The Novel. His explanation of what he means by prophecy helps to clarify the way in which he reads *Moby-Dick*'s mysterious, ungraspable allegory. Prophecy in this context, he tells us, is not about 'foretelling the future', rather, it has to do with 'an accent in the novelist's voice', one telling us that

■ His theme is the universe, or something universal, but he is not necessarily going to 'say' anything about the universe; he proposes to sing, and the strangeness of song arising in the halls of fiction is bound to give us a shock.[13] □

This accent, Forster claims, can be heard in the work of only four writers: Melville, Dostoevsky, Emily Brontë, and D.H. Lawrence. The two major themes of the 'Melville Revival' are thus interwoven in Forster's considerations of *Moby-Dick*, namely, the desire to see its place among the highest of literary achievements recognised, and the struggle to attend properly to its strange allegorical singing of something felt to be universal.

■ *Moby Dick* is an easy book, as long as we read it as a yarn or an account of whaling interspersed with snatches of poetry. But as soon as we catch the song in it, it grows difficult and immensely important. Narrowed and hardened into words the spiritual theme of *Moby Dick* is as follows: a battle against evil conducted too long or in the wrong way. The White Whale is evil, and Captain Ahab is warped by constant pursuit until his knight-errantry turns into revenge. These are words – a symbol for the book if we want one – but they do not carry us much further than the acceptance of the book as a yarn – perhaps they carry us backwards, for they may mislead us into harmonizing the incidents, and so losing their roughness and richness. The idea of a contest we may retain: all action is a battle, the only happiness is peace. But contest between what? We get false if we say it is between good and evil or between two unreconciled evils. The essential in *Moby Dick*, its prophetic song, flows athwart the action and the surface morality like an undercurrent. It lies outside words. Even at the end, when the ship has gone down with the bird of heaven pinned to its mast, and the empty coffin, bouncing up from the vortex, has carried Ishmael back to the world – even then we cannot catch the words of the song. There has been stress, with intervals: but no explicable solution, certainly no reaching back into universal pity and love; no 'Gentlemen, I've had a good dream.'[14]

The extraordinary nature of the book appears in two of its early incidents – the sermon about Jonah and the friendship with Queequeg.

The sermon has nothing to do with Christianity. It asks for endurance or loyalty without hope of reward. The preacher

> kneeling in the pulpit's bows, folded his large brown hands across his chest, uplifted his closed eyes, and offered a prayer so deeply devout that he seemed kneeling and praying at the bottom of the sea.

And he concludes on a note of joy more terrifying than a menace.

> Delight is to him whose strong arms yet support him when the ship of this base treacherous world has gone down beneath him. Delight is to him who gives no quarter in the truth, and kills, burns and destroys all sin though he pluck it out from under the robes of Senators and Judges. Delight – top-gallant delight is to him, who acknowledges no law or lord, but the Lord his God, and is only a patriot to heaven. Delight is to him, whom all the waves of the billows of the seas of the boisterous mob can never shake from this sure Keel of the Ages. And eternal delight and deliciousness will be his, who coming to lay him down, can say with his final breath – O Father! – chiefly known to me by thy rod – mortal or immortal, here I die. I have striven to be Thine, more than to be this world's or mine own. Yet this is nothing: I leave eternity to Thee: for what is man that he should live out the lifetime of his God?

I believe it is not a coincidence that the last ship we encounter at the end of the book before the final catastrophe should be called the Delight; a vessel of ill omen who has herself encountered Moby Dick and been shattered by him. But what the connexion was in the prophet's mind I cannot say nor could he tell us.

Immediately after the sermon, Ishmael makes a passionate alliance with the cannibal Queequeg, and it looks for a moment that the book is to be a saga of blood-brotherhood. But human relationships mean little to Melville, and after a grotesque and violent entry, Queequeg is almost forgotten. Almost – not quite. Towards the end he falls ill and a coffin is made for him which he does not occupy, as he recovers. It is this coffin, serving as a lifebuoy, that saves Ishmael from the final whirlpool, and this again is no coincidence, but an unformulated connexion that sprang up in Melville's mind. *Moby Dick* is full of meanings: its meaning is a different problem. It is wrong to turn the Delight or the coffin into symbols, because even if the symbolism is correct, it silences the book. Nothing can be stated about *Moby Dick* except that it is a contest. The rest is song.[15] □

Forster's essay is difficult, and baffling. *Moby-Dick* is explained only by saying that it cannot be explained. And we witness Forster's major analytic terms – prophecy and song, symbolism and contest – collapse in front of us, and spin off into abstraction. The closing sentence, 'The rest is song', illustrates this problem very clearly. The rhetoric is strong, it makes claims for the power of *Moby-Dick* as a work of art, as a contrivance of language that, mysteriously, goes beyond language. Persuasive as this sounds, though, it is meaningless in terms of an analysis of the book. It merely reconfirms Forster's initial bafflement, by restating that which was already known: *Moby-Dick* is 'difficult and immensely important'.

It is precisely because of this sort of analytic conundrum that Forster's essay is representative of 'Melville Revival' criticism in particular, and of prevailing critical attitudes of the time in general. On the one hand, literature was seen as a tool to enrich our knowledge of the world, to deliver its meaning for us. On the other hand, though, its power was felt to lie in its ability to reach beyond itself, to go 'outside words', and to intimate the ultimate mystery of the universe. The struggle to reconcile these seemingly opposed views of art is typical of the struggle in modernist aesthetics between determinacy and indeterminacy. This can be seen to operate throughout Forster's essay. The great work of art – *Moby-Dick* – occupies a privileged space, he argues, one that is 'full of meanings', but, because of its privileged artistic status as 'prophetic song', it is one that delivers mystery, rather than meaning. In this way art remains a special domain, susceptible only incidentally to everyday concerns. The irony here, of course, is that this view of the autonomy of the work of art is, itself, part and parcel of a culture blown apart (literally and metaphorically) by the experience of the war. Post-war ideology, itself, produces the wish to see art as something unaffected by ideology, a timeless realm of universal, if ineffable, meaning.

Lewis Mumford's *Herman Melville*, published in 1929, is the first book-length analysis of Melville's work that is, in any real sense, useful to the study of Melville. In the following extract, from the book's chapter on *Moby-Dick*, we can see that its critical terms are very close to those of Lawrence and Forster. Mumford attends to *Moby-Dick*'s symbolism, its mythic dimension, and its universal meaning. The 'prophetic song' which Forster heard in Melville is transcribed by Mumford into a rhapsody as he attempts to account for the shimmering power of Melville's great fable of the sea. Mumford's style, rhapsodic and highly charged, may seem now, perhaps, rather quaint and dated. But it is important not to be blinded by this to his sense that Melville's importance lies in the immense pressure *Moby-Dick* puts upon myth and symbol in a struggle to explore what Mumford calls the 'labyrinth' that 'is the universe'. And Mumford's language, always beautifully turned, is sometimes infected by the strangeness he perceives, and is at some pains to describe, in Melville. A prime example of this is his simile of *Moby-Dick* as a flying-boat, which, on reflection, is curiously apt, and startlingly beautiful. Such qualities are indicative of Mumford's desire to read *Moby-Dick* as a text deeply relevant to a 'modern vision of life'.

■ Moby-Dick is a story of the sea, and the sea is life, 'whose waters of deep woe are brackish with the salt of human tears.' Moby-Dick is the story of the eternal Narcissus in man, gazing into all rivers and oceans to grasp the unfathomable phantom of life – perishing in the illusive waters. Moby-Dick is a portrait of the whale and a presentation of the demonic energies in the universe that harass and frustrate and extinguish the spirit of man. We must gather our own strength together if we are to penetrate Moby-Dick: no other fable, except perhaps Dante's, demands that we open so many doors and turn so many secret keys; for, finally, Moby-Dick is a labyrinth, and that labyrinth is the universe.

. . . Once Moby-Dick gets under way, the fable itself belongs to Heaven and Hell – all its naturalism, all its accurate detail, are polarized between these two extremes of being, so that everything which would relieve men's exasperation or take the edge off their lonely delight, disappears, as the land disappears beyond the horizon's edge. The reason for this is not obscure. In terms of Heaven and Hell this comfortable, understandable, tolerable middle portion of existence – that which we agree to call civilized – is the realm of complete illusion: just as, in terms of immediate animal existence, Heaven and Hell are illusions, and reality belongs to the realm of digestion, tropism, reflex action, muscular movement, tactile and visual adjustments. Melville, as we shall see, comprehended both aspects of existence: but he projected them both on the plane of eternity: domestic life and all it implies is seen through reversed glasses.

. . . Before we can take the measure of Moby-Dick we must . . . throw aside our ordinary measuring-sticks: one does not measure Saturn with the aid of an opera-glass and a dressmaker's tape. The conventional critic has dismissed Moby-Dick because it is 'not a novel,' or if it is a novel, its story is marred by all sorts of extraneous material, history, natural history, philosophy, mythological excursions, what not. This sort of criticism would belittle Moby-Dick by showing that it does not respect canons of a much pettier nature than the work itself, or because its colossal bulk cannot be caught in the herring-net of the commonplace story or romance.

. . . The matter is very easily put to rights if we simply abandon these false categories altogether. Moby-Dick stands by itself as complete as the Divine Comedy or the Odyssey stands by itself. Benedetto Croce has correctly taught us that every work of art is indeed in this same position: that it is uniquely what it is, and cannot be understood except in terms of its own purpose.

. . . The fact is that this book is a challenge and affront to all the habits of mind that typically prevailed in the nineteenth century, and still remain, almost unabated, among us: it comes out of a different world, and presupposes, for its acceptance, a more integrated life and consciousness than we have known or experienced, for the most part, these last three centuries. Moby-Dick is not Victorian; it is not Elizabethan; it is, rather, prophetic of another quality of life which Melville had experienced and had a fuller vision of in his own time – a quality that may again come into the world, when we seek to pass beyond the harassed specialisms which still hold and preoccupy so many of us. To fathom this quality of Melville's experience and imagination, we must look a little deeper into his myth and his manner of projecting it. What is its meaning? And first, in what manner is that meaning conveyed to us?

Moby-Dick is a poetic epic. Typographically, Moby-Dick conforms to prose, and there are long passages, whole chapters, which are wholly in the mood of prose: but in spirit and in actual rhythm, Moby-Dick again and again rises to polyphonic verse . . . [Melville] was under no necessity of clipping the emotions or of bleaching the imaginative colours of Moby-Dick: like a flying-boat, he rises from the water to the air and returns to the water again without losing control over either medium. His prose is prose: hard, sinewy, compact; and his poetry is poetry, vivid, surging, volcanic, creating its own form in the very pattern of the emotional state itself, soaring, towering, losing all respect for the smaller conventions of veracity, when the inner triumph itself must be announced. It is in the very rhythm of his language that Ahab's mood, and all the devious symbols of Moby-Dick are sustained and made credible: by no other method could the deeper half of the tale have been written. In these poetic passages, the phrases are intensified, stylized, stripped of their habitual associations. If occasionally, as with Shakespeare, the thought itself is borne down by the weight of the gold that decorates it, this is only a similar proof of Melville's immense power of expression.

. . . Moby-Dick is a symphony; every resource of language and thought, fantasy, description, philosophy, natural history, drama, broken rhythms, blank verse, imagery, symbol, are utilized to sustain and expand the great theme. The conception of Moby-Dick organically demands the expressive interrelation, for a single total effect, of a hundred different pieces: even in accessory matters, like the association of the Parsee, the fire-worshipper, with the death of Ahab, the fire-defier, or in the makeup of the crew, the officers white men, the harpooneers the savage races, red, black, brown, and the crew a mixed lot from the separate islands of the earth, not a stroke is introduced that has not meaning for the myth as a whole. Although the savage harpooneers get nearest the whale, the savage universe, it is Ahab and the Parsee, the European and the Asiatic, who carry the pursuit to its ultimate end – while a single American survives to tell the tale! Melville's instrumentation is unsurpassed in the writing of the last century: one must go to a Beethoven or a Wagner for an exhibition of similar powers: one will not find it among the works of literature.

. . . What is the meaning of Moby-Dick? There is not one meaning; there are many; but in its simplest terms, Moby-Dick is, necessarily, a story of the sea and its ways, as the Odyssey is a story of strange adventure, and War and Peace a story of battles and domestic life. The characters are heightened and slightly distorted: Melville's quizzical comic sense is steadily at work on them, and only Ahab escapes: but they all have their recognizable counterparts in the actual world. Without any prolonged investigation one could still find a Starbuck on Nantucket or a Flask on Martha's Vineyard – indeed, as Mr. Thomas Benton's portraits properly indicate, queerer fish than they.

. . . As a story of the sea, Moby-Dick will always have a call for those who wish to recapture the magic and terror and stress and calm delight of the sea and its ships; and not less so because it seizes on a particular kind of ship, the whaler, and a special occupation, whaling, at the moment when they were about to pass out of existence, or rather, were being transformed from a brutal but glorious battle into a methodical, slightly banal industry. . . . Moby-Dick would have value as first-hand testimony, even if it were negligible as literature. If this were all, the book would still be important.

But Moby-Dick, admirable as it is as a narrative of maritime adventure, is far more than that: it is, fundamentally, a parable on the mystery of evil and the accidental malice of the universe. The white whale stands for the brute energies of existence, blind, fatal, over-powering, while Ahab is the spirit of man, small and feeble, but purposive, that pits its puniness against this might, and its purpose against the blank senselessness of power. The evil arises with the good: the white whale grows up among the milder whales which are caught and cut up and used: one hunts for the one – for a happy marriage, livelihood, offspring, social companionship and cheer – and suddenly heaving its white bulk out of the calm sea, one comes upon the other: illness, accident, treachery, jealousy, vengefulness, dull frustration. The South Sea savage did not know of the white whale: at least, like death, it played but a casual part in his consciousness. It is different with the European: his life is a torment of white whales: the Jobs, the Aeschyluses, the Dantes, the Shakespeares, pursue him and grapple with him, as Ahab pursues his antagonist.

. . . The whole tale of the West, in mind and action in the philosophy and art of the Greeks, in the organization and technique of the Romans, in the precise skills and unceasing spiritual quests of modern man, is a tale of this effort to combat the whale – to ward off his blows, to counteract his aimless thrusts, to create a purpose that will offset the empty malice of Moby-Dick. Without such a purpose, without the belief in such a purpose, life is neither bearable nor significant: unless one is polarized by these central human energies and aims, one tends to become absorbed in Moby-Dick himself, and, becoming a part of his being, can only maim, slay, butcher like the shark or the white whale or Alexander or Napoleon.

. . . Ahab has more humanity than the gods he defies: indeed, he has more power, because he is conscious of the power he wields, and applies it deliberately, whereas Moby-Dick's power only seems deliberate because it cuts across the directed aims of Ahab himself. And in one sense, Ahab achieves victory: he vanquishes in himself that which would retreat from Moby-Dick and acquiesce in his insensate energies and his brutal sway. His end is tragic: evil engulfs him. But in battling against evil, with power instead of love, Ahab himself . . . becomes the image of the thing he hates: he has lost his humanity in the very act of vindicating it. By physical defiance, by physical combat, Ahab cannot rout and capture Moby-Dick: the odds are against him; and if his defiance is noble, his methods are ill chosen. Growth, cultivation, order, art – these are the proper means by which man displaces accident and subdues the vacant external powers in the universe: the way of growth is not to become more powerful but to become more human. Here is a hard lesson to learn: it is easier to wage war than to conquer in oneself the tendency to be partial, vindictive, and unjust: it is easier to demolish one's enemy than to pit oneself against him in an intellectual combat which will disclose one's weaknesses and provincialities. And that evil Ahab seeks to strike is the sum of one's enemies. He does not bow down to it and accept it: therein lies his heroism and virtue: but he fights it with its own weapons and therein lies his madness. All the things that Ahab despises when he is about to attack the whale, the love and loyalty of Pip, the memory of his wife and child, the sextant of science, the inner sense of calm, which makes all external struggle futile, are the very things that would redeem him and make him victorious.

. . . In Moby-Dick, Melville conquered the white whale in his own consciousness: instead of blankness there was significance, instead of aimless energy there was purpose, and instead of random living there

was Life. The universe is inscrutable, unfathomable, malicious, so –
like the white whale and his element. Art in the broad sense of all
humanizing effort is man's answer to this condition: for it is the means
by which he circumvents or postpones his doom, and bravely meets
his tragic destiny. Not tame and gentle bliss, but disaster, heroically
encountered, is man's true happy ending.

. . . The epic and mythic quality of Moby-Dick has been misunderstood because those who examined the book have thought of the epic
in terms of Homer, and the myth itself in relation to some obvious
hero of antiquity, or some modern folk-hero, a Washington, a Boone,
raised to enormous dimensions. 'The great mistake seems to be,' as
Melville said in his essay on Hawthorne, 'that even with those
Americans who look forward to the coming of a great literary genius
among us, they somehow fancy he will come in the costume of Queen
Elizabeth's day; be a writer of dramas founded upon old English
history or the tales of Boccaccio. Whereas, great geniuses are parts of
the times, they themselves are the times and possess a corresponding
colouring.'

Now, Moby-Dick was written in the best spirit of the nineteenth
century, and though it escaped most of the limitations of that period, it
escaped with its finest qualities intact.

. . . Moby-Dick, then, is one of the first great mythologies to be
created in the modern world, created, that is, out of the stuff of that
world, its science, its exploration, its terrestrial daring, its concentra-
tion upon power and dominion over nature, and not out of ancient
symbols, Prometheus, Endymion, Orestes, or mediaeval folk-legends,
like Dr. Faustus. Moby-Dick lives imaginatively in the newly broken
soil of our own life: its symbols . . . are direct and explicit: if the story
is bedded in facts, the facts themselves are not lost in further interpretation. Moby-Dick thus brings together the two dissevered halves
of the modern world and the modern self – its positive, practical,
scientific, externalized self, bent on conquest and knowledge, and its
imaginative, ideal half, bent on the transportation of conflict into art,
and power into humanity. . . . The best handbook on whaling is also –
I say this scrupulously – the best tragic epic of modern times and one
of the fine poetic works of all time.

. . . Each age, one may predict, will find its own symbols in Moby-
Dick. Over the ocean the clouds will pass and change, and the ocean
itself will mirror back those changes from its own depths. All these
conscious interpretations, however, though they serve the book by
approaching its deeper purpose, do not, cannot, quite penetrate the
core of its reality. Moby-Dick has a meaning which cannot be derived
or dissociated from the work itself. Like every great work of art, it
summons up thoughts and feelings profounder than those to which it

gives overt expression. It introduces one, sometimes by simple, bald means, to the depths of one's own experience. The book is not an answer, but a clue that must be carried further and worked out. . . . The book itself is greater than the fable it embodies, it foreshadows more than it actually reflects: as a work of art, Moby-Dick is part of a new integration of thought, a widening of the fringe of consciousness, a deepening of insight, through which the modern vision of life will finally be embodied.[16] □

Mumford's prediction in this final paragraph, about the way *Moby-Dick* will be read by subsequent ages – 'Each age, one may predict, will find its own symbols in *Moby-Dick*'– is uncannily accurate. The critical history of *Moby-Dick* is a peculiarly sharp object lesson in the interestedness of our critical practices. It shows how the texts we read, and the way we read them, reflect back our own ideological assumptions. In the case of the critics involved in the 'Melville Revival', we have seen this demonstrated in a belief in literature's ability to embody universal meanings and mysteries through highly charged symbols. This has been seen to derive from a desire to read *Moby-Dick* as curiously modern, to read its conflicts as ones speaking to the condition of post-war culture. Criticism of *Moby-Dick* in the 1940s and 1950s can again be seen to be reflective of the underlying cultural and ideological concerns of the day. *Moby-Dick* comes to be seen as one of a handful of texts central to the idea of an 'American Renaissance'. Critical evaluations of *Moby-Dick* at this time, therefore, mirror back a concern to plot and explain the growth of American literary ideology, and, by extension, a distinct American culture. It is to such critical evaluations that the next chapter turns.

CHAPTER THREE

The 1940s: *Moby-Dick* and the 'American Renaissance'

IF THE 'Melville Revival' occasioned an upsurge of interest in *Moby-Dick*, it also left subsequent scholars and critics with a distinctly problematic text. As a text rich in symbols and allegory, one of manifold meanings and half-articulated myth, though, *Moby-Dick* was to become the perfect focus for a generation of young American critics who, in the 1940s, were seeking to enlarge the scope and reputation of American Literature. Up to this point in America's literary and critical history, its writers were considered very much as youthful 'second-cousins' – and rather provincial ones at that – to the more serious and mature authors of England. The recognition of *Moby-Dick* as a literary 'classic', of lasting significance and profound complexity in its dealings with the world, meant that this relationship between the literatures of the old and new worlds had to be reassessed. In effect, American critics looked back, pretty much for the first time, into their own literary history, and saw that a century previously American writers were already producing works of immense importance. They saw that other American writers – such as Emerson, Thoreau, Hawthorne and Whitman – could be considered alongside Melville as contributing to this first flowering of a distinctive American literary culture. Works such as *Moby-Dick*, then, came to be seen as declarations of American cultural independence from the aesthetic canons of England and Europe. This flowering of native American literary culture that began around the 1840s was named by critic F.O. Matthiessen the 'American Renaissance'. It is from his hugely influential book *American Renaissance: Art and Expression in the Age of Emerson and Whitman* that the first extracts in this chapter are taken. To introduce these extracts, though, it is worth highlighting some of the main themes and ideas that the notion of an 'American Renaissance' of the 1840s brought to American critical thought of the 1940s, in order to consider the impact such ideas had on the development of *Moby-Dick* criticism.

The very idea of naming America's bid for cultural independence the 'American Renaissance', though, is rather paradoxical. In delineating a peculiarly American literary sensibility it seems strange to call upon an aesthetic model, the Renaissance, that is largely seen as the highpoint of cultural expression in Europe, one that plots the turning of Europe from a medieval into a modern culture. In the opening paragraph of *American Renaissance* Matthiessen is careful to clarify his use of the term 'renaissance':

■ It may not be precisely accurate to refer to our mid-nineteenth century as a *re-birth*; but that was how the writers themselves judged it. Not as a re-birth of values that had existed previously in America, but as America's way of producing a renaissance, by coming to its first maturity and affirming its rightful heritage in the whole expanse of art and culture.[1] □

The 'American Renaissance', then, is less a break with Europe's – specifically England's – literary models, than the rightful culmination of these within the American cultural scene. The tension that is expressed here, between Europe's literary tradition and America's sense of its lack of tradition, is one of the defining motifs of Melville criticism since Matthiessen. And in Matthiessen, as we shall shortly see, and in the other two critical pieces which comprise this chapter, *Moby-Dick* is seen as a product of precisely this tension. *Moby-Dick* arises, for them, out of the collision between the established values of the old world and those, as yet culturally untested, forces of democracy and individualism that were felt to be the defining concepts of the new world in the mid-nineteenth century.

It should not be forgotten, too, that one hundred years later, Matthiessen's own tracing of an 'American Renaissance' arose from a particular set of historical and cultural tensions. Writing in 1941, on the eve of America's entry into the World War Two, he asserts that what unifies the five writers (Emerson, Thoreau, Hawthorne, Whitman and Melville) of his American Renaissance is 'their devotion to the possibilities of democracy'.[2] Matthiessen's idea of an 'American Renaissance', then, demonstrates to America its historical, and continuing, devotion to an ideal of democracy, at exactly the moment when that liberal-humanist ideal was being challenged by the forces of totalitarianism. In arguing the case for America's cultural maturity on the grounds of the devotion of its classic writers to democracy, *American Renaissance* seems also to speak of America's political duties to a world where democracy is under threat. America's rise to political pre-eminence in the post-war years seems, therefore, to go hand-in-hand with its ability, in works such as Matthiessen's, to define and defend itself culturally. Once again *Moby-Dick* can be seen to have been co-opted by its critics to reflect their own cultural concerns. For critics in the early years of the century *Moby-Dick* spoke to modern, post-World War One sensibilities. Seen as central to the idea of an 'American Renaissance' in the 1940s (and later), *Moby-Dick* was now read as a text that reflected the power struggles of a world concerned to uphold democracy, and of a country seeking an identity for itself within that world.

Largely because he seems so clearly to embody such power struggles, it is Captain Ahab who receives the most sustained critical attention from Matthiessen and other critics of this period. Ahab is a problem case, though. For, whilst his monomaniac quest for vengeance, his subjection of the *Pequod*'s crew to his will, and his crazy abuse of rhetorical powers, are all marks of his authoritarian dictatorship, Ahab is also a rugged individual who embodies Emerson's ideal of self-reliance. Ahab is the hero of a truly American epic who speaks words powerful as Shakespeare's. Matthiessen's attempt to untangle these sorts of contradictions in *Moby-Dick* begins with what he calls 'Melville's extraordinary debt to Shakespeare'.[3] Like the paradox at the heart of the notion of an 'American Renaissance', the maturity and power of Melville's expression of a peculiarly American sensibility is affirmed by its debt to the central figure of the English Renaissance, William Shakespeare. The struggle of the American writer with the legacy of Shakespeare was one that Melville had addressed in his 'Hawthorne and His Mosses' essay, but only in Ahab's language is he finally able to formulate this struggle into an expression of American sensibility. It is this struggle that Matthiessen hears, first and foremost, in *Moby-Dick*. This marks a decisive moment in Melville criticism, for it recognises that *Moby-Dick*, and the America for which it speaks, is of as much cultural importance as Shakespeare and his Elizabethan age. This recognition is heard in the following passage from Matthiessen, and it is as if Melville criticism has suddenly discovered the long searched-for words needed to describe *Moby-Dick* as a work of American genius:

■ [Melville's] liberation in *Moby-Dick* through the agency of Shakespeare was almost an unconscious reflex. Unlike Emerson he discussed at no point the origins and nature of language. . . . In his effort to endow the whaling industry with a mythology befitting a fundamental activity of man in his struggle to subdue nature, he came into possession of the primitive energies latent in words. He had already begun to realize in the dream-passages of *Mardi* that meaning had more than just a level of sense, that the arrangement of words in patterns of sound and rhythm enabled them to create feelings and tones that could not be included in a logical or scientific statement.

But he did not find a valuable clue to how to express the hidden life of men, which had become his compelling absorption, until he encountered the unexampled vitality of Shakespeare's language.

. . . The most important effect of Shakespeare's use of language was to give Melville a range of vocabulary for expressing passion far beyond any that he had previously possessed. The voices of many characters help to intensify Ahab's. For instance, as he talks to the blacksmith about forging his harpoon, he finds the old man 'too calmly, sanely woeful . . . I am impatient of all misery . . . that is not mad.' This seems to have drawn upon the mood of Laertes' violent entrance, 'That drop of blood that's calm proclaims me bastard'; or since it has been remarked that 'Ahab has that that's bloody on his mind,' it probably links more closely to Hamlet's 'My thoughts be bloody, or be nothing worth.' The successive clauses, with their insistent repetitions, 'Thou shouldst go mad, blacksmith; say, why dost thou not go mad?' have built upon the cadences of Lear. Finally, as Ahab takes up the blacksmith's statement that he can smooth all dents, and sweeping his hand across his own scarred brow, demands, 'Canst thou smooth this seam?,' Melville has mingled something of Lady Macbeth's anguish with her husband's demand to the physician, 'Canst thou not minister to a mind diseased?'

. . . In Melville's case the accident of reading Shakespeare had been a catalytic agent, indispensable in releasing his work from limited reporting to the expression of profound natural forces. . . .

. . . His practice of tragedy, though it gained force from Shakespeare, had real freedom; it did not base itself upon Shakespeare, but upon man and nature as Melville knew them. Therefore, he was able to handle, in his greatest scenes, a kind of diction that depended upon no source, and that could, as Lawrence noted, convey something 'almost superhuman or inhuman, bigger than life.' . . . Immersed in primitive forces in *Moby-Dick*, Melville soon learned that – as he made Ishmael remark concerning 'the gliding great demon of the seas of life' – there were 'subterranean' levels deeper than his understanding could explain or fathom. But whatever the latent radiations of intuition, . . . they emanate from a core of articulated thought. Here, if Emerson's prejudice against the novel had only allowed him to see it, was the proof that the dialect of mid-nineteenth-century America could rise to dramatic heights. That does not mean that any American ever spoke like this, any more than Elizabethans talked like Lear; but it does mean that the progressions of Melville's prose are now based on a sense of speech rhythm, and not on anybody else's verse. The elaborate diction should not mislead us into thinking that the words have been chosen recklessly, or merely because they sounded well. For they are combined in a vital rhetoric, and thereby build up a defense of one of the chief doctrines of the age, the splendor of the single personality. The matching of the forces is tremendous: the 'placeless,' 'supernal power,' a symbol of the inscrutable mystery which Ahab so hates, is set over against his own integrity, which will admit the intrusion of nothing 'unintegral,' and which glories both in its 'queenly' magnificence and in the terrible violence of its 'earthquake life.' The resources of the isolated man, his courage and his staggering indifference to anything outside himself, have seldom been exalted so high.[4] □

For Matthiessen, then, Ahab's tragedy provides a defence of the Emersonian doctrine of 'Self-Reliance'. For Matthiessen, not only does *Moby-Dick*'s very language match Shakespeare's exaltation of the resources of individualism and humanity, but it does so in a voice that is solely and peculiarly American.

Matthiessen continues, therefore, by looking to the American circumstances out of which *Moby-Dick* arose. Such circumstances, whether a Calvinist sense of innate sin, a democratic hopefulness, or the doctrines of the age of Emerson, are all manifested in the book's symbolism. This, and the 'loose romanticism' upon which it depends, is the key expressive tool of the 'American Renaissance'. And thus Matthiessen's *Moby-Dick* becomes a symbol of Americanness, one which his own age seemed so vociferously to require.

■ . . . We can best approach the meaning of Ahab's tragedy if we leave the Shakespearean strain in abeyance for a while, and try to apprehend Melville's own awakening sense of the meaning of sin, of suffering, and of the 'boundless sympathy with all forms of being,' to which he had responded so eagerly in Hawthorne as well as in Shakespeare. As he wrote to Duyckinck after his first expression of enthusiasm at hearing Emerson lecture: 'Nay, I do not oscillate in Emerson's rainbow, but prefer rather to hang myself in mine own halter than swing in any other man's swing.'[5] As he grew more dissatisfied with Emerson's inadequacy, he seized upon Shakespeare and Hawthorne as allies. Yet his 'sense of Innate Depravity and Original Sin' did not remain just what he found in Hawthorne. A fundamental reason for some transmutation was that, unlike Hawthorne, he did not confine himself to moral and psychological observation, but launched out into metaphysics. The background of Calvinistic thought over which Hawthorne's imagination played served to keep his brooding interpretation within a coherent frame. He dwelt on the contrast between appearance and reality, but his quiet disillusion accepted their inexplicability; he did not expect the hard facts of life to swerve one foot in the direction of the idealists' hopes. Melville could be neither so cool nor restrained. Though deeply impressed by the firmness of the

Puritans' conception of evil, his mind had moved away from any fixed system of theology. Unchecked by formal education, a far more passionate temperament than Hawthorne's drove him to speculate. He felt compelled to search out the truth for himself, even while he recognized, in a growing wildness and turbulence, that it was as unfathomable as the sea.

. . . But although *Moby-Dick* is more notable for abundance than for control or lucidity, Melville had managed to work out his central assumptions about good and evil in ways that are fairly unmistakable.

. . . The preponderating stress on evil in this book is sometimes loosely romantic, as when Ishmael declares that all noble things are touched with melancholy. But the ground is solider when he bases his belief that the man 'who hath more of joy than sorrow in him . . . cannot be true – not true, or undeveloped,' on the proposition that 'the truest of all men was the Man of Sorrows,' and the truest of all books *Ecclesiastes*. Ishmael finds evil in the violent forces of nature, in the 'horrible vulturism' of animals; but he also knows that 'there is no folly of the beasts of the earth which is not infinitely outdone by the madness of men.'

If Melville grants such width of range to unleashed evil, it is important to determine what kind of discriminations he makes between it and good. Some of the more extravagant of the symbolical interpretations of his masterpiece could have been eliminated if the critics had paid stricter attention to Melville's own text, notably to the two chapters where he unfolds his basic conceptions of evil, 'Moby-Dick' and 'The Whiteness of the Whale.' He clearly distinguishes between this whale and all others. The whale in general is one of 'the interlinked terrors and wonders of God,' majestic in its size, portentous in its 'unconscious power.'

. . . But . . . in telling what Moby-Dick had signified for other mariners before Ahab, Melville reiterates that what separates him from the rest of the species is 'that unexampled, intelligent malignity which, according to specific accounts, he had over and over again evinced in his assaults.' How such a creature can be made to symbolize evil in Melville's drama becomes manifest in the long declaration of what the white whale grew to mean for Ahab after the first savage encounter in which he had lost his leg. Ever since then Ahab had cherished 'a wild vindictiveness' against this whale.

. . . At this point Melville shows . . . his awareness that he is dealing with primitive human drives far beyond the scope of the cultivated mind. He expresses this in a remarkable image for Ahab's nature, an image that originated in Melville's having visited the Hotel de Cluny in Paris, and having seen, after 'winding far down' within it, the much earlier remains of 'those vast Roman halls of Thermes; where far beneath the fantastic towers of man's upper earth, his root of grandeur, his whole awful essence sits in bearded state.' In that kind of image Melville asserts the mystery of the elemental forces in man, the instincts that lie deep below his later consciousness.

His emphasis on these forces is an important element in making credible his insistence on malignity. By presenting such a character as Ahab, Melville breaks through the veneer of civilization and reminds the reader that the shallow light of his educated consciousness really penetrates only a very short way into the profundity of the universe.

. . . In projecting Ahab's belief that he had been a victim of 'that intangible malignity,' Melville set the terms for a tragedy of revenge. But it is significant that he did not allow this sense of Moby-Dick's evil to be developed in Ahab's brain alone. Starbuck may protest 'I came here to hunt whales, not my commander's vengeance.' The crew may be swept along by the magnet of Ahab's irresistible will without really understanding what they are about. But Ishmael is explicit: 'What the White Whale was to Ahab has been hinted; what, at times, he was to me, as yet remains unsaid.' Caught up into the reckless mood that followed Ahab's first announcement of his quest, he 'could see naught in that brute but the deadliest ill.' Subsequently that feeling grew upon him, and grew wider in its connotations. He found it almost impossible to put 'in a comprehensible form' why the whiteness of the whale 'above all things appalled me . . . Yet, in some dim, random way, explain myself I must, else all these chapters might be naught.'

To such a depth and breadth does the whiteness become a symbol. All its extraordinary ramifications stem from an assumption antipodal to Emerson's, from what Melville calls the instinctive 'knowledge of the demonism in the world.' Thus, despite even the radiant hue of 'the very veil of the Christian's Deity,' Ishmael is driven to the knowledge that 'though in many of its aspects this visible world seems formed in love, the invisible spheres were formed in fright.' Invisibility connotes to him 'the heartless voids and immensities of the universe,' and stabs him with the thought of annihilation. This 'colorless all-color' suggests too the atheism from which he shrinks; it drives home the feeling that all the vivid tinges of nature herself can be but 'subtle deceits' laid on to conceal the blank charnel house within. As Ishmael heaps instance upon instance, the terrifying indifference of the universe to man's pursuits moves towards the 'vast skepticism and apathy' of existence. . . .

. . . The one thing that could redeem 'the wolfish world,' the Ishmael of *Moby-Dick* found, was sympathy with another human being. . . . [And Melville] gave his fullest presentation of the transforming power of such a feeling in the relation between Ishmael and Queequeg. When Ishmael recognized that 'the man's a human being just as I am,' he was freed from the burden of his isolation, his heart was no longer turned against society. That he rediscovered the sense of Christian brotherhood through companionship with a tattooed pagan was the consequence of Melville's now matured perception of the ironic contradictions between appearance and fact.

. . . Melville's hopes for American democracy, his dread of its lack of humane warmth, his apprehension of the actual privations and defeats of the common man, and his depth of compassion for courageous struggle unite in giving fervor to the declaration of his purpose in writing *Moby-Dick*: a declaration in which he feels most profoundly the Shakespearean lineage of his intent and method. It comes in 'Knights and Squires,' where, summing up his motley cast of characters, he is conscious that he may seem to be endowing ordinary whalemen with too heroic gifts:

> But this august dignity I treat of, is not the dignity of kings and robes, but that abounding dignity which has no robed investiture. Thou shalt see it shining in the arm that wields a pick or drives a spike; that democratic dignity which, on all hands, radiates without end from God; Himself! The great God absolute! The centre and circumference of all democracy! His omnipresence, our divine equality.
>
> If, then, to meanest mariners, and renegades and castaways, I shall hereafter ascribe high qualities, though dark; weave round them tragic graces; if even the most mournful, perchance the most abased, among them all, shall at times lift himself to the exalted mounts; if I shall touch that workman's arm with some ethereal light; if I shall spread a rainbow over his disastrous set of sun; then against all mortal critics bear me out in it, thou just Spirit of Equality, which hast spread one royal mantle of humanity over all my kind! Bear me out in it, thou great democratic God! who didst not refuse to the swart convict Bunyan, the pale, poetic pearl; Thou who didst clothe with doubly hammered leaves of finest gold, the stumped and paupered arm of old Cervantes; Thou who didst pick up Andrew Jackson from the pebbles; who didst hurl him upon a war-horse; who didst thunder him higher than a throne! Thou who, in all Thy mighty, earthly marchings, ever cullest Thy selected champions from the kingly commons; bear me out in it, O God!

This last paragraph-long sentence is one of the summits of Melville's rhetoric: the formal progression of its almost architecturally balanced iterations rises to an eloquence of a purity and sublimity beyond what any other American writer has been able to command. Its crescendo completes his fusion of Christianity and democracy. His unexpected linking of the three heroes would not have surprised Hawthorne, who added to his admiration for Bunyan and for Jackson a warm understanding of 'the profound, pathetic humor' of Cervantes. Through such symbolical figures Melville discloses what wealth of suffering humanity he believed to be pitted in the dynamic struggle against evil. By this full-voiced affirmation of democratic dignity, even of divine equality, he reveals also with what assurance he felt that a great theme could be created from the common stuff of American life. Indeed, he lets us enter the very avenues through which he was then creating one.

. . . Notwithstanding the depth of his feeling for 'the kingly commons,' Melville knew the strength of the contrast between the great individual and the inert mass. He expressed it in Ahab's power to coerce all the rest within the sphere of 'the Leyden jar of his own magnetic life.' Melville himself was caught and fascinated by his hero. He asserted from the outset that he was dealing with 'a man of greatly superior natural force, with a globular brain and a ponderous heart . . . one in a whole nation's census – a mighty pageant creature, formed for noble tragedies.' To such lengths did he go in building up his old whale hunter to the stature of a Shakespearean king. But he was struck at the same time by the obverse side, and concluded his first adumbration of the still unseen captain by adding that 'all men tragically great are made so through a certain morbidness. Be sure of this, O young ambition, all mortal greatness is but disease.'

This electric attraction and repulsion runs through Melville's whole portrayal from the moment when, in this same chapter describing Ishmael's first boarding of the ship, Captain Peleg forewarns him that Captain Ahab is 'a grand, ungodly, god-like man . . .'

. . . The implications of the contrasting terms, 'ungodly' and 'god-like,' come out only as we follow the captain's subsequent career. But their very choice shows Melville's sensitiveness to what was happening in his time. Anyone concerned with orthodoxy holds that spiritual decadence of the nineteenth century can be measured according to the alteration in the object of its belief from God-Man to Man-God, and to the corresponding shift in emphasis from Incarnation to Deification. Melville did not use those terms, but he had been responsive himself to that alteration, from belief in the salvation of man through the mercy and grace of a sovereign God, to belief in the potential divinity in every man. That alteration centered around the Crucifixion. By Melville's time, and especially in protestant, democratic America, the emphasis was no longer on God become Man, on the unique birth and Divinity of the Christ, who was killed and died back into eternal life; but on the rebel killed by an unworthy society, on Man become the

Messiah, become God. That celebration of Man's triumph involved also the loss of several important attitudes: that there was anything more important than the individual; that he might find his completion in something greater than himself; that the real basis for human brotherhood was not in humanitarianism but in men's common aspiration and fallibility, in their humility before God.

The relevance of these reflections to Ahab's tragedy emerges as we see how overwhelmingly he assumes the center of the stage. At the end of the account of what the captain found symbolized in *Moby-Dick*, of why he was intent on an audacious and immitigable revenge, Melville showed how this fixed resolve could sway all before it. There was none who could stand up against him in this crew, composed chiefly 'of mongrel renegades, and castaways, and cannibals – morally enfeebled, also, by the incompetence of mere unaided virtue or right-mindedness in Starbuck, the invulnerable jollity of indifference and recklessness in Stubb, and the pervading mediocrity in Flask.' But Ahab's absolute domination carried Melville even farther; it caused him to drop what had seemed to be one of his major themes – the relation between Ishmael and Queequeg, to abandon all development or even subsequent mention of Bulkington, the barrel-chested demigod whom he had introduced, at the Spouter Inn, as a natural seeker for truth. To a degree even beyond what Melville may have intended, all other personalities, all other human relations became dwarfed before Ahab's purpose.

. . . A concentrated view of Ahab will disclose that he was born from the matrix of Melville's age. He is an embodiment of his author's most profound response to the problem of the free individual will *in extremis*.

Melville's first detailed characterization of him stresses his apartness and his suffering, his 'infinity of firmest fortitude,' and yet the 'crucifixion in his face.' His driven mind has already lost all touch with pleasure of the senses. He can no longer relish his pipe, and tosses it moodily into the sea. He looks at the sunset, and reflects that it soothes him no more: 'This lovely light, it lights not me; all loveliness is anguish to me, since I can ne'er enjoy. Gifted with the high perception, I lack the low, enjoying power; damned, most subtly and most malignantly! damned in the midst of Paradise!' . . .

. . . This cleavage [between perception and feeling] is at the root of Ahab's dilemma. He can see nothing but his own burning thoughts since he no longer shares in any normal fellow-feelings. His resolve to take it upon himself to seek out and annihilate the source of malignity, is god-like, for it represents human effort in its highest reach. But as he himself declares, it is likewise 'demoniac,' the sanity of a controlled madness. The control depends upon 'that certain sultanism of his brain,' which cunningly builds its power over the others into an 'irresistible dictatorship.' At the moment of the initial announcement of his vengeance, he rises to a staggering *hubris*, as he shouts, 'Who's over me?' Starbuck, powerless before such madness, can only think: 'Horrible old man! Who's over him he cries; – ay, he would be a democrat to all above; look how he lords it over all below!' Yet Starbuck is forced not simply to resent but to pity him, since he reads in the lurid eyes the captain's desperation. And in sleep, when alone the grip of the conscious mind has been relaxed, Ahab's tortured soul shrieks out in nightmares, in its frantic effort to escape from the drive of his obsession. At such moments Melville finds an image for his state in calling him a Prometheus whose intense thinking has created the vulture that feeds upon his heart for ever.

. . . Ahab's career, like that of the protagonists of many of the Elizabethan tragedies of revenge, has revealed him as both hero and villain. Ordinary men are no match for him. His superiorities of mind and will, of courage and conviction have exalted him above the sphere of anything petty or ignoble. Yet it is repeatedly affirmed that he is a monomaniac, and that his fixed idea, his hatred of the whale as the symbol of malignity, has carried him into the toils of a diabolic bond. The contrasting halves of his nature cannot be summed up better than in the 'ungodly, god-like' of Captain Peleg's description.

The meaning of his tragedy is involved with his conception of the rigid Fate to which he is chained. This conception runs likewise through Ishmael's comments. The *Pequod* is described as 'the sometimes madly merry and predestinated craft.' In Moby-Dick's final desperate rush against its bow, he vibrated 'his predestinating head': 'Retribution, swift vengeance, eternal malice were in his whole aspect.' The problem of determinism was part of the residue of Puritanism which Melville inherited. . . .

. . . The result of Ahab's Fatalism is that his tragedy admits no adequate moral recognition. The catharsis is, therefore, partially frustrated, since we cannot respond, as we can in *Lear*, to Ahab's deliverance from the evil forces in which he has been immersed. He is held to the end in his Faustian bond to the devil. Moreover, unlike both the sixteenth- and the nineteenth-century Faust, he never really struggles to escape from it. Although his tortured soul cries out in his sleep, during his waking hours his mind and will are dominant, and inflexible. When talking with Pip and Starbuck, he perceives the human consequences of his action. He is momentarily touched, but he is not moved from his insistence that his course is necessary. In his death therefore – a death that engulfs so many others – colossal pride meets its rightful end, and there can be no unmixed pity for him as a human being. . . .

. . . Responsive to the shaping forces of his age as only men of passionate imagination are, even Melville can hardly have been fully aware of how symbolical an American hero he had fashioned in Ahab. The length to which the captain carried his belief in the fixity of Fate makes a searching comment on the theological decay that conditioned Melville's thought. He recognized the inadequacy of transcendentalism on most of the essential problems; but when he tried to reassert the significance of Original Sin, there was no orthodoxy that he could accept. When he examined the dying Calvinism in which he had been brought up, his mind could discover there only the Manichean heresy, which its founders had staunchly repudiated. Its determinism became for him the drastic distortion that he projected in Ahab's career, wherein there was no possibility of regeneration since there remained no effectual faith in the existence of divine grace. The severe, bleak, and uninspired Presbyterian church of Melville's experience had driven him inevitably into questioning even the goodness of the Biblical God.

On the other hand, he could find no security in throwing over all the restraints of dogma, and exalting the god-like man. If the will was free, as the new faith insisted, Melville knew that it was free to do evil as well as to do good. He could not rest happy with Emerson's declaration that if he turned out to be the devil's child, why then he would live from the devil. For Melville had envisaged the fate of just such a man in Ahab. He had also seen in Ahab the destruction that must overtake the Man-God, the self-appointed Messiah. . . . And the captain's career is prophetic of many others in the history of later nineteenth-century America. Man's confidence in his own unaided resources has seldom been carried farther than during that era in this country. The strong-willed individuals who seized the land and gutted the forests and built the railroads were no longer troubled with Ahab's obsessive sense of evil, since theology had receded even farther into their backgrounds. But their drives were as relentless as his, and they were to prove like him in many other ways also, as they went on to become the empire builders of the post-Civil War world. They tended to be as dead to enjoyment as he, as blind to everything but their one pursuit, as unmoved by fear or sympathy, as confident in assuming an identification of their wills with immutable plan or manifest destiny, as liable to regard other men as merely arms and legs for the fulfilment of their purposes, and, finally, as arid and exhausted in their burnt-out souls. Without deliberately intending it, but by virtue of his intense concern with the precariously maintained values of democratic Christianity, which he saw everywhere being threatened or broken down, Melville created in Ahab's tragedy a fearful symbol of the self-enclosed individualism that, carried to its furthest extreme, brings disaster both upon itself and upon the group of which it is part.

. . . Ahab's savagery, not unlike that of a Hebrew prophet, has rejected the warmly material pantheism of the Greeks; but Melville's breadth has effected, not a fusion, but a unique counterpoint of both. The reason why the values of both Pan and Jehovah were not merely words to him, as they are to most men, is that he had relived them for himself in his own body and mind, and especially in his imagination. This means that he had cut through the dead tissues of the culture of his day, and had rediscovered the primitive and enduring nature of man. . . . it is significant of Melville's difference from Emerson that he did not conceive of art as an ever higher and more refined ascent of the mind. He wanted nothing less than the whole of life. He symbolized its vast and terrifying forces when he likened Ahab's 'darker, deeper' part to those hidden antiquities beneath the Hotel de Cluny, where man's 'root of grandeur, his whole awful essence sits in bearded state.' The flavor of that image is even more Biblical than Greek. It takes man beyond history to the source of his elemental energies.[6] □

To go 'beyond history' to the source of such 'elemental energies' is to enter the realm of myth. Largely under the influence of Matthiessen, American literary criticism was dominated by the study of myth from the 1940s up to the 1970s (and beyond). The primary concern of critical writing about America was the examination and explication – in relation to a fairly narrow set of 'classic' American texts – of the founding myths upon which American ideology was felt to be based. As one of these key documents, *Moby-Dick* was read as a reflection of American myths of the frontier, of rugged individualism, of the land of opportunity, of freedom and democracy, among many others. Examples of this type of 'myth-criticism' are given in the next chapter. The further two pieces in this chapter are important because they can be seen to be setting up some of the mythic terms applied to *Moby-Dick* by later criticism. Interestingly, their examples derive from both 'high' and 'popular' cultures. They thus articulate a sense of Melville's America as a hybrid culture, one where Shakespeare and Homer can co-exist with Frontier Tales, Barnum's Circus and the forces of emerging capitalism.

Space is the starting myth for the next extract, which is selected from the magnificently eccentric, yet scholarly and poetic study of Melville, *Call Me Ishmael*, by Charles Olson. A one-time aspiring politician in the Democratic Party, Olson had, after the war and at around the time that he wrote his study of Melville, given up politics in favour of poetry. In the 1950s he was Rector of the famous Black Mountain College in North Carolina, a position which means that he is probably the single, most influential figure in the experimental arts of post-war America. Olson was born in Worcester, and spent most of his life in Gloucester, Massachusetts, a small fishing town near Boston. This accounts for his acute ear for *Moby-Dick*'s seafaring language, and his deep understanding of the tensions of whaling as an industry. Along with these 'native' resources, he also brought to Melville studies the first serious and scholarly work on Melville's use of Shakespeare. As the first scholar to carefully read, and make critical use of, the annotations that Melville himself had made in his copy of Shakespeare's plays, his researches had a deep influence on Matthiessen's reading of *Moby-Dick*. As we shall see, though, Olson's writing on *Moby-Dick* is anything but dry and scholarly. In its energy, playfulness and high intelligence his voice is a perfect match for that which he hears throughout *Moby-Dick*:

■ I take SPACE to be the central fact to man born in America, from Folsom cave to now. I spell it large because it comes large here. Large, and without mercy.

It is geography at bottom, a hell of a wide land from the beginning. That made the first American story (Parkman's):[7] exploration.

Something else than a stretch of earth – seas on both sides, no barriers to contain as restless a thing as Western man was becoming in Columbus' day. That made Melville's story (part of it).

PLUS a harshness we still perpetuate, a sun like a tomahawk, small earthquakes but big tornadoes and hurrikans [sic], a river north and south in the middle of the land running out the blood.

The fulcrum of America is the Plains, half sea half land, a high sun as metal and obdurate as the iron horizon, and a man's job to square the circle.

Some men ride on such space, others have to fasten themselves like a tent stake to survive. As I see it Poe dug in and Melville mounted. They are the alternatives.

Americans still fancy themselves such democrats. But their triumphs are of the machine. It is the only master of space the average person ever knows, ox-wheel to piston, muscle to jet. It gives trajectory.

To Melville it was not the will to be free but the will to overwhelm nature that lies at the bottom of us as individuals and a people. Ahab is no democrat. Moby-Dick, antagonist, is only king of natural force, resource.

I am interested in a Melville who decided some time in 1850 to write a book about the whaling industry and what happened to a man in command of one of the most successful machines Americans had perfected up to that time – the whaleship.

This captain, Ahab by name, knew space. He rode it across seven seas. He was an able skipper, what the fishing people I was raised with call a highliner. Big catches: he brought back holds barrel full of the oil of the sperm, the light of American and European communities up to the middle of the nineteenth century.

This Ahab had gone wild. The object of his attention was something unconscionably big and white. He had become a specialist: he had all space concentrated into the form of a whale called Moby-Dick. . . .

. . . I am interested in a Melville who was long-eyed enough to understand the Pacific as part of our geography, another West, prefigured in the Plains, antithetical.

The beginning of man was salt sea, and the perpetual reverberation of that great ancient fact, constantly renewed in the unfolding of life in every human individual, is the single important fact about Melville. Pelagic.

He had the tradition in him, deep, in his brain, his words, the salt beat of his blood. He had the sea of himself in a vigorous, stricken way, as Poe the street. It enabled him to draw up from Shakespeare. It made Noah, and Moses, contemporary to him. History was ritual and repetition when Melville's imagination was at its own proper beat.

It was an older sense than the European man's, more to do with magic than culture. Magic, which, in contrast to worship, is all black. For magic has one purpose: compel men or non-human forces to do one's will. Like Ahab, American, one aim: lordship over nature.

I am willing to ride Melville's image of man, whale and ocean to find in him prophecies, lessons he himself would not have spelled out. A hundred years gives us an advantage. For Melville was as much larger than himself as Ahab's hate. He was a plunger. He knew how to take a chance.

The man made a mess of things. He got all balled up with Christ. He made a white marriage. He had one son die of tuberculosis, the other shoot himself. He only rode his own space once – *Moby-Dick*. He had to be wild or he was nothing in particular. He had to go fast, like an American, or he was all torpor. Half horse half alligator.

Melville took an awful licking. He was bound to. He was an original, aboriginal. A beginner. It happens that way to the dreaming men it takes to discover America.

. . . Beginner – and interested in beginnings. Melville had a way of reaching back through time until he got history pushed back so far he turned time into space. He was like a migrant backtrailing to Asia, some Inca trying to find a lost home.

We are the last 'first' people. We forget that. We act big, misuse our land, ourselves. We lose our own primary.

Melville went back, to discover us, to come forward. He got as far as *Moby-Dick*.

... He had a pull to the origin of things, the first day, the first man, the unknown sea, Betelgeuse, the buried continent. From passive places his imagination sprang a harpoon.

He sought prime. He had the coldness we have, but he warmed himself by first fires after Flood. It gave him the power to find the lost past of America, the unfound present, and make a myth, *Moby-Dick*, for a people of Ishmaels.

The thing got away from him. It does, from us. We make AHAB, the WHITE WHALE, and lose them.

... Whitman we have called our greatest voice because he gave us hope. Melville is the truer man. He lived intensely his people's wrong, their guilt. But he remembered the first dream. The White Whale is more accurate than *Leaves of Grass*.[8] Because it is America, all of her space, the malice, the root.

... Don't think whaling was any different from any other American industry. The first men in it, the leaders, explorers, were WORKERS. The money and the glory came later, on top with the exploiters. And the force went down, stayed where it always does, at the underpaid bottom. Where the worker is after the leader is gone.

Whaling started, like so many American industries, as a collective, communal affair. See any history of Sag Harbour or Nantucket. And as late as 1850 there were still skippers to remember the days when they knew the fathers of every man in their crew. But it was already a sweated industry by the time Melville was a hand on a lay (1841–3).

THE TRICK – then as now:

reduce labor costs lower than worker's efficiency – during the 1840s and '50s it cost the owners 15 cents and 30 cents a day to feed each crew member

combine inefficient workers and such costs by maintaining lowest wages and miserable working conditions. ...

THE RESULT: by the 1840s the crews were the bottom dogs of all nations and all races. Of the 18,000 men (Melville above) *one-half* ranked as green hands[9] and more than *two-thirds* deserted every voyage.

There were so many Pacific natives like Queequeg, the second colored harpooner, that a section of Nantucket came to be known as New Guinea.

There were so many Portuguese from the Islands that a section of New Bedford was called Fayal.

The third of Melville's harpooneers was the imperial African Negro Ahasuerus Daggoo.

For bottom dogs made pretty SEE the balletic chapter called MID-NIGHT, FORECASTLE, in *Moby-Dick*.

. . . So, if you want to know why Melville nailed us in *Moby-Dick*, consider whaling. Consider whaling as FRONTIER, and INDUSTRY. A product wanted, men got it: big business. The Pacific as Sweatshop. Man, led, against the biggest damndest creature nature uncorks. The whaleship as factory, the whaleboat the precision instrument. The 1840s: the New West in the saddle and Melville No. 20 of a rough and bastard crew. Are they the essentials?

. . . Melville didn't put it all on the surface of *Moby-Dick*. You'll find the frontier all right, and Andrew Jackson regarded as heavyweight champion (READ end of first KNIGHTS AND SQUIRES chapter for finest rhetoric of democracy). And the technic of an industry analysed, scrupulously described. But no economics. Jefferson and John Adams observed that in their young days very few men had thought about 'government', there were very few writers on 'government'. Yes, the year *Moby-Dick* was being finished Marx was writing letters to the N. Y. *Daily Tribune*. But Melville . . .

Lear and *Moby-Dick*

It was *Lear* that had the deep creative impact. In *Moby-Dick* the use is pervasive. That its use is also the most implicit of any play serves merely to enforce a law of the imagination, for what has stirred Melville's own most is heaved out, like Cordelia's heart, with most tardiness.

In the Hawthorne-Mosses article it is to Lear's speeches that Melville points to prove Shakespeare's insinuations of 'the things we feel to be so terrifically true':

Tormented into desperation, Lear, the frantic king, tears off the mask, and speaks the same madness of vital truth.

His copy of the play is marked more heavily than any of the others but *Antony and Cleopatra*. Of the characters the Fool and Edmund receive the attention. . . . For Melville sees the Fool as the Shakespeare he would have liked more of, not one who refrained from hinting what he knew.

Melville is terrified by Edmund who took his fierce quality in the lusty stealth of nature and who, in his evil, leagued with that world whose thick rotundity Lear would strike flat.

 . . . Melville is dumb with horror at the close, blood-stop double meaning of Shakespeare's language in the scene of the blinding of Gloucester. His comment is an exclamation: 'Terrific!' When Regan calls Gloucester 'Ingrateful fox!'[10] Melville writes:

Here's a touch Shakespearean – *Regan* talks of *ingratitude*!

First causes were Melville's peculiar preoccupation. He concentrates on an Edmund, a Regan – and the world of *Lear*, which is almost generated by such creatures, lies directly behind the creation of an Ahab, a Fedallah and the White, lovely, monstrous Whale.

Melville found answers in the darkness of *Lear*. Not on the weak goodness of an Albany who thinks to exclude evil from good by a remark as neat and corrective as Eliphaz in the Book of Job:

Wisdom and goodness to the vile seem vile;
Filths savour but themselves.[11]

The ambiguities do not resolve themselves by such 'rightmindedness'. Albany is a Starbuck.

Melville turned rather to men who suffered as Job suffered – to Lear and Edgar and Gloucester. Judged by his markings upon the scene in which Edgar discovers, with a hot burst in his heart, his father's blindness, Melville perceived what suggests itself as a symbol so inherent to the play as to leave one amazed it has not been more often observed – that to lose the eye and the capacity to see, to lose the physical organ, 'vile jelly', is to gain spiritual sight.

The crucifixion in *Lear* is not of the limbs on a crossbeam, but of the eyes put out, the eyes of pride too sharp for feeling. Lear himself in the storm scene senses it, but Gloucester blind speaks it: 'I stumbled when I saw.'

 . . . What moves Melville is the stricken goodness of a Lear, a Gloucester, and Edgar, who in suffering feel and thus probe more closely to the truth. Melville is to put Ahab through this humbling.

Shakespeare drew *Lear* out of what Melville called 'the infinite obscure of his background'. It was most kin to Melville. He uses it as an immediate obscure around his own world of *Moby-Dick*. . . .

Shakespeare, concluded

Melville was no naive democrat. He recognized the persistence of the 'great man' and faced, in 1850, what we have faced in the twentieth century. At the time of the rise of the common man Melville wrote a tragedy out of the rise, and the fall, of uncommon Ahab.

. . . A whaleship reminded Melville of two things: (1) democracy had not rid itself of overlords; (2) the common man, however free, leans on a leader, the leader, however dedicated, leans on a straw. He pitched his tragedy right there. America, 1850, was his GIVEN:

'a poor old whale-hunter' the great man;
fate, the chase of the sperm whale, plot (economics is the administration of scarce resources);
the crew the commons, the captain over them;

EQUALS

tragedy.

. . . As the strongest literary force Shakespeare caused Melville to approach tragedy in terms of the drama. As the strongest social force America caused him to approach tragedy in terms of democracy.

It was not difficult for Melville to reconcile the two. Because of his perception of America: Ahab.

It has to do with size, and how you value it. You can approach BIG America and spread yourself like a pancake, sing her stretch as Whitman did, be puffed up as we are over PRODUCTION. It's easy. THE AMERICAN WAY. Soft. Turns out paper cups, lies flat on the brush. N.G.[12]

Or recognize that our power is simply QUANTITY. Without considering purpose. Easy too. That is, so long as we continue to be INGENIOUS about machines, and have the resources.

Or you can take an attitude, the creative vantage. See her as OBJECT in MOTION, something to be shaped, for use.

. . . Melville did his job. He calculated, and cast Ahab. BIG, first of all. ENERGY, next. PURPOSE: lordship over nature. SPEED: of the brain. DIRECTION: vengeance. COST: the people, the Crew.

Ahab is the FACT, the Crew the IDEA. The Crew is where what America stands for got into *Moby-Dick*. They're what we imagine democracy to be. They're Melville's addition to tragedy as he took it from Shakespeare. He had to do more with the people than offstage shouts in a Julius Caesar. This was the difference a Declaration of Independence made.[13]

. . . To MAGNIFY is the mark of *Moby-Dick*. As with workers, cast-aways, so with the scope and space of the sea, the prose, the Whale, the Ship and, OVER ALL, the Captain. It is the technical act compelled by the American fact. Cubits of tragic stature. Put it this way. Three forces operated to bring about the dimensions of *Moby-Dick*: Melville, a man of MYTH, antemosaic; an experience of SPACE, its power and price, America; and ancient magnitudes of TRAGEDY, Shakespeare.[14] □

In many ways, Olson's essay can be seen to be a development of the concerns that D.H. Lawrence had noticed in *Moby-Dick* a quarter of a century earlier. For what underlies Olson's reading of Melville is a concern with the myths of the American people. The urge of these 'last "first" people' to carve out space for themselves on the continent is expressed in Ahab's mythical pursuit of the white whale. But, Olson sees that *Moby-Dick* also analyses this urge in the attention it gives to whaling as a declining industry. The excitement of Olson's reading of Melville stems from his ability to animate a sense of how *Moby-Dick* is an accomplished literary realisation of the political and cultural tensions of antebellum America. *Moby-Dick* is, for Olson, the 'last "first"' exploration of America's growing capitalist economy.

The final extract in this chapter is from Richard Chase's book *Herman Melville: A Critical Study*. The myth sustaining Chase's eloquent argument about *Moby-Dick* is one of the heterogeneity of American culture. If *Moby-Dick* is an epic, moreover *the* American epic, then this is because its mythic models are both European and American, derived from an idea of America as a cultural 'melting-pot'. Ahab is, again, the problematic hero in this reading. Whilst he is described as a Christ-like figure, his depiction, for Chase, also makes him seem to be a native American *shaman*, or healing magician. If Ahab is a modern Prometheus, the figure who, in classical myth, stole fire from the Olympian gods to benefit mankind, then he is also a charlatan showman like Phineas T. Barnum who, in the mid-nineteenth century, stole the credulity of his audiences across America to benefit his bank balance. These are all important cultural images not simply *of* America in the nineteenth century, but *for* America following World War Two. With them Chase furnishes post-war America with an epic of complexity and genius, a *Moby-Dick* whose mythic heart confirms, though belatedly, America's arrival as a culture of world-class importance.

■ I should say that Ahab is as much the American of his time as was Homer's Odysseus the Greek of his time or Joyce's Leopold Bloom the Jew of his time. He is the American cultural image: the captain of industry and of his soul; the exploiter of nature who severs his own attachment to nature and exploits himself out of existence; the good progressive American; the master of the most beautifully contrived machine of his time; the builder of new worlds whose ultimate spiritual superficiality drives him first to assume an uneasy kingship and a blind, destructive motive of revenge, and then gradually reduces him to a pure, abstract fury on whose inhuman power he rides off into eternity, leaving nothing behind but disaster for the races of the world and an ambiguous memory of the American flair which accompanied the disaster and was the only hint of moral meaning or of solace for the future or for the dead at the bottom of the Pacific. . . . Thus Melville constructs Ahab out of many myths and many men.

Ahab is a primitive magician who tries to coerce man and the universe by compulsive ritual; and again like the magicians, he insults and castigates his god. He is the *shaman*, that is, the religious leader (common among certain tribes of American Indians) who cuts himself off from society to undergo his private ordeal, through which he attains some of the knowledge and power of the gods. The *shaman* is usually deeply neurotic and sometimes epileptic – the saviour with the neurosis. Again, Ahab is the culture hero (though a false one) who kills monsters, making man's life possible.

But Ahab also resembles an even more momentous mythical being: Christ. Were he not so committed to his 'monomaniac' pursuit of the whale, Ahab might have been the source of genial spirits and reviving life. He is 'stricken' and 'blasted,' says Captain Peleg, but 'Ahab has his humanities.' And in the beautiful chapter called 'The Symphony,' Ahab, overcome for a moment by the insinuating feminine vitalities of the Pacific air, is seen to shed a tear into the sea, a tear of compassion for the suffering in the universe. . . . Like the Saviour, Ahab is preceded by a prophet; namely, the demented Elijah, who so persistently importunes Ishmael and Queequeg with his divinations shortly before the *Pequod* sets sail. . . . we are told that Ahab sleeps 'with clenched hands, and wakes with his own bloody nails in his palms.' The pun is unavoidable. But there is this difference between Ahab and Christ: these are Ahab's own nails. He is not a sacrifice; he is a suicide.

. . . But Ahab's is [a] Promethean task, and as the *Pequod* searches for Moby-Dick, Ahab becomes more and more the Promethean type of hero. Modern classical scholars suppose that Prometheus was a fire-god; and so Melville considers him. . . . [He knows that] fire is a double principle: it can create and it can destroy; and without perpetual tending, the act of creation becomes itself an act of destruction.

Ahab has learned this lesson well. And, like Prometheus, he is the possessor of a secret which God, whom he addresses as 'my fiery father,' does not know. In the tortured and difficult chapter called 'The Candles,' Ahab hurls his challenge at God, who has laid His 'burning finger' on the *Pequod* as it sails through an electric storm.

'   . . . Ahab knows that his fiery father, though in fatal control of the *Pequod*, is transcended by a greater power from which the fiery father derives whatever of creativeness he has. Again we hear the suffering Prometheus who taunts Zeus: 'there is some unsuffusing thing beyond thee, thou clear spirit, to whom all thy eternity is but time, all thy creativeness mechanical.' . . . At these times, he [Ahab] is able to defy the annihilating god with the only weapon which can conquer him – the assertion of humanness. 'In the midst of the personified impersonal, a personality stands here.' Yet his premonition tells him that the act of defiance will finally rob him of personality, will turn out to be the act of suicide – that where the true Prometheus succeeded, Ahab, the false Prometheus, will fail.

. . . The predicament of Ahab as Prometheus is, in certain senses, the Puritan predicament; and his failure is the Puritan failure. Having cut himself off from society, having become in his 'radical protestantism' . . . an 'individualist,' Ahab turns in upon himself and eats away his own vitality.

. . . Once Melville had conceived and created Ahab, the story of the disintegration of his personality, symbolizing, as it does, the primeval and universal father-son relationship, could not fail to be a spectacle that was unique in its magnificence and its evocation of pity and wonder. What was needed to complete the picture was a compelling, external symbol of the father.

Moby-Dick is God incarnate in the whale. . . . The inscrutable secrecy, the profound wisdom of God are in Moby-Dick. . . . The horror, too, of God as tyrant and annihilator is in Moby-Dick. . . . Imagining an American Olympus, Melville says that if we ever people our naked, overbearing heaven with divinities, . . . 'the great Sperm Whale shall lord it.'

. . . The White Whale does not represent evil, as is usually said. As a divinity, he is an exceedingly complex being. Yet the question of what Moby-Dick represents can be answered very simply. He represents purity, the purity of an inviolable spiritual rectitude which, since it cannot be discovered among the imperfections of life, must be sought in death. Ahab's purpose is to die in one final heraldic gesture of righteousness – pure, meaningless, inhuman, violent. All the terrific action of his career is directed toward this ultimate stasis, this perfect objectification of his own inner image of self-destruction in which all of life freezes into the representation of death, in which, finally, all the colours of the rainbow disappear into the whiteness of the whale.

. . . Melville correctly pictures the soul of Ahab as the contested battleground of the gods, saviours, and heroes of the Western world. . . . There is a magnificent felicity in the final image of *Moby-Dick* – this purifying act of annihilation which, it may be, recalls from the dim past some awful white nakedness of flesh that blotted out the mind and petrified the hapless beholder and which, with a tender lyricism, translates this fierce encounter into a symbolic smash-up of the American world. . . . The American ship, with the tribes and complexions of the world aboard, thus meets its doom. And the very flag undulates through the final scene: the red of Tashtego's pennant; the whiteness of the whale; the roofless blue of the Pacific spaces. And then, nothing is left save the whiteness of Death in its appalling domesticity with Space. But the heraldic tableau is broken and by some obscure saving grace the resurrected life wills to set the world in motion again. Ishmael floats on the coffin-lifebuoy, a lost American brooding over the vast and timeless sea.

. . . *Moby-Dick*, it does the book no disservice to admit it, is a literary-scientific extravaganza with very clear affinities to Barnum's showmanship. The fact that the tale winds up in anything but a hoax does not invalidate the relationship. Indeed, that is Melville's point: it looks like a hoax, but woe to him who allows himself the comfortable belief that it *is* a hoax.

. . . At its lower levels, *Moby-Dick* is pure showmanship of the peculiarly American kind, science tacitly tending toward the fabulous, normality subtly misshaping itself into monstrosity, fact covertly throwing off images of itself and creating an elusive world of fantasy.

. . . Yet Moby-Dick is no hoax, or rather, the emotions and ideas he excites are no hoax. Looking back after one hundred years, we perceive a certain unity in American culture which embraces the kinds of thought and feeling represented by Barnum's scientific museum and Melville's *Moby-Dick*. Yet the difference is that most important of all differences: the one between art and other forms of organizing experience. Barnum's use of the peculiarly American amalgam of fact and fantasy served in effect to affirm that the high and difficult emotions of wonder and exaltation did not really exist or did not need to be taken seriously, for he always dispersed troublesome phantoms by the hoax, which came upon the stage like a *deus ex machina* to wind up the play. . . . But *Moby-Dick* uses the folk spirit differently. If there is a hoax, it is directed against those who are looking for a hoax. Like any work of art, it is uncompromising in its emotions and intellectual quality. It is as resolutely against the American grain as it is resolutely with it.

. . . *Moby-Dick* is an American epic; so far it seems to be *the* American epic. An epic is the response of a poet to the body of received and implicit myth which his culture bequeaths to him. The myth his society bequeathed to Homer was a good deal more complete, more established, more complex, more elegant than the myth Melville's culture bequeathed to him. It is fortunate that Melville had the American knack of exploitation, which allowed him to find more in the folk myths of his country than one might have thought was there . . .

. . . But there *is* a received and implicit myth in *Moby-Dick*. The high perception makes it into the universal allegory; the low enjoying power establishes it as the folk foundation. This myth is capitalism. *Moby-Dick* remains intransigently a story of the whaling industry; a hymn to the technical skill of the heroes and the marvelous perfection of their machine and to the majesty of what they appropriate from the sea – the sheer weight, mass, wealth, power, and beauty of the whale's body; a saga of the exploitation of nature and man for profit or for righteousness (for our American capitalism has had spiritual motives and spiritual weaknesses and strengths never imagined by Marx). There is no doubt that the voyage is an industrial enterprise bossed by Ahab, the nineteenth-century type of the manager of an absentee-owned plant. All the facts are there: the wage of the sailor, the occupational hazards, the deployment of the personnel in the field, the precautions to be taken and the risks to be calculated in each operation, the nature and care of the various kinds of equipment – all the intricate parts and economy of the machine which reduced the whale by a series of lovingly described processes to the useful oil in the casks. Almost every process included the possibility that a man might be killed; if so, his death was at once the murder of an industrial worker and the ritual sacrifice of a hero.

The hunt for the White Whale is anything but an abandonment of the capitalist myth. Ahab may hoot at the Nantucket market, but he never hoots at capitalism. Quite the contrary, he accepts its full disastrous implications. Ahab is the epic transmutation of the American free enterpriser, and the White Whale is the transmutation of the implicit spiritual meaning of free enterprise. The meaning is clear: the American who exploits nature soon learns to pursue a mysterious and dangerous ideal, and this pursuit transforms him into the likeness of what he pursues.

. . . 'I try all things,' says Melville in *Moby-Dick*. 'I achieve what I can.' His plight as an epic writer was less desperate than his words might imply, for he did not have to invent the central epic theme. That was given to him by his culture; he had merely to recognize it, though that was no doubt difficult enough. What he had to do was adduce the body of supporting mythology, clothe the skeleton with flesh and the habiliments of style. For this purpose 'all things' were grist for the mill – jokes, puns, dances, ceremonies, side shows, catalogues, scientific discourses, orations, meditations, confessions, sermons, tall tales, redactions of Old World mythologies, and literary conventions. Much more so than the Homeric epic, *Moby-Dick* remains the willed, self-generating, and idiosyncratic act of a partly lost and un-cultured man. But this is the typical act of the American genius.[15] □

We have seen in this chapter that critical readings of *Moby-Dick* in the 1940s, by placing the novel as a central text within an American Renaissance that took place in the mid-nineteenth century, all attempt to use *Moby-Dick* to unlock and examine what they assume to be fundamental myths of American identity. Chase's appeal, in his final sentences quoted above, to the image of America as a cultural melting-pot is an example of this. Such readings, however, fail to acknowledge the extent to which myths and images like this derive from the powerfully persuasive perspective of a white, Anglo-Saxon, protestant, and male version of American culture. In much the same way that the image of America as a cultural melting-pot has been used to promote a particular political version of America, based on Hector St Jean de Crèvecoeur's romantic and Eurocentric view of American democracy, *Moby-Dick* criticism has promoted a particular version of America as a land of mythic heroes, bent on taming the wilderness on a mission for democracy. The problems of reading *Moby-Dick* in this way have received concerted critical attention only since the 1980s, when, as a result of post-structuralist and postmodern critical practices, the ideological tensions involved in reading, and writing about, *Moby-Dick* have been made more explicit. The next chapter, however, will look at the continuing use of 'the mythic method' in critical reactions to *Moby-Dick* throughout the 1950s, and to the place of *Moby-Dick* in the growth and development of American Studies.

CHAPTER FOUR

The 1950s: 'Myth Criticism' and the Growth of American Studies

WRITING IN 1957, Henry Nash Smith was one of the first critics to discuss the newly emerging academic discipline of American Studies. He noted that American Studies represented the 'desire to study American culture as a whole', rather than within discrete disciplines that are (particularly) sociological or literary.[1] Because, Nash argues, of its attempts to assess the 'ambiguous relation between works of art and the culture in which they occur', American Studies must develop a new method of inquiry, one of 'principled opportunism' that draws from a variety of different disciplinary methods and resources.[2] He calls, then, for an American Studies that is as heterogeneous as American culture itself. What underpins this study of America 'as a whole' is a belief that myth and symbol are cultural phenomena. The underlying pattern of American culture can therefore be discovered through the proper reading and analysis of its dominant myths and symbols.[3] Given the steady growth of serious academic interest in *Moby-Dick* after the war, and the boost this received with the 1951 centenary of its publication, it is not surprising that across the 1950s critical discussion of *Moby-Dick* came to be seen as highly important in the growth and development of American Studies. In this period of its critical history, *Moby-Dick*'s use of myth and symbol, and its own seemingly opportunistic drawing upon heterogeneous resources, were the focus of a plethora of literary, cultural and sociological interpretations.

All three pieces which make up this chapter share the assumption that the analysis of myth and symbol is the key to an understanding of *Moby-Dick*. As exercises in 'myth criticism', though, they vary greatly in methodology and focus. The first piece, by Henry Murray, is a psychoanalytic reading of *Moby-Dick*: its myths and symbols are those of the unconscious mind. Charles Fiedelson's study sees the book's symbols as exclusively literary, and is thus firmly planted in a 'New Critical' idea of the autonomy of art which dominated American critical practice at the time. And the final piece, by R.W.B. Lewis, is perhaps the closest to real-ising the aspirations of Henry Nash Smith for American Studies. Lewis' controlling myth which sees Americans as Adams in a new Garden of Eden, is one felt to be fundamental to American culture as a whole. Seen together, such works testify to the susceptibility of *Moby-Dick* to a huge range of different, and sometimes competing, critical readings. What is not in dispute, though, is that *Moby-Dick* is a masterpiece of extraordinarily powerful expression. Exactly what it expresses seems, as we have seen again and again throughout its history, largely dependent upon assump-tions about literature, culture and America that are brought to the text by each particular critic. If the history of *Moby-Dick* criticism in the 1950s tells us anything, it tells us that despite the best efforts to read American culture as a whole – a single unified body – that finds expression through a set of shared myths, symbols and assumptions, it is, in fact, a culture of dis-unity, one of competing myths, all of which struggle to express the particular idea of America held by each critic.

The image of America, then, which emerges in *Moby-Dick* criticism of the 1950s sounds rather pathologically unstable in its attempt to describe unity where in fact it discovers division and fracture. This is not entirely surprising: the 1950s were a time of acute and wholesale reassessment of the nature and meaning of American culture. On the one hand America was booming politically, economically and socially. Not only had the war precipitated a complete re-thinking of America's role within world politics, but post-war America, far from needing the sort of austerity measures that plagued Europe, was enjoying unprecedented prosperity. The mass consumer culture that fuelled this boom was fed images, particularly through advertising, of 'all-American values': the happy family, the refrigerator, a suburban lifestyle, and middle-class conformity. But, on the other hand, such conformity to material progress, and to such ideals of Americanness, was felt to be 'phoney' by an increasingly vociferous, and rebellious, youth culture. The booming economy served only to disguise a culture of social division, in which paranoia and suspi-cion were played out on a grand scale within the Cold War. Whilst these tensions were to lead to the upheaval of American values that took place in the civil rights movement of the 1960s, it is underneath the appar-ently calm surface of 1950s America that many of the founding myths of American ideology were already being re-examined. With its dramatic tensions, its rhetoric of freedom and compulsion, its examination of obsessive madness, and its grounding in myth and symbol, *Moby-Dick* was to play a vital role in such re-examinations of American culture.

Henry A. Murray's reading of *Moby-Dick* is the first to deal with the book in any really rigorous psychoanalytic manner. The Freudian model which he employs to illuminate the book is one of the aggression that results from the repression of 'Eros' (or sexual drive). He uses this, as it were, 'Freudian mythology' to mirror the tensions that were inherent in Melville's own psyche resulting from his moralistic, Presbyterian upbringing. This seems rather uncanny because the tension between repression and freedom to which he points seems so clearly to express the tensions of America in the 1950s as much as it does those of the puritan legacy in 1850s America. The paper was first read at William College, on 3 September 1951, as part of events commemorating the centennial of the publication of *Moby-Dick*.[4] Part of this essay's importance is the fact that it is written by a psychoanalyst, and not a literary critic. The seeming naivety of its critical methodology is balanced by the force of conviction in its reading of *Moby-Dick* as a text struggling with conceptions of evil and goodness. It provides, in this regard, then, a refreshingly new direction in Melville criticism:

■ To me, *Moby-Dick* was Beethoven's *Eroica* in words: first of all, a masterly orchestration of harmonic and melodic language, of resonating images and thoughts in varied metres. Equally compelling were the spacious sea-setting of the story, the cast of characters and their prodigious common target, the sorrow, the fury, and the terror, together with all those frequent touches, those subtle interminglings of unexampled humor, quizzical and, in the American way, extravagant, and finally the fated closure, the crown and tragic consummation of the immense yet firmly-welded whole. But still more extraordinary and portentous were the penetration and scope, the sheer audacity of the author's imagination. Here was a man who did not fly away with his surprising fantasies to some unbelievable dreamland, pale or florid, shunning the stubborn objects and gritty facts, the prosaic routines and practicalities of everyday existence. Here was a man who, on the contrary, chose these very things as vessels for his procreative powers – the whale as a naturalist, a Hunter or Cuvier, would perceive him, the business of killing whales, the whale-ship running as an oil factory, stowing-down, in fact, every mechanism and technique, each tool and gadget, that was integral to the money-minded industry of whaling. Here was a man who could describe the appearance, the concrete matter-of-factness, and the utility of each one of these natural objects, implements, and tools with the fidelity of a scientist, and, while doing this, explore it as a conceivable repository of some aspect of the human drama; then, by an imaginative tour de force, deliver a vital essence, some humorous or profound idea, coalescing with its embodiment. But still more. Differing from the symbolists of our time, here was a man who offered us essences and meanings which did not level or depreciate the objects of his contemplation. On the contrary, this loving man exalted all creatures – the mariners, renegades and castaways on board the *Pequod* – by ascribing them 'high qualities, though dark' and weaving round them 'tragic graces'. Here, in short, was a man with the myth-making powers of a Blake, a hive of significant associations, who was capable of reuniting what science had put asunder – pure perception and relevant emotion – and doing it in an exultant way that was acceptable to skepticism.

Not at first, but later, I perceived the crucial difference between Melville's dramatic animations of nature and those of primitive religion-makers: both were spontaneous and uncalculated projections, but Melville's were in harmony, for the most part, with scientific knowledge, because they had been recognized as projections, checked, and modified. Here, then, was a man who might redeem us from the virtue of an incredible subjective belief, on the one side, and from the virtue of a deadly objective rationality, on the other.

For these and other reasons the reading of *Moby-Dick* – coming before Psychology – left a stupendous reverberating imprint, too lively to be diminished by the long series of relentless analytical operations to which I subsequently subjected it. Today, after twenty-five years of such experiments, *The Whale* is still *the* whale, more magnificent, if anything, than before.

Before coming to grips with the 'mystery' of *Moby-Dick* I should mention another providential circumstance to which all psychologists are, or should be, forever grateful, and literary critics too, since without it no complete understanding of books like *Moby-Dick* would be possible today. Ahead of us were two greatly gifted pioneers, Freud and Jung, who, with others, explored the manifold vagaries of unconscious mental processes and left for our inheritance their finely-written works. . . . Some of us psychologists have been devoting ourselves to the study of dreams, fantasies, creative productions, and projections – all of which are primarily and essentially emotional and dramatic, such stuff as myths are made of. Thus, by chance or otherwise, this branch of the tree of psychology is growing in the direction of Herman Melville.

. . . This brings me to the problem of interpreting *Moby-Dick*. Some writers have said that there is nothing to interpret: it is a plain sea story marred here and there by irrelevant ruminations. But I shall not cite the abundant proof for the now generally accepted proposition that in *Moby-Dick* Melville 'meant' something – something, I should add, which he considered 'terrifically true' but which, in the world's judgement, was so harmful 'that it were all but madness for any good man, in his own proper character, to utter or even hint of.' What seems decisive here is the passage in Melville's celebrated letter to Hawthorne: 'A sense of unspeakable security is in me this moment, on account of your having understood the book.' From this we can conclude that there *are* meanings to be understood in *Moby-Dick*, and also – may we say for our own encouragement? – that Melville's ghost will feel secure forever if modern critics can find them, and, since Hawthorne remained silent, set them forth in print. Here it might be well to remind ourselves of a crucial statement which follows the just quoted passage from Melville's letter: 'I have written a wicked book.' The implication is clear: all interpretations which fail to show that *Moby-Dick* is, in some sense, wicked have missed the author's avowed intention.

. . . My version of the main theme of *Moby-Dick* can be . . . limited to two hypotheses.

The first of them is this: Captain Ahab is an embodiment of that fallen angel or demi-god who in Christendom was variously named Lucifer, Devil, Adversary, Satan. The Church Fathers would have called Captain Ahab 'Antichrist' because he was not Satan himself but a human creature possessed of all Satan's pride and energy, 'summing up within himself,' as Irenaeus said, 'the apostasy of the devil.'

That it was Melville's intention to beget Ahab in Satan's image can hardly be doubted. He told Hawthorne that his book had been boiled in hell-fire and secretly baptized not in the name of God but in the name of the Devil. He named his tragic hero after the Old Testament ruler who 'did more to provoke the Lord God of Israel to anger than all the Kings of Israel that were before him.' King Ahab's accuser, the prophet Elijah, is also resurrected to play his original rôle, though very briefly, in Melville's testament. We are told that Captain Ahab is an 'ungodly, god-like' man who is spiritually outside Christendom. He is a well of blasphemy and defiance, of scorn and mockery for the gods – 'cricket-players and pugilists' – in his eyes. Rumor has it that he once spat in the holy goblet on the altar of the Catholic Church at Santa. 'I never saw him kneel,' says Stubb. He is associated in the text with scores of references to the Devil. He is an 'anaconda of an old man.' His self-assertive sadism is the linked antithesis of the masochistic submission preached by Father Mapple.

. . . There is some evidence that Melville was re-reading *Paradise Lost* in the summer of 1850, shortly after, let us guess, he got the idea of transforming the captain of his whale-ship into the first of all cardinal sinners who fell by pride. Anyhow, Melville's Satan is the spitting image of Milton's hero, but portrayed with deeper and subtler psychological insight, and placed where he belongs, in the heart of an enraged man.

. . . Stated in psychological concepts, Ahab is captain of the culturally repressed dispositions of human nature, that part of personality which psychoanalysts have termed the 'Id.' If this is true, his opponent, the White Whale, can be none other than the internal institution which is responsible for these repressions, namely the Freudian Superego. This then is my second hypothesis: Moby-Dick is a veritable spouting, breaching, sounding whale, a whale who, because of his whiteness, his mighty bulk and beauty, and because of one instinctive act that happened to dismember his assailant, has received the projection of Captain Ahab's Presbyterian conscience, and so may be said to embody the Old Testament Calvinistic conception of an affrighting Deity and his strict commandments, the derivative puritan ethic of nineteenth-century America, and the society that defended this ethic. Also, and most specifically, he symbolizes the zealous parents whose righteous sermonizings and corrections drove the prohibitions in so hard that a serious young man could hardly reach outside the barrier, except possibly far away among some tolerant, gracious Polynesian peoples.[5] The emphasis should be placed on that unconscious (and hence inscrutable) wall of inhibition which imprisoned the puritan's thrusting passions. 'How can the prisoner reach outside,' cries Ahab, 'except by thrusting through the wall? To me the White Whale is that wall, shoved near to me . . . I see in him outrageous strength, with an inscrutable malice sinewing it.' As a symbol of a sounding, breaching, white-dark, unconquerable New England conscience what could be better than a sounding, breaching, white-dark, unconquerable sperm whale?

. . . Since Ahab has been proclaimed 'Captain of the Id,' the simplest psychological formula for Melville's dramatic epic is this: an insurgent Id in mortal conflict with an oppressive cultural Superego. Starbuck, the First Mate, stands for the rational realistic Ego which is overpowered by the fanatical compulsiveness of the Id and dispossessed of its normally regulating functions.

. . . In *Civilization and its Discontents* Freud, out of the ripeness of his full experience, wrote that when one finds deep-seated aggression – and by this he meant aggression of the sort that Melville voiced – one can safely attribute it to the frustration of Eros. In my opinion this generalization does not hold for all men of all cultures of all times, but the probability of its being valid is extremely high in the case of an earnest, moralistic, nineteenth-century American, a Presbyterian to boot, whose anger is born of suffering, especially if this man spent an impressionable year of his life in Polynesia and returned to marry the very proper little daughter of the Chief Justice of Massachusetts, and if, in addition, he is a profoundly creative man in whose androgynic personality masculine and feminine components are integrally blended.

If it were concerned with *Moby-Dick*, the book, rather than with its author, I would call *this* my third hypothesis: Ahab-Melville's aggression was directed against the object that once harmed Eros with apparent malice and was still thwarting it with the presentiments of further retaliations. The correctness of this inference is indicated by the nature of the injury – a symbolic emasculation – that excited Ahab's ire. Initially, this threatening object was, in all likelihood, the father, later, possibly, the mother. But, as Melville plainly saw, both his parents had been fashioned by the Hebraic-Christian, American Calvinist tradition, the tradition which conceived of a deity in whose eyes Eros was depravity.

. . . If this line of reasoning is as close as I think it is to the known facts, then Melville, in the person of Ahab, assailed Calvinism in the Whale because it blocked the advance of a conscience beneficent to evolutionary love. And so, weighed in the scales of its creator, *Moby-Dick* is not a wicked book but a *good* book, and after finishing it Melville had full reason to feel, as he confessed, 'spotless as the lamb.'

But then, seen from another point, *Moby-Dick* might be judged a wicked book, not because its hero condemns an entrenched tradition, but because he is completely committed to destruction. Although Captain Ahab manifests the basic stubborn virtues of the arch-protestant and the rugged individualist carried to their limits, *this* god-defier is no Prometheus, since all thought of benefitting humanity is foreign to him. His purpose is not to make the Pacific safe for whaling, nor, when blasting at the moral order, does he have in mind a more heartening vision for the future. The religion of Eros which might once have been the secret determinant of Ahab's undertaking is never mentioned. . . . The truth is that Ahab is motivated solely by his private need to avenge a private insult. His governing philosophy is that of nihilism, the doctrine that the existing system must be shattered. . . .

If we grant that Ahab is a wicked man, what does this prove? It proves that *Moby-Dick* is a *good* book, a parable in epic form, because Melville makes a great spectacle of Ahab's wickedness and shows through the course of the narrative how such wickedness will drive a man on iron rails to an appointed nemesis. Melville adhered to the classic formula for tragedies. He could feel 'spotless as the lamb,' because he had seen to it that the huge threat to the social system, immanent in Ahab's two cardinal defects – egotistic self-inflation and unleashed wrath – was, at the end, fatefully exterminated, 'and the great shroud of the sea rolled on as it rolled five thousand years ago.' The reader has had his catharsis, equilibrium has been restored, sanity is vindicated.

. . . *Moby-Dick* may be taken as a comment on the strategic crisis of Melville's allegorical life. In portraying the consequences of Ahab's last suicidal lunge, the hero's umbilical fixation to the Whale and his death by strangling, the author signalized not only his permanent attachment to the *imago* of the mother, but the submission he had foreseen to the binding power of the parental conscience, the Superego of middle-class America. Measured against the standards of *his* day, then, Melville must be accounted a *good* man.

But does this entitle him to a place on the side of the angels? He abdicated to the conscience he condemned and his ship *Pequod*, in sinking, carried down with it the conscience he aspired to, represented by the sky-hawk, the bird of heaven. With his ideal drowned, life from then on was load and time stood still. All he had denied to love he gave, throughout a martyrdom of forty years, to death.[6] □

The speculative nature of Murray's Freudian reading of Melville has its counterpoint in the close textual analysis of *Moby-Dick* encountered in Charles Fiedelson's *Symbolism and American Literature*, from which the next extracts are taken. As with Murray, Fiedelson's interest is in the patterns of myth and symbolism in the book. Unlike Murray, though, Fiedelson does not see such patterns as indicative of concerns, be they personal or cultural, that are extrinsic to the text. If *Moby-Dick* has a mythic and symbolic structure, he argues, then this is because it is a highly wrought work of art, and should be read as such. To attempt to read its symbolism as an index – whether conscious or unconscious – of its society, or its author's state of mind, is to do a disservice to its aesthetic worth. This ideal of aesthetic autonomy, the belief, or at least the hope, that the importance of literary works of art is unaffected by social and cultural circumstances, is typical of the school of thought that dominated American literary criticism of the 1950s, the so-called 'New Criticism'. Under the influence of the critical writings of T.S. Eliot and I.A. Richards, American New Critics such as John Crowe Ransom, W.K. Wimsatt, and Cleanth Brooks believed that literary texts were able to deliver universal 'truths' of experience. They believed that a text was complex and ambiguous, not because the author's own particular emotional experience was complex and ambiguous, but because the unchanging nature of human experience is one of complexity and ambiguity.[7] Any critical response that tried to deduce the author's state of mind from a text was, they felt, bound to fail: it could only ever amount to a second-guessing of the author's intentions. Such a mistake in critical practice, the 'Intentional Fallacy' as it was named in 1946 by Wimsatt and Beardsley, indulges romantic views of authorship rather than critical and objective criteria of reading. For New Critics, then, the literary text becomes an aesthetic icon, something that is self-contained and isolated, detached from the world of everyday concerns. Fiedelson's use of such New Critical models leads him to dismiss Matthiessen's *American Renaissance*, which he feels to be too concerned with cultural, as opposed to aesthetic, matters. This is seen in the short passage that follows, from the 'Introduction' to his *Symbolism and American Literature*:

■ The first large-scale attempt to define the literary quality of American writing at its best was Matthiessen's *American Renaissance*, which is 'primarily concerned with *what* these books were as works of art,' with 'the writers' use of their own tools, their diction and rhetoric, and . . . what they could make with them.' Yet even in this magnificent work, which reorients the entire subject, the sociological and political bent of studies in American literature makes itself felt indirectly. Despite Matthiessen's emphasis on literary form, his concern with the 'artist's use of language' as 'the most sensitive index to cultural history' tends to lead him away from specifically aesthetic problems. The 'one common denominator' which he finds among the five writers treated in his book is not, in the final analysis, a common approach to the art of writing but a common theme – 'their devotion to the possibilities of democracy.'[8] □

Fiedelson's argument throughout his book is neatly encapsulated in this statement. The value of American literature is not, for him, because it reveals something about democracy, or American culture, but because it works, through its use of symbolism, as literature. If the determining myth for Matthiessen is democracy, then for Fiedelson it is aesthetics.

In his chapter on *Moby-Dick*, from which the following extract is taken, Fiedelson attempts a reading of *Moby-Dick* that attends to its 'specifically aesthetic problems'. He reads its symbolism, for example, as evidence of the book's carefully wrought artistry, through which Melville sets before the reader a 'complex of logical oppositions'. Despite his New Critical standards, however, he appears troubled by the role of Melville himself in the narration of the text. His rather makeshift solution, to claim that the voices of Melville and Ishmael 'often merge into one' in their acts of narration, does not solve the question of narrative inconsistency that his New Critical instincts tell him is one of the text's greatest aesthetic problems. However, this does mean that he devotes much critical attention to the role of Ishmael. In this respect, his reading – alongside that of Walter Bezanson which appears in the next chapter – sounds a new note in the history of *Moby-Dick* criticism. Up to this point critical attention had focused almost exclusively on Ahab, and had, consequently, read the text as a tragic drama, wherein Ahab struggles with forces of madness and vengeance, good and evil. Fiedelson sees Ishmael's role in *Moby-Dick* to be as important as that of Ahab. This lays the foundations for a gradual shift in critical attitudes toward the text that took place over the following decades. As we shall see in later chapters, Ishmael comes to greater and greater prominence, and Ahab has an increasingly backstage role in critical readings of the book. Here, Fiedelson sees, in Ishmael's Narcissistic water-gazing, a symbol of *Moby-Dick*'s aesthetic double-bind. The text reflects back our own image, but to enter the text will annihilate that image. Perhaps, unconsciously, Fiedelson here places a question-mark against the possible narcissism of his own New Critical practices:

■ . . . The voyage of Ishmael, though it lacks the desperation of Ahab's outlook, is crossed by a doubt similar to his. Water-gazing is a paradoxical activity – a search for absolute unity with objects of thought, only to discover that immediate knowledge destroys the thinker. This is the 'still deeper . . . meaning' of the story of Narcissus – to return to the first chapter [of *Moby-Dick*]. 'Because he could not grasp the tormenting, mild image he saw in the fountain, [he] plunged into it and was drowned. But that same image, we ourselves see in all rivers and oceans. It is the image of the ungraspable phantom of life; and this is the key to it all.' The image is not merely a self-reflection but the embodiment of thought, the matching phantom in the sea of forms. The phantom is ungraspable as long as we stand on the bank; and the ocean is annihilative once we dive into it.

Whatever hazards Ishmael may perceive in the alliance of 'meditation and water,' the impossibility of resolving the dilemma by simply returning to land is even more obvious in his case than in Ahab's. To send the visionary back home would be to invalidate the whole book. Ishmael is at once a character and the narrator of *Moby-Dick*, and he is a 'voyager' in both respects. The concluding paragraphs of the first chapter are not only an explanation of the sailor's motives in going to sea but also a kind of rationale of the book itself as a 'voyage.' The narrator is immersed in a drama of which the Fates, in a manner of speaking, are the 'stage managers,' since he performs a part having nothing to do with his own 'unbiased free will and discriminating judgement.' Will is the essence of self, and judgement is objective knowledge; but he is governed by the symbolic imagination, which moves in still another plane. Before him swims 'the overwhelming idea of the great whale.' In the sea, which is the field of his vision, the White Whale is the mightiest image, the summation of all the myriad shapes that succeed one another through infinite change:

The great flood-gates of the wonder-world swung open, and in the wild conceits that swayed me to my purpose, two and two there floated into my inmost soul, endless processions of the whale, and, midmost of them all, one grand hooded phantom, like a snow hill in the air.

The 'endless processions of the whale' are transitive forms that issue out of a fecund center; each procession comes 'two and two,' for each shape implies an opposite. To go whaling is to entertain these symbolic perspectives. It is significant that the narrator himself is flooded as he sets out to invade the sea. For, properly speaking, the moment of imagination is a state of becoming, and the visionary forms simultaneously are apprehended and realize themselves.

In 'The Whiteness of the Whale' the ambiguity of whiteness – its mingled beauty and horror, as exemplified in countless ways – repeats the doubleness of 'endless processions,' and 'whiteness' becomes a synonym for fluid reality, like the 'grand hooded phantom' of the earlier account. In this chapter Ishmael solicits the reader's understanding of his method; he must explain himself, he says, 'else all these chapters might be naught.' He is trying to define not only 'what the White Whale . . . was to me' but also the kind of thinking which generates that ambiguous creature: 'How is mortal man to account for it?' The apparent answer is that the double meaning of whiteness is a product of imaginative perception: 'To analyze it would seem to be impossible . . . In a matter like this, subtlety appeals to subtlety, and without imagination no man can follow another into these halls.' He who would follow Ishmael must exert the symbolic imagination, for Ishmael's 'pursuit' of the whale is the evolution of an image. Although the meanings that develop are disquieting, and the whole process tends to become a 'fiery hunt,' he has no other approach.

Ishmael, unlike most fictive narrators, is not merely a surrogate for an absentee author. Behind him, always present as a kind of *Doppelgänger*, stands Herman Melville. As Ishmael the narrator enters more deeply into his symbolic world, he increasingly becomes a presence, a visionary activity, rather than a man; we lose interest in him as an individual, and even Ishmael the sailor almost drops from the story. Ishmael the visionary is often indistinguishable from the mind of the author himself. It is Melville's own voice that utters the passage on the heroic stature of Ahab. This apparent violation of narrative standpoint is really a natural consequence of the symbolic method of *Moby-Dick*. The distinction between the author and his alter ego is submerged in their common function as the voyaging mind. In fact, the whole book, though cast in the form of historical narrative, tends to the condition of drama, in the sense that it is a presentation, like Ishmael's vision of the whale processions, in which both Melville and Ishmael lose themselves. The frequent references to drama and the actual use of dramatic form in a number of chapters reflect the visionary status of the entire action. In the sequence of chapters (xxxvi–xl) from 'The Quarter-Deck' to 'Midnight, Forecastle,' there is no narrator, to all intents and purposes; Ishmael has to re-establish his own identity at the beginning of chapter xli. At the same time the drama does not take place *in vacuo*; the symbolic nature of the action depends on its being perceived. This is the reason why Ishmael is necessary in the book, despite the fact that he and Melville often merge into one. Ishmael is the delegated vision of Melville: he can enact the genesis of symbolic meaning, whereas Melville, speaking solely as an omniscient author, could only impute an arbitrary significance. Unlike Hawthorne, the Melville of *Moby-Dick* does not verge toward allegory, because he locates his symbols in a unitary act of perception. Moreover, the symbolic vision of Ishmael is repeated by the dramatis personae. From Father Mapple's interpretation of Jonah to Ahab's blasphemous rituals, the symbols take on meaning in the course of perception. The pattern of 'The Doubloon' is the scheme of the book: under the overhanging consciousness of Ishmael, with Melville looking over his shoulder, the several characters envisage the meaning of the coin. As the various meanings multiply, we hear the chant of Pip: 'I look, you look, he looks; we look, ye look, they look.'

Melville, first and last, assumes that 'some certain significance lurks in all things.' There is no other justification for the survival of Ishmael at the end of *Moby-Dick*. 'The drama's done. Why then does anyone step forth?' Ishmael survives as the voyaging mind, the capacity for vision, the potentiality of symbolic perception. He floats on the ocean to which he is dedicated, just as the entire narrative assumes the necessity of water-gazing. The white shroud of the sea, the plenum of significance, remains an eternal challenge. Yet the very fact that Ishmael and the sea are left as mere potentiality indicates the deep distrust interwoven with Melville's faith. The translation of man and world into sheer process, which satisfies Emerson and Whitman, does not content him. The doubloon is evidence of the reality of symbolic meaning; the significance is in the world, and the significant world is generated by 'looking.' But the meaning suffers a fragmentation as it comes into being, and Pip's commentary is an assertion of real multiplicity. The diversity that Emerson and Whitman easily accept as new 'frontiers' of exploration presents itself to Melville as a network of paradox. Travelling with Whitman down the open road, 'the earth expanding right hand and left hand,' Melville notes that right and left are opposites.

Not only does symbolism imply a complex of logical oppositions but it also tends to obscure these real and important differences. While Melville hardly contemplates, except as a lost hope, any return to the substance of the land, he is uncomfortably aware of the irrationality of the fluid sea. The ultimate horror of whiteness is 'its indefiniteness,' the merging of distinctions in the insubstantial medium. For 'whiteness is not so much a colour as the visible absence of colour, and at the same time the concrete of all colours,' so that a snowy landscape, though 'full of meaning,' is 'a dumb blankness, . . . a colourless, all-colour of atheism from which we shrink.' The totality of symbolic meaning is intensely present, but destroys individuality; its 'atheism' is that of transcendentalists like Whitman, who, in order to become god-possessed, deny a personal God. By the same token, in order to unite themselves with nature, they also deny personal identity. Melville follows in evident dismay. Seen rationally, as an object, the world is inaccessible; but, seen as accessible, the world swallows up the visionary. Ishmael's presentiment of the danger of water-gazing is verified by the fate of the 'Pequod,' which disappears in to the ambiguity and formlessness of the sea. Only by self-annihilation does the 'Pequod' penetrate the whiteness, which closes above it in 'a creamy pool.' Ishmael, as though to epitomize Melville's position, almost follows, but does not. He is drifting toward the 'vital centre' of the swirling vortex when the 'coffin life-buoy' suddenly emerges. Ishmael's status remains provisional. He accepts ambiguity and indefiniteness – he is 'buoyed up by that coffin' – and yet somehow manages to retain his own 'identity.'

If the inconclusive fate of Ishmael evinces a double attitude in Melville – an acceptance of 'voyaging' and a fear of its full implications – the fate of Ahab results from a refusal to remain in suspense. Ahab's motives, which are dramatized as vengeance against nature and revolt from God, lie deeper than mere satanic pride. Beneath his ferocious mood is the 'little lower layer' which he confides to Starbuck: he seeks a kind of value not to be measured by the arithmetical methods of accountants. Money, the medium of exchange, is for him a symbolic medium; and his repudiation of the 'Nantucket market' is a rejection of rational thought, just as Melville's doubloon is opposed to the commerce of Boston. When Starbuck continues to protest this irrational 'profit,' Ahab counters with a still 'lower layer.' He draws a contrast between 'visible objects' and the world in process – the 'event,' the 'living act,' the 'undoubted deed.' Ahab has taken quite seriously Emerson's dictum, 'But man thyself, and all things unfix, dispart, and flee.' The visible object is only a 'pasteboard mask'; the wall should open, as Emerson says, 'into the recesses of being'; the living act is fraught with meaning. And in one sense the death of Ahab is the necessary outcome of these premises. For him 'the White Whale is that wall, shoved near.' He does manage to penetrate, hurling his harpoon, and he disappears into the sea, 'still chasing . . . though tied to' the whale. In another sense, indicated by the wreck of the 'Pequod,' Ahab dies because the object is impenetrable and his assumptions are wrong. As he remarks long before the final chase, 'the dead, blind wall butts all inquiring heads at last.' He simultaneously carries the voyage to an extreme, losing himself to gain reality, and is forced to accept the rational distinction between the human intellect and the world it explores. In either case he is faced with an 'inscrutable' world: a mask whose meaning is enticing but destructive, or a wall without any human significance. 'That inscrutable thing,' he declares, 'is chiefly what I hate.' He hates both the ambiguity of the meanings that lure him on and the resistance of objects to the enquiring mind. As the mood of the voyager alters, from love to hate, the world of the Emersonian journey changes from hospitality to malice, and the 'living act' becomes an act of defiance.

All this does not imply, however, that Melville washes his hands of Ahab. If Ahab persists in the face of an obvious dilemma, and is thereby destroyed, the dilemma is the same as Melville's own, and Melville has not resolved it for himself. Melville can reprobate Ahab only as part of his self-reprobation, for Ahab's fury is the last stage of Melville's malaise. Actually, no final condemnation is possible. The largest paradox in *Moby-Dick*, prior to any moral judgement, is the necessity of voyaging and the equal necessity of failure. . . . The voyage . . . issues in the satanism of Ahab, the wilfully destructive pursuit of a knowledge that dissolves into nothingness. Melville feels involved in what happens to Ahab. That is why he could write Hawthorne that Ahab's great blasphemy was 'the book's motto (the secret one)': 'Ego non baptizo te in nomine patris, sed in nomine diaboli!'[9] □

So, in ending up with this motto ('I baptise you, not in the name of the father, but in the name of the devil'), Fiedelson seems as troubled by the question of evil in *Moby-Dick* as was Henry Murray in the first critical extract of this chapter.

R.W.B. Lewis' analysis of *Moby-Dick*, with which this chapter concludes, though troubled by similar questions of evil, has a myth of innocence – and its corruption – as its starting point. For Lewis, this represents *the* fundamental American myth, and is encapsulated in the story of Adam's expulsion from the garden of Eden. The figure of Adam, he believes, provides America with a mythic personality, a hero who is the embodiment of those forces which underpin American culture. American culture, he argues, is founded upon the twin ideas of newness and hope. In the colonial imagination of its early settlers the American continent was a New World that promised a new chance for mankind. But by the mid-nineteenth century, the historical period upon which Lewis' study focuses, that promise had more or less evaporated. The story of Adam in the Garden of Eden is repeated, according to Lewis, by this pattern of innocence and hope corrupted. He notes that the literary texts of his chosen period (which for Matthiessen, as we have seen, were devoted to democracy) repeatedly portray rugged figures of romantic individualism, which he terms 'American Adams'.

The figure of the 'American Adam', then, provides Lewis with a myth, and a set of symbols, for reading mid-nineteenth-century

American culture as a whole. This, in turn, answers a need of mid-twentieth-century American culture. It helps to articulate some of the tensions in 1950s America between, on the one hand, the hopeful prosperity with which America emerged from World War Two, and, on the other hand, the guilt, suspicion and paranoia which this disguised. Unsurprisingly, Lewis' *The American Adam* has come to be seen as one of the first 'classics' of American Studies. *Moby-Dick* plays an absolutely vital role in Lewis' book. He describes Melville as 'the apotheosis of Adam', and *Moby-Dick* as 'a novel ablaze with anger'.[10] This sense of anger suffuses the whole of *The American Adam*, and it expresses the anger of a culture disillusioned with its dreams of innocence. The following extract, which closes this chapter, is from Lewis' reading of *Moby-Dick* in *The American Adam*. By asking how American culture can escape the tragic sensibility that characterises European tradition, it sums up, neatly, Lewis' aim throughout his book.

■ What had been a mere rustle of resentment over a world false to the promises of hope had grown, by 1851, into a fury of disenchantment: Adam gone mad with disillusion. *Moby-Dick* manages to give very clear voice to that fury. If Melville could not yet overcome his anger, he was able to do something which a number of his critics would regard as better. He was able to hold his anger in balance, which may have been the only way to bring it alive and make it clear. Melville had discovered how to establish an attitude toward his own sense of outrage or, inversely, how to establish his outrage in relation to a comprehensive and in some ways traditional attitude. The relation expresses itself in *Moby-Dick* in the actual dramatic relation between frenzied Ahab and far-seeing Ishmael; and psychologizing critics might tell us that what happens in the novel is the 'splitting-off' of a personality first introduced as Ishmael into fragments of itself – one still called Ishmael, others called Ahab and Starbuck and Pip and so on. But we can regard the achievement in terms of the materials of narrative. From this viewpoint, it may be argued that the success of *Moby-Dick* and the clarity of its anger are due to Melville's peculiar, yet skilful, exploitation of the legacy of European literature – and 'the tradition' which that literature has made manifest.

The legacy was the greatest of Melville's resources as, in his own way and according to his own needs, he gradually came into possession of it. The anger in *Moby-Dick* becomes resonant in the tension it creates with the legacy and the tradition. And, conversely, it is the tradition which – in the choral voice of Ishmael and for what it is worth within the ironic frame of the novel – transvaluates the values implicit in the anger.

For the author of *Moby-Dick*, the central strain in the European tradition was tragic. The tragic sensibility defined in . . . the 'Try-Works' is attributed to books as well as to men: 'That mortal man who hath more of joy than sorrow in him, that mortal man cannot be true – not true or undeveloped. With books the same.' There, plainly enough, is an antihopeful judgement, and almost the reverse of it can be read on many pages of Emerson and Thoreau. But there is a point beyond that, which has to do with the creative process itself; and we should recall the actual experience out of which Ishmael's meditation rises, for the enterprise of trying-out was an explicit trope for Melville of the act of creativity. He wrote Dana, while at work on *Moby-Dick*, that the novel would be 'a strange sort of book . . . blubber is blubber you know; though you might get oil out of it, the poetry runs as hard as sap from a frozen maple-tree.' And since trying-out was associated in the story with so hellish a scene and nightmarish an experience, it is hard to resist the inference that creativity for Melville was closely, dangerously, associated with the monstrous vision of evil. You have to go through hell, he suggests, either to get the oil or to write the book.

Melville, that is to say, belongs to the company of gifted romantics from Blake and Baudelaire to Thomas Mann, who have supposed that art is somehow a flower of evil and that the power through which the shaping imagination is raised to greatness may also be a power which destroys the artist; for it is the strength derived from the knowledge of evil – not the detached study, but perhaps a very descent into the abyss. At some stage or other, Melville felt, art had to keep an appointment with wickedness. He believed with Hawthorne that, in order to achieve moral maturity, the individual had to engage evil and suffer the consequences; and he added the conviction that, in order to compose a mature work of literature, the artist had to enter without flinching into the 'spheres of fright.' For Melville, the two experiences happened not to be separable.

But how, having looked into the fire, was the artist to articulate his vision of evil in language? Still another clue is provided by the 'Try-Works.' It can scarcely be a coincidence that, after the slices of blubber (the source of oil) have been pointedly referred to as 'Bible leaves,' the insight gained from the spectacle is conveyed by Ishmael in a cluster of biblical references. The 'Bible leaves' are passed through the furnaces, and oil is the result; similarly, Melville hints, the formed and incrusted language of the past must be 'tried-out' in the trans-forming heat of the imagination, and the result is the shaped perception which can light up the work of art.

The transforming process was crucial, for Melville never simply echoed the words of the great books of the past; he subjected them to tremendous pressure and forced them to yield remarkable new revela-tions. His characterizing 'relation to tradition' was extremely ambiguous: it was no more the willing enslavement exemplified by the nostalgic than it was the blithe patriotic indifference manifested by the hopeful.

... And even the lumpiness of the traditional elements included is significant: significant, anyhow, that his relation to the tradition was American. For the American writer has never (if he is honest and American) been able to pretend an authentic initial communion with the European past; and especially not if he begins, as Melville did, imbued with the antitraditional principles of the party of Hope. He can know a great deal, even everything, about the past; he can go after it, which is just the demonstration that he is not in communion with it. And if he establishes a communion, it is one of a quite different order from that which most European writers – until 1939, at least – possessed as their birthright. The American kind of communion will usually be a sort of tussle, and the best of our writers (like Melville) can convert the tussle into drama. At the same time, since the American writer is outside the organic world of European literature to start with, there is no limit to how much of the world he can draw upon. He has the Protestant's contempt for the long line of commentary and influence; he can go directly to the source and find it anywhere. Nothing is his by right; and so nothing constrains him; and nothing, ultimately, is denied him. Such has been and such must continue to be the actual relation between the American writer and the European tradition: a queer and vigilant relation, at once hospitable and hostile, at once unlimited and uneasy.

... Our first glimpse of Ahab in *Moby-Dick* may further illustrate Melville's practice. .... Ahab is animated within a density of suggestive and echoing language that carries us into the outsize world of heroic legend, without wholly detaching us from the hard wood of the quarter-deck. But the substance of that heroic dimension is a fusion of violently contradictory 'visions' – the vision vitalized by anger and vengeance and pride and wilfulness, on the one hand, and the vision of Christian-cum-Greek tragic acceptance, on the other.

It is in the interplay, the so to speak open-ended dialectic, of the visions that Melville's 'relation to tradition' is to be found and where his expanded resources reveal themselves. Ahab's heroic pride, his wilfulness, his defiance of God and his destruction of the world make sense within our imaginative recollection (constantly prodded throughout the novel) of Christian heroism – meekness, submission, obedience, and the salvation of mankind. Annihilation at sea makes sense within our stimulated recollection of the homecoming myth, the *Odyssey*. *Moby-Dick*'s sustained mood of impending disaster sharpens itself against the Homeric echo of impending triumph. The cosmic anger of Ahab at betrayal, by God, by the father, is correlative to

Melville's anger at the devastating betrayal by experience of the promises of hope. All this rage assumes its full dimension because it is established in opposition to the traditionally comprehensive acceptance voiced by Father Mapple and by Ishmael.

Moby-Dick is an elaborate pattern of countercommentaries, the supreme instance of the dialectical novel – a novel of tension without resolution. Ishmael's meditation, which transfigures the anger and sees beyond the sickness and the evil, is only one major voice in the dramatic conversation; and not until *Billy Budd* does this voice become transcendent and victorious. In *Moby-Dick*, Melville adopted a unique and off-beat traditionalism – a steadily ambiguous re-rendering of the old forms and fables once unequivocally rejected by the hopeful – in order to recount the total blasting of the vision of innocence. He went beyond a spurious artistic originality to give narrative birth to the conflict with evil: that evil against which a spurious and illusory innocence must shatter itself. In doing so, he not only achieved a sounder originality but moved a great step toward perceiving a more durable innocence.[11] □

CHAPTER FIVE

Formalist Approaches, Humanist Readings

THE ESSAYS in this chapter range from the 1950s up to the 1980s.
Despite this wide time frame, though, two key critical approaches to
Moby-Dick – formalist and humanist – are shared by these essays. Though
these two modes of formalism and humanism represent distinct critical
practices, they coalesce within *Moby-Dick* criticism. They are thus broadly
representative of the development and redefinition of Melville studies
during the period from World War Two to the mid-1980s. Building on
the sort of thinking that was outlined in the previous chapter, they can
also be seen to underpin the development and redefinition of American
Studies over this period, for they mark an increasing emphasis on
America's role as a liberal democracy.

The first of these modes is what might be termed a 'formalist'
approach to the text. Such an approach shares with New Criticism the
belief that a literary text should be read as a conscious contrivance, a
'work of art'. It is also influenced by 'structuralist' views, within which
language and literature are seen as 'signifying systems'. In both cases –
New Critical, and structuralist – the critic is concerned with a text's *formal*
properties, with how meaning is generated from its shaping of language
into a literary form. A text is, therefore, seen as a structured literary
experience, and not a reflection of reality, or the means of accessing the
solid things of the world.

And the second mode is the attempt of critics to use such formalist
critical tools to deliver a 'humanist' reading of *Moby-Dick*. This may,
initially, sound rather paradoxical. For, if a formalist approach implies a
retreat from the world into the realm of art, then it is surely incompatible
with being able to deliver meanings about the world, and about *humanity*.
Indeed, much post-war *Moby-Dick* criticism is the product of precisely
this struggle to reconcile its formalist approach with its reading of the
book as a humanist text. However, these two modes are not as antithetical

to each other as they may at first appear. Both strive to uncover the *idea* underlying the object of their attention: in the same way that formalism exposes an *idea* of literature, humanism is about an *idea* of humanity, and not about specific individual experiences. Formalism, therefore, sees literature as conveying a concept of human nature and culture. Texts may not imitate the world in a realist manner, but they do present, as formalist critic *par excellence* Northrop Frye insists, 'the total dream of man'.[1]

Within this conjunction of formalist and humanist modes are sketched the terms of an emerging critical consensus about *Moby-Dick* that held powerful sway over discussions of the book until well into the 1980s. The book's intense concern with language itself, and its self-reflective speculations about literature, were commonly taken to be the markers of its liberal and humanist concerns. Because it was felt to 'say' something of profound importance about the human condition, it was to become established as a key text in the liberal arts programmes at (especially American) universities, schools and colleges. Its concerns are read as exemplary, those of a liberal democracy, struggling to entertain heterogeneity in its attempts to realise a 'total dream of man'. In such readings *Moby-Dick* becomes, so to speak, a symbol of America. Clearly influenced very deeply by such ways of thinking, the following short extract from Richard Brodhead's 'Introduction' to the 1986 book *New Essays on Moby-Dick*, indicates the extent to which *Moby-Dick* criticism was still, in the 1980s, dominated by formalist-humanist concerns:

■ *Moby-Dick* delights in being heterogeneous – a work of mixed and discordant kinds, amalgamating into itself every form of writing (so it would seem) that strikes its fancy. Formally, *Moby-Dick* is always becoming something else, always deciding what kind of book it will be next; and its hectic shape shiftings bespeak, again, the peculiar idea of literature that governs this work.

. . . As *Moby-Dick* presumes to practice it, literature is not simply a secular art. First and last things, the state of the world and our place in it, are not the province of some other cultural system called religion, *Moby-Dick* asserts. They are instead literature's province, questions literature is empowered to address and explore. Moreover, Melville presumes that literature has the power not just to retell religious truth already arrived at but to deliver religion's realm *to* knowledge, to grasp and speak it into comprehensible form.

More persistently than anything else – more persistently than it is heroic, or philosophic, or whatever – *Moby-Dick* is a book in love with language. It is so in love with the sound of words that it savors their spoken heft as it writes them. It is so in love with the infinitude of language that it always wants to use more of it, to heap high all the actual or conceivable words that any textual space will support. . . . But it is peculiarly the case with *Moby-Dick* that its addiction to the act of putting things in words, or what we could call its sheer indulgence in language, serves as the means by which it drives its insights into knowledge. *Moby-Dick* loves to amplify. Having half-said something, its urge is always to stop and say it again. And this process of rhetorical elaboration is, on page after page, how it finally manages to say what at first eluded its grasp. If we end up with some idea of the spiritual torments that fuel Ahab's quest for revenge, it is because Melville keeps naming what exasperates Ahab. . . . If we finally begin to understand the dreadful blankness Ishmael associates with the white whale's whiteness, it is because he keeps renewing his surmise, more and more ingeniously naming the nothing he addresses. . . . If we come more fully to realize the blind, unmindful destructiveness embodied in the beautifully deadly sea, it is because Melville's repetitions drive through our usual obliviousness. . . . If we begin to grasp the mixed and quite elusive motives that drive Ishmael to that sea in the first place, it is because he does not just name his reasons, but rhetorically elaborates them.[2] □

Brodhead, here, is typical of the sort of critical thinking that, after the war, finally guaranteed, and maintained, *Moby-Dick*'s place in the American literary canon. He is typical in another sense, though. Writing in 1986, Brodhead says nothing that would surprise a Melville critic of the 1950s. The sheer powerful persistence of these ways of thinking about *Moby-Dick* can be seen, therefore, to have led to a sense of stalemate in Melville criticism up to the mid-1980s. There was, it seemed, little new to be said about *Moby-Dick*. This critical dearth notwithstanding, the three essays selected in this chapter are exceptions in that they all offer new insights into *Moby-Dick*. Working within fairly formalist modes, they each offer readings that further humanist interpretations of the book. And for all three, it is Ishmael who is the text's key figure.

The next extract is from Walter Bezanson's essay '*Moby-Dick*: Work of Art', an essay which is essential in setting out the formalist and humanist terms which dominated readings of *Moby-Dick* over the following three decades. This is, perhaps, the single-most important essay to emerge from the celebrations of the centenary of *Moby-Dick*'s publication.[3] It is worthy of high praise because its clarity and apparent simplicity convey a subtle and complex reading of *Moby-Dick*. Bezanson's insistence upon seeing Ishmael as the book's most important character marks – along with the essay by Fiedelson in the previous chapter – a crucial shift in *Moby-Dick* criticism. And whilst this change of focus results from a formal consideration of the book's narrative strategies, it also serves to promote a humanist vision. Bezanson sees Ishmael as the representative figure of a liberal, pluralist humanism. The delight in heterogeneity, that is noted by Brodhead above, is Ishmael's distinguishing quality. Bezanson argues that, as the book's narrator, Ishmael controls many different, and often competing, voices. Ishmael's narrative power rests in his ability to arrange those voices into an effective, yet dynamic, artistic form. According to Bezanson, when thus arranged, the work of art, through its energies of form, can speak to the condition of humanity: 'Art is an enabling act for mankind without which life may easily become meagre, isolated; with it the mind can be cleared and the spirit refreshed.' Such a turn-around towards a consideration of Ishmael's role, then, signifies an attempt to accommodate readings of *Moby-Dick*'s multivocal indeterminacy to a pluralist American political ideal, an ideal that has latterly come to be known as multiculturalism. Ishmael's philosophising, which implies that thought is conditional upon language, is far more congenial to a liberal, humanist imagination than Ahab's monomaniacal essentialism.

■ Interest in *Moby-Dick* as direct narrative, as moral analogue, as modern source, and as spiritual autobiography has far outrun commentary on it as a work of art. A proper criticism of so complex a book will be a long time in the making and will need immense attention from many kinds of critics. In the meantime I am struck by the need just now [1951] for contributions toward a relatively impersonal criticism directed at the book itself. The surrounding areas – such as *Moby-Dick* and Melville, *Moby-Dick* and the times in which it was made – are significant just because the book is a work of art. To ask what the book means is to ask what it is about, and to ask what it is about is in turn to ask how art works in the case at hand.

My remarks are therefore in this direction. Beginning with a look at the materials out of which *Moby-Dick* is created, we shall explore the means of activation and some of the forms that contain and define them. The three roadmarks we shall follow are *matter*, *dynamic*, and *structure*.

By *matter* I mean here the subject (or subject matter) in the gross sense. *Moby-Dick* has as its gross subject not Indian fighting or railroad building but whaling.

Any book about mid-nineteenth-century American whaling must in some fashion or other deal with certain phenomena, artifacts and processes. There they are, and they must be used or the book is not about whaling. . . .

Looking back into nineteenth-century Anglo-American history, we find at least four different levels of communication on whaling.

The first was that of the typical whaling logbook. A whaleman's log was a record kept for the owners by the mates or captain; it consisted of daily entries giving the ship's position, weather, landfalls, ships sighted or hailed, whales taken and their size (expressed in barrels of oil), crew desertions, injuries, deaths, etc. . . .

A second level was that of the standard histories. The aim here was the compilation of reliable data on the natural history of the whale (as part of the zoological record) or on the happenings in the fishery (as a contribution to economic history). . . .

A third level of communication was the simple transcription of generalized personal experience. Americans who had never been whaling were interested to know something of the representative experiences of the seventeen thousand men engaged in the American fisheries in the 1840's. So came [such] reports of scenes and adventures, of duties and dangers . . .

A generous distance beyond these logbooks, histories, and personal narratives lies in the problem of fiction. When Melville was composing *Moby-Dick* in 1850 and 1851 he did not hesitate to make quite shameless use of all [such] books . . . in the preparation of his own. Reading for facts and events, for recall and extension, he took on an enormous cargo of whaling matter. But facts are not fiction. In *Moby-Dick* the inert matter of whaling has been subjected to the purposes of art through a dynamic and a structure.

By the term 'dynamic' I mean the action of forces on bodies at rest. The whaling matter in *Moby-Dick* is in no sense at rest, excepting as here or there occurs a failure in effect. For the most part the stuff and data of whaling are complexly subject to the action of a force which can be defined and illustrated. So too is the whole narrative base of the book, which is something far more than a record of what anyone aboard the *Pequod* would agree had happened. There is a dynamic operating on both matter and narrative which distinguishes *Moby-Dick* from logs, journals and histories.

One of two forces, or their combination, is commonly assumed to provide the dynamic of *Moby-Dick*. The first, of course, is Captain Ahab, the dark protagonist, the maimed king of the quarter-deck whose monomania flows out through the ship until it drowns his men – mind and (finally) body. That he is the dominant 'character' and the source of 'action' seems obvious. The reader's image of him is a lasting one. Is Ahab the dynamic?

The alternative force, it is commonly assumed, is Moby Dick himself, that particular white 'spouting fish with horizontal tail' about whom legend and murmured lore have woven enchantments, so that he looms a massive phantom in the restless dreams of the *Pequod*'s captain and crew. His name gives the novel its title. He is prime antagonist of the tale. Is Moby Dick the dynamic?

Both these interpretations have their uses, especially when taken together in a subject-predicate relation. But there is a third point of view from which neither Ahab nor the White Whale is the central dynamic, and I find it both compelling and rewarding, once recognized. This story, this fiction, is not so much about Ahab or the White Whale as it is about Ishmael, and I propose that it is he who is the real center of meaning and the defining force of the novel.

The point becomes clearer when one realizes that in *Moby-Dick* there are two Ishmaels, not one. The first Ishmael is the enfolding sensibility of the novel, the hand that writes the tale, the imagination through which all matters of the book pass. He is the narrator. But who then is the other Ishmael? The second Ishmael is not the narrator, not the informing presence, but is the young man of whom, among others, narrator Ishmael tells us in his story. He is simply one of the characters in the novel, though to be sure a major one whose significance is possibly next to Ahab's. This is forecastle Ishmael or the younger Ishmael of 'some years ago.' . . . Narrator Ishmael is merely young Ishmael grown older. He is the man who has already experienced all that we watch forecastle Ishmael going through as the story is told.

. . . The distinction between the function of the two Ishmaels is clear. Yet it would be a mistake to separate them too far in temperament. Certainly young Ishmael is no common sailor thoughtlessly enacting whatever the fates throw his way. He is a pondering young man of strong imagination and complex temperament; he will, as it were, become the narrator in due time. But right now he is aboard the *Pequod* doing his whaleman's work and trying to survive the spell of Ahab's power. The narrator, having survived, is at his desk trying to explain himself to himself and to whomever will listen. The primary use of the distinction is to bring the narrator forward as the essential sensibility in terms of which all characters and events of the fiction are conceived and evaluated. The story is his.

. . . Every reader of *Moby-Dick* can and will want to enlarge and subtilize the multiple attributes of Ishmael. The prime experience for the reader is the narrator's unfolding sensibility. With it we have an energy center acting outward on the inert matter of nature and experience, releasing its possibilities for art. Whereas forecastle Ishmael drops in and out of the narrative with such abandon that at times a reader wonders if he has fallen overboard, the Ishmael voice is there every moment from the genesis of the fiction in 'Call me Ishmael' to the final revelation of the 'Epilogue' when 'The drama's done.' It is the narrator who creates the microcosm and sets the terms of the discourse.

But this Ishmael is only Melville under another name, is he not? My suggestion is that we resist any one-to-one equation of Melville and Ishmael. Even the 'Melville-Ishmael' phrase, which one encounters in critical discussions, though presumably granting a distinction between autobiography and fiction, would seem to be only a more insistent confusion of the point at stake unless the phrase is defined to mean either Melville or Ishmael, not both. For in the process of composition, even when the artist knowingly begins with his own experience, there are crucial interventions between the act that was experience and the re-enactment that is art – intrusions of time, of intention, and especially of form, to name only a few. Which parts of Ishmael's experience and sensibility coincide with Melville's own physical and psychological history and in just what ways is a question which is initially only tangential to discussions of *Moby-Dick* as a completed work of art.

But what of structure? That there is a dynamic excitation in *Moby-Dick* sympathetic readers have not denied. Is the effect of Ishmael's energy, then, simply to fling the matter in all directions, bombarding the reader with the accelerated particles of his own high-speed imagination? Is Ishmael's search for 'some dim, random way' to explain himself not merely a characterization of the complexity of his task but also a confession of his inadequacy to find form? The questions are crucial, for although readers will presumably go on reading *Moby-Dick* whichever way they are answered, the critical reader will not be encouraged to keep coming back unless he [sic] can 'see' and 'feel' the tension of controlling forces.

To an extraordinary extent Ishmael's revelation of sensibility is controlled by rhetoric. Throughout the tale linguistic versatility and subtle rhythmic patterns exploit sound and sense with high calculation. . . .

Of the narrative's several levels of rhetoric the simplest is a relatively straightforward *expository* style characteristic of many passages scattered through the cetological accounts. But it is significant that such passages are rarely sustained, and serve chiefly as transitions between more complex levels of expression. . . .

A second level of rhetoric, the *poetic*, is well exemplified in Ahab's soliloquy after the great scene on the quarter-deck. . . .

Quite different in effect is a third level of rhetoric, the *idiomatic*. Like the poetic it occurs rather rarely in a pure form, but we have an instance in Stubb's rousing exordium to his crew:

'Pull, pull my fine hearts-alive; pull my children; pull, my little ones . . . Why don't you break your backbones, my boys? . . . Easy,

easy; don't be in a hurry – don't be in a hurry. Why don't you snap
your oars, you rascals? Bite something, you dogs! . . .'

. . . The passage is a kind of rowing song and hence is exceptional; yet
it is related in tone and rhythm to numerous pieces of dialogue and
sailor talk, especially to the consistently excellent idiom of both Stubb
and young Ishmael.

One might venture a fourth level of rhetoric, the *composite*, simply
to assure the inclusion of the narrator's prose at its very best. The
composite is a magnificent blending of the expository, the poetic, the
idiomatic, and whatever other elements tend to escape these crude
categories. . . .

Beneath the rhetoric, penetrating through it, and in a sense rising
above it, is a play of symbolic forms which keeps the rhetoric from
dropping into exercise or running off in pyrotechnics. The persistent
tendency in *Moby-Dick* is for facts, events, and images to become
symbols. . . .

. . . The symbolism in *Moby-Dick* is not static but is in motion; it is
in process of creation for both narrator and reader. Value works back
and forth: being extracted from objects, it descends into the consciousness; spiralling up from the consciousness, it envelops objects.

Symbolism is so marked a characteristic of the narrator's microcosm that it is possible to use the phrase Ahab's tragedy not only in
moral, social, and psychological terms, but in 'structural' terms as
well. Clearly Ahab accepts the symbolic as a source of cognition and of
ethics. It was a symbolic vision that brought him on his quest, as no
one senses with stronger discomfort than Starbuck, who stands alone
in his sturdy, limited world of facts and settled faith. Yet the tragedy of
Ahab is not his great gift for symbolic perception, but his abandonment of it. Ahab increasingly reduces all pluralities to the singular.
His unilateral reading of events and things becomes a narrow translation in the imperative mood. Unlike young Ishmael, who is his equal
in sensitivity but his inferior in will and authority, Ahab walls off his
receptiveness to the complexities of experience, replacing 'could be' or
'might be' with 'must.' His destruction follows when he substitutes an
allegorical fixation for the world of symbolic potentialities.

Ishmael's predilection for keying his narrative in the symbolic
mode suggests another aspect of structure. *Moby-Dick* lies close to the
world of dreams. We find the narrator recalling at length a remembered dream of his childhood. Stubb attempts a long dream-analysis
to Flask after he has been kicked by Ahab. It is not strange, then, that
young Ishmael's moment of greatest crisis, the night of the try-works
when he is at the helm, should be of a traumatic order. More subtly,
numerous incidents of the narrative are bathed in a dream aura: the

trancelike idyll of young Ishmael at the masthead, the hallucinatory vision of the spirit spout, the incredible appearance on board of the devil himself accompanied by 'five dusky phantoms,' and many others. The narrator's whole effort to communicate the timeless, spaceless concept of 'The Whiteness of the Whale' is an act of dream analysis. . . .

. . . *Moby-Dick* is like Emerson's *Essays and Poems*, like *Walden*, like *Leaves of Grass*, in its structural principles. In the literature of the nineteenth century it is the single most ambitious projection of the concept of organic form.

Recharting our explorations we can see now where we have been. The matter of *Moby-Dick* is the organic land-sea world where life forms move mysteriously among the elements. The dynamic of the book is the organic mind-world of Ishmael whose sensibility rhythmically agitates the flux of experience. The controlling structure of the book is an organic complex of rhetoric, symbols and interfused units. There is no over-reaching formal pattern of literary art on which *Moby-Dick* is a variation. To compare it with the structure of the Elizabethan play, or the classical epic, or the modern novel is to set up useful analogies rather than congruous models. It is a free form that fuses as best it can innumerable devices from many literary traditions, including contemporary modes of native expression. In the last analysis, if one must have a prototype, here is an intensively heightened rendition of the logs, journals, and histories of the Anglo-American whaling tradition.

Organic form is not a particular form but a structural principle. In *Moby-Dick* this principle would seem to be a peculiar quality of making and unmaking itself as it goes. The method of the book is unceasingly genetic, conveying the effect of a restless series of morphic-amorphic movements. Ishmael's narrative is always in process and in all but the most literal sense remains unfinished. For the good reader the experience of *Moby-Dick* is a participation in the act of creation. Find a key word or metaphor, start to pick it as you would a wild flower, and you will find yourself ripping up the whole forest floor. Rhetoric grows into symbolism and symbolism into structure; then all falls away and begins over again.

Ishmael's way of explaining himself in the long run is not either 'dim' or 'random.' He was committed to the organic method with all its possibilities and risks. As he says at the beginning of one chapter: 'There are some enterprises in which a careful disorderliness is the true method.' And at the beginning of another chapter we have an explicit image whose full force as a comment on method needs to be recognized: 'Out of the trunk, the branches grow; out of them, the twigs. So, in productive subjects, grow the chapters.'

From our considerations of *Moby-Dick* a few simple, debatable propositions emerge. More accurately they are, I suppose, the assumptions which underlie what has been said. The first is that *nature*, ultimately is chaos. Whatever order it has in the mind of God, its meaning is apparent to man only through some more or less systematic ordering of what seems to be there. The second is that *experience* is already one remove from nature; filtered through a sensibility, nature begins to show patterns qualified by the temperament and the culture of the observer. And the third is that *art*, which is twice removed from nature, is a major means for transforming experience into patterns that are meaningful and communicable. As in part it is the function of religion to shape experience for belief and conduct, and of science to organize nature for use and prediction, so it is the business of art to form man's experience of nature for communication. In art the way a thing is said is what is being said. To the maker the form is completion; to the receiver it is possibility. Art is an enabling act for mankind without which life may easily become meagre, isolated; with it the mind can be cleared and the spirit refreshed; through it memory and desire are rewoven.

The great thing about fiction, which is simply the telling of a story in written words, is that it is fiction. That it is 'made up' is not its weakness but, as with all art, its greatest strength. In the successful work of fiction certain kinds of possibilities, attitudes, people, acts, situations, necessities, for the first and last time exist. They exist only through form. So it is with *Moby-Dick* – Ishmael's vast symbolic prose-poem in a free organic form. From *olim erat* to *finis* is all the space and time there is.[4] □

Along with the shift of attention from Ahab to Ishmael comes a different set of 'crucial' passages from the book upon which critics focus, and a change in critical terminology too. Previously, critics had tended to focus on Ahab's histrionics, his heroic individualism, and how seemingly Shakespearean was his 'tragedy'. Such analyses looked to key dramatic scenes in the text: Ahab's bending of the crew to his will in the chapter 'The Quarter-Deck'; his Promethean rage in 'The Candles'; or the eventual sinking of the *Pequod*. With Ishmael as the centre of attention, though, critics started to look at other parts of the book, for example: the so-called 'cetology chapters' that deal with the natural history of the whale; Ishmael's 'Loom of Time' in the chapter 'The Mat-Maker'; and the chapters 'The Monkey-Rope' and 'The Doubloon'. Increasingly, critical discourses talk about the text in terms of its relativism and complexity of form, and rather than seeking to resolve its dualities, critics describe them as conveying the irreconcilable oppositions inherent in our apprehension of the world. For Bezanson, above, these new sorts of tensions discovered in *Moby-Dick* result from its organic form. And this provides a link back to Emerson, whilst it indicates a change in attitude, within Melville criticism, towards nature. If Ahab exemplifies the urge to control the forces of nature, then Ishmael comes to embody the realisation that mankind is part of nature, subject to the 'flux of experience'.

Writing nearly twenty years after Bezanson, John Seelye describes this conflict of world views between Ahab and Ishmael as the fundamental pattern to an understanding of *Moby-Dick*. A notion of organic form is replaced by one of irony. Rather than *Moby-Dick* bringing different discourses together into one organic whole, Seelye sees the novel's basic pattern of irony as one that, simultaneously, presents us with 'paired possibilities and unreconcilable opposites'. But, like organicism, the idea of an 'ironic pattern' that Seelye traces through Melville's work is rooted in the romanticism of the mid-nineteenth century. This 'ironic diagram', as Seelye puts it, betrays a romantic 'double consciousness', one that stems from the conviction that art 'should be all-inclusive . . . a unity of totality, an organic composite'.[5] In its very form, then, as an 'ironic diagram', *Moby-Dick* is a reading of human nature. Its irony makes apparent the conflicts that sustain romantic consciousness:

■ Both Ahab and Ishmael are spokesmen for a troubled consciousness. Melville created in Ahab a Byronic figure to express his profound pessimism about the goodness of divine purpose. In Ishmael, he created a more complex vehicle, a voice which varies from a sage appreciation of Solomon to a smug recommendation of home and heart as man's best felicity. Melville could not be completely an Ahab, nor could he subscribe to the excesses of Ishmael's kind regard for the sunnier aspects of life, but both voices serve as instruments to express his wanderings between these antipodes of light and shadow.[6] □

Leaving aside the tendency here to romanticise Melville himself, as a figure caught in a struggle between light and shadow, we have a clear exposition of how Seelye's formalism leads him towards a humanist reading of *Moby-Dick*. It serves, therefore, as a useful introduction to the next extract, which is taken from the chapter '*Moby-Dick*: Line and Circle', in Seelye's book *Melville: The Ironic Diagram* (1970). Seelye's reading of *Moby-Dick* builds upon the assumption, hinted at in the imagery of 'light and shadow' in the above passage, that patterns of metaphor and of irony are inextricably linked in a literary text. For him, *Moby-Dick* is built around the opposition between Ahab and Ishmael. This is expressed in the novel's imagery of the line and the circle, which he maintains represents the conflict between Ahab's indomitable will, and Ishmael's all-embracing humanity.

■ The device of countering Ishmael's adventurous urgings by a series of ominous episodes gives way to a much more complicated arrangement, in which Ahab's absolutistic quest is qualified by the various attitudes towards the White Whale voiced by the *Pequod*'s crew . . . and the several world views suggested by the various whalers with which Ahab's ship has contact. But the most important planetary device is provided by the cetology chapters. Ahab's quest is associated with the kinetic, linear element of the story – the onrushing narrative. The cetology chapters, with their relatively static, discursive movements, act to block and impede the forward movement of the narrative, much as the ideas which they contain qualify Ahab's absolutism.

At first glance, the encyclopedic cetology chapters seem to promote the macrocosmic significance of Moby Dick. By marshalling historical and mythological materials associated, however remotely, with whales and whaling, they act as epic similes to elevate the subject of whales until the object-Whale of Ahab's quest becomes one with the universe. As Ahab's mad subjectivity creates a symbol of universal malignity, Ishmael's rational relativity creates a universe of being, of *All*, which inflates even further the importance of Moby Dick, the giant among whales. But even as they built up the White Whale's significance, assisting in the metamorphosis of phenomenon to noumenon, the cetology chapters act to negate the validity of Ahab's hunt. Much of what Ishmael says about whales is factitious, from his insistence that the whale is a fish to his insistence that Perseus was the first whaleman.

This direction is mock heroic, mock epical, and qualifies the validity of Ahab's heroic character and the epical nature of his quest. Moreover, by collective implication these chapters suggest the Whale can never be 'known' (i.e., caught), that as a symbol of the universe he shares the puzzlelike nature of the universe and is shadowy, elusive, paradoxical, inscrutable. Ahab, who tries to impose an absolute interpretation on Moby Dick, fails to read the puzzle rightly, and yet Moby Dick's savage retaliation suggests that the captain is not entirely wrong, either. Like the Whale, the book is a cipher also, the result of paired possibilities and unreconcilable opposites.

Though Ishmael and Ahab never meet face to face, they are engaged in a long debate, and, as in a debate, their arguments enhance yet refute one another. Ahab reduces Moby Dick to an analogy of his mad idea of nature, making inscrutable blankness a mask of universal malice. Ishmael, though suspecting a fearful contingency, suspects nature to be at base a hollow sham, hiding absolutely nothing. He discourses not only on the whiteness that is to him symbolic of the 'atheistical' void behind appearances, but on man's many futile attempts to arrive at some common agreement as to the nature of appearances, attempts which, when opposed one to one, add up (like the implications of whiteness) to absolute zero. Whereas Ahab hopes to end his pursuit with the capture of Moby Dick, Ishmael fears that the chase has but three possibilities, none fruitful: it will end where it began; it will lose itself in the world-maze; it will end in disaster.

The opposition of Ahab and Ishmael is one of character type (misanthrope and philanthrope), ontology (absolutist and relativist), and psychology (head and heart). Ahab's reasoning is deductive; Ishmael's is inductive. Ahab's personality is fixed, virtually unwavering, while Ishmael is moody, contradictory. The scheme is not perfect (thank goodness!), for Ishmael is fascinated by the 'idea' of the Whale and is swayed by Ahab's rhetoric into joining the fiery hunt. Ahab, on the other hand, has his 'humanities' and his moments of self-doubt. But these exceptions serve only to achieve a larger end, to dovetail points of view, welding the opposition of attitudes into an impervious unity, an organic puzzle which contains the complexity of the world. . . .

This opposition of character traits is part of the ironic diagram, an association that extends even to metaphor. Relativistic Ishmael with his relativistic cetology chapters is an exponent of circular views. He hopes 'to include the whole circle of the sciences, and all the generations of whales, and men, and mastodons, past, present, and to come, with all the revolving panoramas of empire on earth, and throughout the whole universe, not excluding its suburbs' within his book (p.452).[7] Not only may the cetology chapters be seen as circular in implication, but Ishmael's journey, unlike Ahab's, is a round trip. He is often associated with circular objects, like the tubs of sperm, or holistic events, like the invasion of the whale circle. At the outset, he identifies himself with the 'insular city of the Manhattoes, belted round by wharves as Indian isles by coral reefs – commerce surround[ing] it with her surf,' a centrifuge on whose outer rim 'all around' stand thousands of sea dreamers, and which is an emblem of the 'round world itself.' And at the end of the book, Ishmael is found bobbing on the rim of the creamy vortex left by the sinking *Pequod*.

Absolutistic Ahab, contrarily, is associated with lines. According to the prophetic old carpenter, Ahab is 'always under the Line – fiery hot, I tell ye!' (p. 520), an analogy echoed in the mad captain's plan to meet with Moby Dick during the 'Season-on-the-Line.' His figure, too, is linear, a quixotic leanness that suggests the intensity of his enthusiast conviction. . . . The mark of his casting is a 'slender, rod-like scar' which is rumoured to run the length of his body and which terminates in the ivory stick-leg fixed in an auger hole bored into Ahab's quarter-deck. Stationed there, his body fastened to the body of his ship, Ahab presents a figurehead portrait of single-mindedness. . . .

. . . Ahab imagines himself master of his fate. He compares himself to an express train, that technical marvel, and, with his faith in himself and his ship, is an insane epitome of Western man, whose faith is in linear progress, whose wisdom is based upon analogies. For Ahab, the world is an allegory in which Moby Dick is a personification of malignity, a dragon needing a knight to slaughter it. But for Ishmael, whose consciousness has an Eastern awareness of relativity, of the endlessly revolving cycles of time, the Whale (whose very name means 'roundness or rolling') is a totality of meaningless impressions, a something that is nothing, a symbol of the void at the center of material reality. . . .

. . . Circle and line merge in the symbolism of the doubloon which Ahab nails to the mast as a prize for the man who first sights Moby Dick. All the major characters (save Ishmael) confront the coin, and all interpret it in the light of their particular biases, for like the Whale, the doubloon is an index of truth's relativity. It is the 'white whale's talisman' and takes its significance from his essential mystery. Both by its 'thingness' and by its predominant symbol – 'the keystone sun entering the equinoctial point at Libra' – the coin is an emblem of transcendent, planetary power, a sun token, made from gold mined and minted under the equator (p. 428). But this token of balance has been nailed to the mast by a monomaniac who regards the equator as a 'line,' and who confronts the coin's golden roundness with a dark intensity of purpose. . . . As he has nailed it, so would he like to nail Moby Dick, to pierce him with the harpoon that is the chief instrument of his 'pointed intensity.'

So monomaniacal is Ahab that to him even the symbols on the coin correspond to aspects of his ego. In his view, it is an absolute, not a relativistic token – as Moby Dick seems to him a symbol of universal malevolence, so the various signs on the coin stand for various aspects of his own personality. But the coin (like the Whale) transcends Ahab's interpretation of it. The generic symbols on its face draw together the various ontological strands of the book into one mysterious Gordian knot: the 'Andes' summit, crowned by a flame, suggests the hell-fire of the tryworks episode, the madness of introversion, while the mountain bearing a tower hints at the airy pantheism of the masthead incident. And the crowing cock on the third mountain is a blazon of egotism, a 'cock-of-the-walk.' Each of the three suggests some extreme viewpoint, but all three 'heaven-abiding' peaks are joined at a common base in the 'dark valley' of doubt, and the dominant sun is frozen in the balance sign of Libra. Minted under the equator, the doubloon gathers and equates the disparate opinions of the crew towards the Whale and contains (joins) antipodes of existential attitude. A unity forged of disunities, the coin is a puzzle whose meaning can only be read by little Pip, for whom the heroic captain is an object of jeering laughter.

Ahab may have nailed the coin to the mast, but Pip prophesies that it is the captain who will be nailed by Moby Dick. Pip has experienced the huge extremity of the ocean, a golden circle of infinity 'flatly stretching away, all round . . .' (p. 412). . . . To the mad, withdrawn, and indifferent Pip, the mad reasonableness of Ahab's analogies seems like the plan of a fool . . .

. . . According to Pip, the doubloon is 'the ship's navel . . .' (p. 432). The coin is a navel, 'contemplated' by each member of the crew in turn – fixed to the center of the ship, it is dominated by 'Libra,' the navel sign of the zodiacal Great Man. The talisman of the Whale, token of Ahab's quest, the coin is fundamental to the structure of the book and a sign of the universal ambiguity which the book is designed to accommodate. If it should, like the navel of the fabled Hindu which Pip seems to have in mind, be unscrewed, the results would be disastrous.

No one is more on fire to unscrew the golden navel than old Ahab, who wants both Whale and talisman. And in attacking the Whale, in arousing that mystery to show its dark, malevolent side, he attempts to violate the circle of existence, to penetrate the Omphalos, the navel of God. In the end, he does succeed in penetrating the divine helix, but by the only means available to mortal man. Caught in the spiralling threads of a maelstrom, Ahab, his ship, and his crew are drawn down into the depths to death, providing a final configuration of the paradoxical force with which Ishmael has been dealing throughout – the circle which is the antithesis of the line, and its synthesis as well, here on this round globe.

The circular view is transcendental and holds that 'Nature is intricate, overlapped, interweaved, and endless.' It is tokened by the doubloon, but it is also figured in the sword mat woven by Ishmael and Queequeg. The warp of the loom is necessity, the shuttle is free will, but the pattern of the mat's weave is determined by the blows of 'Queequeg's impulsive, indifferent sword' (p. 213), the careless weapon of chance. . . . It is chance which determines the pattern of fate, and it is by chance that Ishmael survives the sinking of the *Pequod*, as it is a chance loop of the whale line that snatches Ahab into eternity.

But Ahab's solipsistic view precludes chance. He has chained it to the instruments of his will, the compass needle and his harpoon. . . . As Ishmael's stoicism has its diagram in the sword mat, so Ahab's wilfulness is mapped by the 'pointed intensity of his charts,' the sane means by which his mad object is to be accomplished.

Emblematically, the 'lines and shadings' on the chart are matched by the 'shifting gleams and shadows of lines' thrown on Ahab's wrinkled brow by the heavy lamp 'suspended in chains' overhead. . . .

And Ahab's pale brow, in turn, is reflected in the hieroglyphic markings on the snow-white forehead of the White Whale, suggesting (as with his bone leg) a link of shared identity between fierce Ahab and his ferocious adversary. The lines also indicate a plan of calculated analogies of which the wilful Ahab is only a subsidiary part, and of which, because of his single-minded purpose, he is not aware.

The lines on the chart differ from those of the mat in that they disregard the element of chance, and it is here that Ahab makes his fatal mistake. He has put his faith in rational means, in the statistics and records from which his ingenious chart has been constructed, but he has ignored the vagaries of chance. Part of a totality, Ahab cannot transcend the pattern; nor, like Jonah, can he escape it. As Fedallah darkly foresees, Ahab will be strangled by a cord woven in part by himself and compounded of the same strands that go to make up the sword mat – free will, necessity, and chance. The ironic pattern is completed when Ahab, having braved all dangers, conquered all souls, disregarded all portents, encounters his adversary only to be dragged down by his true antagonist, a 'chance' loop in the instrument of his revenge – not the dedicated harpoon, but the humble, hempen rope attached to it, the last unravelling of Ahab's linear voyage. That deadly, prophetic hemp, formed of the same stuff as the shroud to which the captain has clung for so long, pulls him down beneath the 'great shroud of the sea,' which rolls on unheeding, 'as it rolled five thousand years ago.' . . .

Thus, while constantly reminding us of the eternal flux, of the absolute of absolutes, Melville nevertheless returns to the relatively fixed structure of contrasts, line and circle, which lies at the heart of his narrative. The circle may be broken, but to a circle it returns, and the line soon becomes taut again. For Ahab throughout has eyes only for darks and depths, for leviathans and sharkish thoughts – like Narcissus, he mistakes his own dark reflection for truth, 'and this is the key to it all.' Having converted himself, like his razors, into an instrument of his ruling passion, the captain has become his own fate indeed, but in a sense not realized by himself. The world is a fluid loom through which he drives the shuttle of his quest, but the wilful pattern of his plan is ultimately absorbed by the whole, the Whale, the fabric of being constructed from the matched contraries of existence.[8] □

Finally, though, Seelye's reading of *Moby-Dick* seems to expose the shortcomings of its own formalist methodology. Despite its wonderfully eloquent and assured tone, its close reading of the text, and its sense of verbal play, Seelye's reading tends to reduce the whole of *Moby-Dick* to the controlling figures of line and circle. And though a fascinating, and in many respects convincing analysis of the text, its ultimate ploy is to

ⱴr to the text's mystery, to 'the eternal flux, of the absolute of
ⱴs', which its controlling figures can neither fully express nor
ⱴely encompass. The essay repeats, therefore, the idea of *Moby-*
ⱴscrutability that has been heard throughout its critical history.

In his book *The Power of Blackness: Hawthorne, Melville, Poe* (1976),
Harry Levin attempts one solution to this critical impasse. His reading of
Moby-Dick, which returns to the use of myth and symbol as critical tools,
is based in what might be termed a 'pessimistic humanism'. For him,
Moby-Dick reveals that the human condition is, like the symbol of Moby
Dick, the white whale himself, 'ungraspable':

■ If Moby-Dick holds any answer to the enigmas that perplex
mankind, . . . he disappears into the depths without yielding it up.
Perhaps the secret may be that there is no secret, Melville speculated
in one of his letters to Hawthorne. And again: 'Why, ever since grand-
father Adam, who has got to the meaning of this great allegory – the
world?' Since, in sober fact, there is no such animal as an albino
whale, Moby-Dick is utterly unique by definition. Since he is an irre-
ducible symbol, an archetype of archetypes, there is no cogency in the
varying labels with which his interpreters have attempted to tag him.
To evade reduction into categories is the essence of his character. As a
sperm-whale he concretely embodies a generative principle, which is
intimated by the sexual interplay of the ninety-fourth and ninety-fifth
chapters. But as a sport . . . he is a preternatural being; he is everything
and nothing, the absolute, 'the great gliding demon of the seas of life.'
Doubtless, to apprehend him would be to understand the ways of
God. . . . Melville's book is not a mystery, . . . it is a book about a
mystery.[9] □

Such deliberate mystification, though, does not really further an understanding of the text, or of the particular circumstances and
understandings of the human condition from which it arose. A more
successful reading is that of Lawrence Buell, whose essay – from which
the final extract of this chapter is taken – re-locates *Moby-Dick* within the
religious discourses of nineteenth-century America. If, he implies, *Moby-
Dick* seems mysterious, that is because it emerges from
mid-nineteenth-century America, a culture steeped in a language of religious mystery. Buell's *Moby-Dick* is deeply a product of its age, its tensions
are those of a culture struggling to explain its apprehension of the transcendent in a language that can scarcely begin to express such an
apprehension. His analysis of *Moby-Dick* as a 'sacred text' remains
formalist in the attention it gives to narrative strategies, to the extent to
which *what* the book says is dependent upon *how* the book says it.

■ In certain ways *Moby-Dick* is a sort of scripture. It is, to begin with, indisputably one of the works of the American literary 'canon,' as scholars like to call it, read and taught by the professional priesthood with a more genuinely religious zeal than most of that priesthood probably feel toward the literal sacred texts of their own ethnic traditions – the Torah, the New Testament, or whatever. In my field, to write a commentary on *Moby-Dick* is more respectable than to write a commentary on the book of Job or Jonah. One reason for this is the depth of the waters in which Melville fished, the fact that this particular fish story becomes ultimately in some sense a record of an encounter with the divine. The book's language is drenched in sacramentalism, 'brimming over with signals of the transcendent.'[10] When the white whale rises out of the water on the first day of the chase, it does not merely breach [but, we are told that] 'the grand god revealed himself' (Chap. 133). Here and at innumerable other points metaphor seems to convert story into myth.

. . . One of the major intellectual forces behind the whole so-called American literary renaissance to which Melville's work contributed was a religious ferment and anxiety resulting from the breakdown of consensual dogmatic structures and particularly the breakdown of biblical authority in Protestant America. This had both 'negative' and 'positive' aspects. Negatively, the rise of the 'higher criticism' in biblical studies, which began to make inroads in America during the decade of Melville's birth, seemed threatening and destructive in its approach to the Bible (and by extension, to institutionalized Christianity as a whole) as a culture-bound, historical artifact subject to the same methods of interpretation and susceptible to the same errors and obsolescence as any other ancient artifact. This threatened to reduce holy scripture to myth in the bad sense – to quaint superstitious fabrication. Concomitantly, however, a less parochial and more creative understanding of the religious imagination now became possible, an affirmative reading of myth as the expression of spiritual archetypes informing not only the Bible but the scriptures of all cultures, and not only ancient texts but – at least potentially – the literature of one's own day as well. At least partially offsetting the disillusioning sense that prophets were no more than poets was the exciting dream that poets might be prophets. This indeed was one of the great themes of the romantic movement in both England and America. It was wholly in keeping with this thrust of romanticism that its first major American exemplar, Ralph Waldo Emerson, was an ex-minister who, in reaction against contemporary theology and denominationalism, turned to the vocation of freelance lecturer-writer, defining it as a secular priesthood.

. . . But it is high time to look at Melville more closely. His general orientation is aptly characterized by Robert Richardson as 'mythic investiture': the infusion of what we know to be natural phenomena with a sense of mystic otherness.[11] . . . What is especially interesting and distinctive about the investiture process is how the narrative builds this impression in the face of the narrator's disclaimers and even discreditation. . . . Ishmael's discourses generally . . . testify . . . to the quixoticism of the myth-making process; and we . . . ascribe to Melville or at least to Ishmael the debunking conception of myth as fabrication. This leads, on the level of symbol interpretation, to a reading of *Moby-Dick* as an allegory of reading and particularly as an allegory of unreadability: the undecipherability of the whale as text. . . . This . . . leads ultimately to a reading of *Moby-Dick* as about an encounter with the realm of the transcendent that dramatizes parallel failures of human striving (Ahab) and knowing (Ishmael). In this reading, Ishmaelean mockery . . . starts to look like self-protective compensation for the frustration and anxiety of failing to grasp the elusive, mysterious, and therefore threatening Other. It is through the eyes of this second reading that *Moby-Dick* begins to look somewhat like a sacred text.

That this second reading is more persuasive as well as more powerful than the first is strongly suggested by the book's narrative structure. The narrative 'proves' Ahab to have been a false prophet, but it does not disown the framework of supernaturalism established by his shadow Fedallah's three *Macbeth*-like prophecies, which uncannily come to pass. The narrative leaves open the question of whether the White Whale is a divine or demonic agent, and in leaving this question open leaves us in a state of wonder rather than with a confident reduction of the whale to the status of material object or (on the symbolic level) narcissistic projection.

. . . the book plays an interesting double game. Because its central subject is an absent object of obsession for nearly the entire narrative, the text continually signals to the reader that 'This is not yet quite reality; this is only preparatory information or interpretation.' Not until a third of the book is over does an encounter with even an ordinary whale take place. During this long buildup, the repetitious quality of the cetology chapters and of Ishmael's meditations in general, combined with the fundamental fact of Moby Dick's absence, reinforce the plausibility of the frequent hints that the quest is empty of meaning except for what is read into it.

. . . the plethora of foreshadowings and the repeated admissions of intellectual defeat and skepticism create intense frustration for the reader as well as the narrator (as every teacher of undergraduates knows) and with this a great longing for closure, which the text in the long run pretty much provides. Near the end, the narrative becomes much more linear; the whale's eruption into the text and disposal of the *Pequod* dissipates the haze of speculation in the sense of providing a resolution, at least on the plot level, to the prior state of indefiniteness. . . . The narrative structure is reminiscent of the tale of Job without the frame. In each work, redundant expostulation and soul searching build up to an intolerable pitch of uncertainty until abruptly resolved by authoritative, repressive intervention – except that in Melville the whale speaks only on the level of the action.

. . . Insofar as the *Pequod*'s encounter with the monster of the deep is a mysterious, deeply inexplicable, and magic-suggesting event that gives rise to the telling of the story in the first place and also, at the end of the tale, supersedes the telling in the sense that reflective commentary becomes largely displaced by the force of narrative relation – insofar as all this is true, *Moby-Dick* begins to reemerge on the narrative level as sacred text even as it might have seemed that any pretences to revelation had been contained by wily Ishmael. I take it that one of the reasons, maybe the main reason, for the inconsistency of Ishmael's disappearance from the later stages of the narrative may be to dramatize this very effect: the effect of what seems *comparatively* like a pure, unmediated vision of successive mysterious events bursting through the power of both commentary (Ishmael) and false prophecy (Ahab) to contain them. It is interesting in this regard that when Ishmael does reappear in the Epilogue, he seems to have been coopted by the discourse of revelation. He now speaks in the role of Job's messenger-servant, whose function is simply to serve as the reporter of the demonically arranged and divinely permitted catastrophe: 'I only am escaped alone to tell thee' (Epilogue).

. . . The prospect of the authority of revelation at the prophetic level, eroded by Ishmael's critique of Ahab, is thus partially recovered at the level of plot through the agency of the whale and through the move toward greater objectification of the narrative voice. The narrative method of having the tale eventually seem to reabsorb and outstrip its teller reflects and repeats the romantic impulse both to demythologize and remythologize. In this it reflects, but with a difference, Emerson's dictum to the newborn bards of the Holy Ghost to 'cast behind you all conformity, and acquaint men at first hand with Deity.' The *form* of this prescription is enacted faithfully in *Moby-Dick* by Ishmael's exposure of the arbitrariness of all particular readings of the divine (starting with the juxtaposition of Father Mapple-ism and Yojo worship as equivalent rituals) in a narrative pattern in which all speculation about the divine is abruptly displaced by the revelation of that which might actually be a mark of the divine. Yet then again, it might not. This is Melville's aesthetics of doubt; and as every

Melvillean knows, the issue becomes progressively more clouded and doubtful in Melville's later novels, *Pierre* and *The Confidence-Man*.

. . . This reading establishes *Moby-Dick* as a document in the history of the clash in American and specifically northeastern post-Puritanism between Reformation-Calvinist and Enlightenment-Unitarian cross-currents, with Melville emerging as a sort of disaffected Calvinist. . . . *Moby-Dick* . . . stands as a great pioneering work of comparative religion and as one of the most ambitious products of the religious imagination that American literature is likely to produce.[12] □

Buell's essay is important because it stresses the importance of understanding what were the cultural conditions of nineteenth-century America from which *Moby-Dick* arose. This way of thinking, given impetus by the advent in the mid-1980s of 'cultural materialism' and generally 'deconstructive' critical practices, provides Melville criticism with a strategy for rescuing *Moby-Dick* from the critical dead-end into which formalist analyses had tended to lead it. The final two chapters of this book examine the ways in which *Moby-Dick* has been rehabilitated by such 'postmodern' critical strategies, and their readings of *Moby-Dick*'s ideological agenda.

CHAPTER SIX

Cultural Materialism and 'Reconstructive' Readings

THE FINAL two chapters of this book chart the development of *Moby-Dick* criticism from the mid-1980s up to the present day. Both chapters demonstrate a fundamental change of direction – not only in Melville criticism, but in critical practice generally – towards reading practices that are more ideologically aware. Such a tendency leads, in this chapter, to a series of essays which can be broadly termed 'cultural materialist'. That is, they seek to examine the way in which *Moby-Dick* is a product of the cultural materials of mid-nineteenth-century America. It is this ideology which defines what *Moby-Dick* is, and any understanding of Melville's book, they would argue, is dependent upon recreating and examining, so far as this is possible, the cultural environment from which it is produced. The essays in the next chapter, the final one of this book, push this mode of critical enquiry further. In seeking to 'deconstruct' the ideological conditions that underpin *Moby-Dick*, the essays in the closing chapter of this Guide raise questions about the extent to which *Moby-Dick* is the product, not simply of the cultural forces at play in America during the last century, but also of the structures of ideological power which have determined the ways in which the book has been read throughout the course of its critical history. In short, then, the essays which comprise these final two chapters bring *Moby-Dick* criticism up to date by emphasising that the act of reading *Moby-Dick* is never ideologically innocent, they stress that the way in which *Moby-Dick* is read betrays a reading of America and its culture.

In all cases, the critical pieces in this chapter are important in that they challenge us to go back to *Moby-Dick* and read it afresh. The essays that follow in this chapter signal a new – or returned – sense of excitement in criticism of the book. They do not, necessarily, see *Moby-Dick* as important because it is a classic *per se*, but rather because it offers some radical and invigorating insights into American culture, our own liberal humanist assumptions, and, indeed, our own reading practices. These readings (especially in comparison with the essays that follow in the next chapter) are at the 'softer' end of the critical-theoretical spectrum. Rather than out-and-out post-structuralist deconstructions of the text, they are better thought of as 'reconstructive' readings. David S. Reynolds, whose vitally important essay on *Moby-Dick* and antebellum popular culture closes this chapter, describes what he terms 'reconstructive criticism' in the *Epilogue* to his book *Beneath the American Renaissance* (1988). According to Reynolds, such 'reconstructive criticism' brings together the best (formalist) practices of close textual reading with a scholarly knowledge, and examination, of the sociopolitical environment from which the text is produced:

■ Applied to the internal workings of literary texts, reconstructive criticism views the literary work as simultaneously self-sufficient *and* historically shaped by environmental factors in society and personal life. In the case of the literary masterpieces of the American Renaissance, textual self-sufficiency does not constitute a rejection or evasion of socioliterary forces but rather a full assimilation and willed transformation of these forces. This process of assimilation and transformation – which might be called artistic or aesthetic – is another important aspect of reconstruction. The literary text reconstructs disparate socioliterary elements from its contemporary culture. In effect it tries to save the society by giving certain popular elements new emotional resonance and artistic meaning.[1] □

Such a 'reconstructive criticism' does not hide its humanist agenda, then. Indeed, its persuasive power lies in its ability to see the materials of a text's contemporary culture transformed within literary texts, given a depth and texture that is 'universal', something that, it is assumed, speaks to the human condition. Reynolds continues: 'The "meaning" of a text lies in the richness of its texture, the emotions its stirs, the metaphysical speculations it instigates.'[2] Theoretical objections may be raised to this way of thinking by arguing that the very notion of a universality of human experience – especially literary experience – is, in itself, ideologically determined. But, objections to such a belief in literature's humanising power notwithstanding, Reynolds' critical model does seem to re-open the radical and subversive potential of texts such as *Moby-Dick*. He notes, further, that

■ The literary text can be distinguished from other types of text both by its openness to the most subversive forces in its immediate socioliterary environments and by its simultaneous endeavor to lend depth and artistry to these forces. Both the radical openness and the instinct to restructure must be present, or the literary text will not appear. The literary text fully confronts the subversive – plunges wholly into it, as it were – but at the same time it removes itself through an assertion of the humanizing artistic imagination.[3] □

Though the relationship between 'literature' and 'the subversive' that Reynolds sets up here seems rather fraught and uneasy, it conveys, perhaps, an accurate sense of the pressures from which *Moby-Dick* and other works of the American Renaissance were produced. Whereas Matthiessen's model of the American Renaissance dealt exclusively with works of 'high' literary merit, Reynolds' critical model prises open such exclusivity. This allows him to get beneath, so to speak, the surface of the culture which gave rise to the American Renaissance. Not only, therefore, does this provide him with a critical model for reading *Moby-Dick* as a book deeply influenced by the popular culture of Melville's day, but it also paves the way for other critics to read *Moby-Dick* as a product of ideological and cultural forces in nineteenth-century America that extend beyond the exclusively literary. And though earlier criticism had noted the influence of American popular culture on *Moby-Dick* (see, for example, Richard Chase's discussion of Barnum in chapter three above), this had been seen to mark the book out as anomalous. *Moby-Dick*'s cultural hybridity had thus been seen as problematic, something that distinguished it from 'proper' literature. Taken as illustrating a wider concern, such a problematic seemed to embody the lack of a critical language for talking about American literature itself. In a sense, then, Reynolds' 'reconstructive' model discovers a critical language, so long lacking, for discussing the Americanness of American literature in general, and, as we shall see at the end of this chapter, of *Moby-Dick* in particular.

All four essays which make up this chapter seek to reconstruct and examine the cultural environment from which *Moby-Dick* arose. The first two essays, those by Paul Royster and David Leverenz, focus on *Moby-Dick*'s relationship to a specifically defined topic, and how this throws light upon the culture of nineteenth-century America. The following essays by Leo Bersani and David S. Reynolds, however, take a more general view of the American ideology which a reading of *Moby-Dick* can expose. Through both specific and general terms of inquiry, then, this chapter shows critics using *Moby-Dick* as a means of re-reading nineteenth-century America.

The first extended extract in this chapter is from Paul Royster's essay 'Melville's Economy of Language', and looks specifically at the impact of a rhetoric of labour and emerging capitalism upon *Moby-Dick*. This theme had been touched on in earlier Melville criticism, notably that of D. H. Lawrence and Charles Olson that appears earlier in this book, but it was only with the publication of Michael T. Gilmore's book *American Romanticism and the Marketplace* (1985) that the importance of capitalist discourses to America in the last century was given any full, detailed and serious consideration. The fact that such considerations now seem so essential to any understanding of writers of the American Renaissance demonstrates the groundbreaking importance of Gilmore's study. However, the chapter on *Moby-Dick* is a weak point in his book. It amounts to little more than a plot summary which points out some of the (rather obvious) references in the text to labour, industry, the market-place, and an alienated workforce. However, before we get to the extract from Royster's essay, which develops a slightly more sophisticated, quasi-Marxist, reading of such themes in the text, a short passage from Gilmore is given below. This helps to underline two things that Royster's essay, published a year later, will develop. Firstly, that Melville's America was a culture in transition from an agricultural to an industrial economy. And, secondly, that the great pressure Melville felt to produce books for a massively expanding literary marketplace, has a deep effect on the language and imagery of *Moby-Dick* itself.

■ The background to *Moby-Dick* is the critical juncture in American history when a fundamental reordering took place in men's relation to each other and their surroundings. 'Are the green fields gone?' Ishmael asks as early as the third paragraph of his narrative, and his question points to the moment of transition from an agricultural to a commercial and industrial society. . . . Joint-stock ventures like the whaling industry set the pattern for a new economic order in which nature is systematically exploited for profit.

. . . This immense novel about the whaling industry delights in showing how goods are made, literary wares included. At the book's heart is the elaborately described process whereby a living part of nature is transformed into an object of human consumption. Hundreds of pages of dense and often technically detailed prose are devoted to the fashion-ing of a commodity; the climactic battle with Moby Dick, by contrast, gets a scant three chapters out of a hundred and thirty-five. Ishmael relates – or rather sings, to adopt his own word – how the great leviathan is sighted from the masthead and slaughtered on the deep; . . . and how his oil is decanted into casks and finally stowed in the hold. At each step of this extended process the reader is shown working men carrying out the operation of turning nature into merchandise. If *Moby-Dick* is a commercial epic, it is an epic much like *Walden* in which human labor is not marginalized but situated at the center.[4] □

The apprehension that *Moby-Dick* is a 'commercial epic' similarly manifests itself in Royster's essay. This essay is taken from the collection of essays edited by Sacvan Bercovitch and Myra Jehlen entitled *Ideology and Classic American Literature* (1986). This is one of the first major works to begin to question some of the ideological assumptions which, since Matthiessen in 1941, can be seen to underpin the very notion of a Classic American Literature that is supported by the idea of an American Renaissance. Royster, like much post-war Melville criticism, sees Ishmael as the key to the text. However, it is Ishmael's 'liberalism' that he sees as problematic. Despite *Moby-Dick*'s apparent radicalism – of form and of theme – it delivers, according to Royster, a less than radical critique of the forces of emerging capitalism.

■ No other novel of the nineteenth century is so concerned with the actions and relations of the workplace or so committed to describing the processes of production as *Moby-Dick*. Yet *Moby-Dick* is no ordinary industrial novel, because of its conscious attention to the task of constructing itself as language. The interaction of these two processes – industrial production and literary construction – produces a work rich in the metaphorical interplay of language and labor. . . .

. . . *Moby-Dick* is an exuberant paean to labor, an elaborate celebration of the human energy and industry of nineteenth-century America. Yet what it converts to metaphor is a particular set of economic relations: Whaling is a capitalist enterprise, an industry that produces commodities for a market and employs labor to return a profit on investment. Ishmael's advocacy of 'the honor and glory of whaling' does not separate labor from capital, as being distinctive parts of the industry. He is as proud of the number, size, and efficiency of the American whaling fleet as of the skill, productivity, and dedication of its seamen. Both the labor and the physical means of production emerge from Ishmael's account in favorable colors. Meanwhile, he invests the process of producing whale oil with additional symbolic meanings, which make it an extended metaphor for various social and metaphysical referents. Ishmael is never so happy as when he is finding in some dull, arduous, or onerous task an allegory of universal truth. Work takes on extra value when Ishmael can interpret it symbolically, when it assumes the pattern of some larger structure or condition of human life.

With Ishmael, this rhetoric of labor is in part a defensive strategy, an ideology that allows him to cope with the embarrassments or unpleasantness of his working-class position. For example, he dexterously explains away the kick administered by Captain Peleg as a sample of 'the universal thump,' passed the whole world round and imaginatively linking the entire race of men in the vast circuit of taking one's lumps. Ishmael's rhetoric transforms this striking example of class relations (owner/employee) into an illustration of higher democracy. Of course, the incident need not have been mentioned at all, and Ishmael's explication of it is noticeably ironic. Nonetheless, it supports his construction of whaling as an occupation representative of the universal human condition, even if this blurs the distinction between industrial discipline and human equality.

In general, Ishmael's rhetoric of labor does not dwell on such relations of production or on the social structure of the workplace. Most often it finds in some feature of the job at hand analogies for the universe of absolutes. In the chapter 'The Mat-Maker,' the job of weaving mats figures as an explanation of metaphysics: 'It seemed as if this were the Loom of Time, and I myself were a shuttle mechanically weaving and weaving away at the Fates.'[5] Ishmael analogizes the fixed threads of the warp as necessity or fate, the threads of the woof that he weaves with his own hand as free will, and the wooden sword with which Queequeg drives home the yarns as chance. . . . Necessity, free will, chance – Ishmael's labor contains these elements even as it represents them: Weaving mats participates in the structure of metaphysics that it signifies. This works out very neatly: Ishmael's understanding of his task illuminates the larger process of events – the parameters of human history brought together on the Loom of Time. The metaphor rests not on the product (the mat) but on the process, the labor, the weaving, the act of production. Ishmael's labor partakes of the historical process it represents, as Ishmael's labor both produces the symbol and is produced in turn by the things it signifies – necessity, free will, and chance.

In a later chapter, 'The Monkey-Rope,' Ishmael again introduces labor as a symbolic reproduction; this time when he finds in the work of 'cutting-in' (or stripping the layers of blubber from the dead whale) an emblem of the social networks of human interdependence. The 'monkey-rope,' tied around the waists of Queequeg on the slippery back of the whale and Ishmael on the ship's deck, forces Ishmael to realize 'that my own individuality was now merged in a joint stock company of two: that my free will had received a mortal wound; and that another's mistake or misfortune might plunge innocent me into unmerited disaster and death' (p. 1135). In this case, the rope serves as the figure, representing the ties among men because it *is* one – an outward and visible sign of the mutual dependence and linked fates of men. The monkey-rope is a material example of what it represents; it simply conforms (in a remarkable degree) to the pattern of other social relations. Its bond is an economic relation, dictated by the process of production. The structure of interdependence it stands for is also a set of economic relations: Ishmael suggests that the failure of one's banker or apothecary would be as disastrous as if Queequeg should slip and fall off the whale. Here again the figure represents by synecdoche rather than pure metaphor; the rope's extended meaning is produced by universalizing it, by identifying one particular economic relation with the total structure of relations in society. At bottom Ishmael insists, his situation is no different from any other: 'I saw that this situation of mine was the precise situation of every mortal that breathes; only, in most cases, he, one way or other, has this Siamese connexion with a plurality of other mortals' (p.1135). In Ishmael's case, his connections are concentrated and made symbolically manifest through the act of production.

. . . In *Moby-Dick*, labor represents and becomes part of nature; whereas the other side of economy – money – represents and becomes part of language. Ishmael repairs this division in economy (and in semantics) by unfolding correspondences that reinstate the symbolic unity of the experienced world and authorize language and money as representatives of a single integrated whole, consisting of man and nature. Money and language become authentic signs by virtue of their multivocalness and their ability to mediate between a singular objective world and a diversity of imaginative ones. In a central chapter that dramatizes this theory of signs, all the various characters confront a talismanic object and read themselves in a piece of money – 'The Doubloon' – the Spanish-American gold piece that Ahab nails to the mast as the reward for the first to sight the white whale. All the major characters (except Ishmael) attempt to interpret the doubloon's significance, and this progression of imaginative encounters centralizes the issues of perception and motivation that so concern the novel. The chapter arrays a multiplicity of meanings around a central sign or text, and the pattern of the different readings illuminates the differences among the observers and suggests the semi-magical properties that adhere to the sign of money.

The coin described by Ishmael is an eight escudo gold piece (or doubloon) actually minted in Ecuador from 1838 through 1843. The obverse, showing a 'Liberty' head, is nailed toward the mast, so that it is never seen. But the reverse, showing a sun flanked by the zodiac over three mountains, capped by a tower, fowl, and volcanic cloud, proves a fertile text. Ahab, Starbuck, Stubb, Flask, the Manxman, Queequeg, Fedallah, and Pip, each sees his own portrait on the coin and constructs his own particular relation to the value it represents. . . . The doubloon's manifold uses as a figure derive from its doubleness, or reflective function, its separation of individualized meanings, so that no one reading excludes or impinges on another, and its accumulation of significance from the procession of observers. The coin multiplies the fetish quality of money by making many different systems of value reside in a single material object.

The doubloon is ultimately a fit symbol of symbols – its worth proves its significance, while its value is defined through its symbolic meanings. The coin is not involved in any transaction; it is not the product of labor, nor part of the system of capital that commissioned the ship. Of 'purest, virgin gold . . . untouchable and immaculate to any foulness,' the *Pequod*'s doubloon 'was set apart and sanctified to one awe-striking end; . . . the mariners revered it as the white whale's talisman.' Through various tropes (synecdoche, metonymy, typology, symbolism) the doubloon's system of representation expands to include the entire world; from Ahab to Moby Dick, from the trinity to the zodiac, from cigars to signs and wonders, from the life of man to the language of interpretation. As money and as symbol the doubloon serves as a pledge of Ahab's will; it represents the debt he owes Moby Dick. The coin also seals Ahab's unholy bargain with the crew; it represents the abrogation of the social contract expressed in the ship's articles; it is the token of the diabolical covenant to hunt the white whale.

The doubloon presents a reflective surface to each observer. Ahab declares: 'This round gold is but an image of the rounder globe, which, like a magician's glass, to each and every man in turn but mirrors back his own mysterious self.' Queequeg's perspective (like Stubb's and Starbuck's) is much the same: He sees his identity with the coin – its value is representative of himself; the coin is his own reflected double. Perhaps this is why Melville chose the 'doubloon' as his figure, for its doubling effect is its most characteristic function. The coin is a figure that both divides and reunites, bifurcating the world and reintegrating it by reflective correspondences. Pip, the last speaker, must recognize something of this, for his jingle implies that reality resides not in the coin but in the progression of its observers: 'I look, you look, he looks; we look, ye look, they look.' Not the thing that is seen, but the ways of seeing it and the connections among the observers determine for Pip the doubloon's value or significance. 'I, you, he, we, ye, they' imply a range of human relations, relations, moreover, that are mediated by language. Pip's conjugation of looking brings together the different readings just as the coin itself does, except that Pip's emphasis is on the human subjects and not, like the coin's, on the reflective world of signs. Pip looks, so to speak, on the other side of the coin, the obverse side, which is never seen, and from that perspective he announces the identity of all the observers.

The different values that Pip, Ahab, Starbuck, and the others place on the doubloon become in some sense equivalent, being mutually represented by the same thing. The chorus of readings locates the doubloon's meaning not in the coin but in the different observers; the doubloon's abundance of signs accommodates all interpretations and offers a language to each understanding. But even though the coin eventually conflates all these meanings, it does not work, as currency should, to mediate the relations among its human observers. None of the interpreters speaks to another. Each has a separate encounter with the substance of value and a different reading of its name. Stubb, who overhears them all musing aloud, narrates the episode and allows each reader to take away his own proper meaning without impinging on the meanings attributed by the others. As Stubb says, 'There's another rendering now; but still one text. All sorts of men in one kind of world, you see.' Eight ways of looking at a gold coin (nine if we count Ishmael's, ten if we count the crew's) do not upset its reality; no one questions the coin's value or authenticity. The doubloon remains a substantial and definite object; its multiplicity, although ambiguous, is cumulative and reassuring; its value is not neutralized by contradictory appraisals. The meanings that are concentrated in the coin can coexist without conflict because the doubloon itself is fixed and static, never becoming part of the system of exchanges or a token of men's economic relations. The coin's elaborate dual structure of supply and demand, of desire and object, of man and his reflections, refers each observer in turn to an alternate version of himself. The value of the coin is achieved in each case only by way of an imaginative exchange or symbolic transaction.

. . . Viewing *Moby-Dick* as a less than radical critique of American capitalism coincides with one of the plot's central features: Ahab's rebellion against God, economy and nature. Ahab has no respect for the commercial purposes of the *Pequod*'s voyage, yet the form of his opposition to the system of economic relations serves ultimately to reinforce the values of the bourgeois order. Ahab's madness, his usurpation of power, and his rigid authoritarianism all deflect criticism away from the economic system that launched the *Pequod*. Ahab is more dangerous than the ship's owners; and although he is also more sympathetic and even admirable in his grand self-reliance, it is a self-reliance run amok. Ahab sets up a false opposition – between his own wild romanticism and the commercial values of Starbuck and the owners. These emerge as the two formal choices; while Ishmael, who, if anyone, would seem to represent an alternative to this dichotomy of capitalism straight or capitalism perverted, declines to choose and so serves both sides. Ahab radiates the grandeur of the heroic individual; Starbuck, the conventional values of business, family and home. Ahab, with his demonic power and enormous attractiveness, is represented as a demagogue who usurps the system of production for his own private mission of vengeance. His revolt against the system of profit diverts Ishmael's criticism away from the whaling industry itself, which in its pristine form regularly sacrifices human life to the production of capital.

Ishmael's ideology of labor offers no effective antithesis to the system of production; the novel is balanced rather than dialectical. Ishmael's ideology combines comic resignation with democratic rhetoric; his perspective on events is emphatically not subversive of whaling as a capitalist industry. Ishmael often has his reveries and epiphanies of mystical transcendence – not only squeezing sperm, but also at the masthead, or floating serenely among schools of whales. But while each of these occurs in a social context – that is, during some form of labor – the content of Ishmael's meditations is distinctly asocial, concerning not the relations among men but those imaginary relations between the individual mind and the universe at large. The rhetoric of labor and the types and figures through which production corresponds to its universal referents make Ishmael's work inseparable from what it represents. The relations of production are sanctioned by their symbolic qualities. Ishmael is reminded of nature, Providence, time, society, and human life processes because they are both symbolized and literalized in his labor. This redoubling or inner reflection characterizes all his tropes: Each illuminates itself and effectively eliminates the distance between the sign (labor) and whatever it signifies.

Melville remained enthusiastic about his practice of representation in *Moby-Dick*, even though he was fast becoming aware of its potential limitations. . . . By pondering the different possible meanings of the coin, the whale, or the labor, Melville emphasizes the man-made or artificial quality of his signs. Yet the central symbol always predates any of its interpretations, each of which is incomplete and inferior insofar as it partial or personal. The signs themselves remain seemingly unmotivated, though displayed within a structure of motivated meanings. There is clearly a sense in which Ahab invents Moby Dick, even though, significantly, Moby Dick is already there, ubiquitous in space and time. In much the same way, Ishmael does not merely invent any of the labor he finds so meaningful. It awaits his discovery, and its independence from himself lends additional authority to his symbolic readings. This is also true more generally of Ishmael's relation to language (his other means of production); for he is ever protesting that he has found, and not originated, such arcane whaling terms as 'squilgee,' 'specksynder,' 'white-horse,' 'plum-pudding,' or 'slobgollion.' The things and the words for them are always there, but signification awaits the conception that links the object or person to its name, a situation emphasized from the novel's very beginning – 'Call me Ishmael' – where the symbol ('Ishmael') applies to the self ('me') in a relation produced by an act of language. The ambiguity of symbols such as money and labor revolves around this question of whether signs are discovered or invented, whether economy is natural or artificial. Ishmael's discovery of chains of analogies throughout the economic process must always be balanced against competing interpretations. The signs themselves, however, are solid, definite, unmistakable, and authoritative in their own right. Upon this literal level of economic fact Ishmael rests with confidence, doubting neither the material world nor its connection to other worlds beyond. Similarly, Ishmael's philosophy, his irony, and his vision of human and cosmic nature depend on the values of a certain way of life – American democratic free enterprise. This ideology gives substance to Ishmael's language, and he benefits from going with rather than against the grain of his rhetoric.[6] □

Royster's reading of *Moby-Dick* is quite clearly influenced by post-structuralist theory. His discussion, for example, of the act of self-naming with which Ishmael opens the book's narrative – wherein selfhood is seen as a product of language – seems drawn from discussions of subjectivity by the French theorist Jacques Lacan. Similarly, Lacan has pointed to the 'split subject' in a text, where the 'I' who speaks is felt to be split from the 'I' of the text, the subject of the discourse.[7] For Royster such anti-essentialism – the insistence that selfhood is produced by language rather than being grounded in an idea of the self as fixed and unchanging, an essence at the heart of being – sits uneasily with his materialist reading of the 'Doubloon' chapter. Each observer of the doubloon, he notes, sees their own essential individuality reflected back to them by it. By stressing Pip's 'reading' of the doubloon, Royster reconfirms an ideology of self-reliance, one in which an emphasis 'on the human subjects and not . . . on the reflective world of signs' assumes that 'the identity of all the observers' is a material fact rather than something constituted within language.

Royster's essay represents a refreshing and challenging new direction in *Moby-Dick* criticism in the attention it throws upon the problematic relationship between selfhood and representation that the text exposes. His reading is also, however, rather disappointing in not fully analysing how such a problematic results from pressures within the discourses of capitalism and individualism in Melville's time. Finally, then, Royster's essay seems to veer away from the socio-political reconstruction of mid-nineteenth-century America as a burgeoning capitalist economy that it promises at the outset.

The next extract is more successful in its use of a close reading of *Moby-Dick* to illuminate the more general state of mind of Melville's America. Whilst its specific focus is entirely different from that of Royster, it again revolves around questions of selfhood, social relations, and power. In the following extract, taken from his fascinating book *Manhood and the American Renaissance* (1989), David Leverenz's reading of

-Dick draws on psychoanalytic models to explore the tension ᴅetween self and society that underpins antebellum American ideology. Using a broadly Freudian conception of the self – as one of repressed desires – Leverenz expressly attempts to 'return the book to Ahab'.[8] His study, then, represents a double return in Melville criticism. Firstly it returns to an examination of Ahab (rather than Ishmael) as the book's controlling centre. This, as we shall see in the next chapter, provides *Moby-Dick* criticism with a strategy for usefully deconstructing the discourses of power and persuasion that operate in the text. And secondly, it returns to an examination of the text's troublesome doubleness and ambiguity, something Royster never quite seems to manage. For Leverenz, the seat of such ambiguity is the very concept of selfhood, and its expression in the figure of Ahab. He argues that 'Ishmael and Ahab are doubles of a self that loathes itself',[9] and that such self-loathing is the key to understanding the constitutive forces of nineteenth-century America. In Leverenz's analysis, then, the doubling of Ahab and Ishmael comes to signify the pressures of a society feeling itself to be being slowly torn apart by internal divisions, divisions between, say, individualism and democratic responsibility, male and female roles in a rapidly changing culture, conformity and rebellion, and economic power and powerlessness within the emerging capitalist economy.

Leverenz's use of psychoanalytic theory also allows him, for the first time in *Moby-Dick* criticism, to make a virtue of the reader's own 'contradictory feelings'[10] towards the text. We are both fascinated and appalled by Ahab's coercive power over us, Leverenz argues. And our delight in – even desire for – such helplessness when faced with the book, he believes, exposes the book's main structuring principle. According to Leverenz, Ahab's craving for power is also a craving to be submissive. His desire for absolute dominance over his crew displays, in Freudian terms, his repressed desire to be dominated by a pure power. His defiance of God in the chapter 'The Candles' exposes, therefore, what Leverenz calls his 'ecstatic yet terrified passivity',[11] in which he asks to be beaten by a masterful father-figure. This, in turn, discloses the terms within which an ideology of entrepreneurial manhood can be seen to have been operating in Melville's America:

■ Melville exposes the chaos of narcissistic needs and fears in the American middle-class marketplace – the same marketplace that drove his patrician father to bankruptcy, insanity, and perhaps unconscious suicide. *Moby-Dick* is obviously a man's book, about a man obsessed with avenging his shattered manhood.[12] □

Though Leverenz's specific focus is an analysis of manhood in *Moby-Dick*, his reading is thus one of the first to develop a coherent critical practice for measuring the extent to which the text's contradictions and tensions are a product of, as he puts it, 'the sex-segregated world of American capitalism in its most predatory individualistic phase'.[13] Similarly, but to varying degrees, *Moby-Dick* criticism has followed Leverenz by using a reading of the book as the means to analyse (or even deconstruct) the social, political and cultural tensions underlying the formation of American ideology during the nineteenth century. The extract from Leverenz starts where Royster seemed, earlier, to get stuck: with the troublesomeness of an American ideology of individualism and freedom.

■ At one level, Ishmael's narrative exposes the craving for dominance and the fears about being beaten that underlie the conventional American rhetoric of freedom and individualism. At a more confused and primal level of feeling, his narrative exposes not a fear but a *craving* to be humiliated and thus to be passively fused with manly power. With Queequeg, Ishmael's loving, submissive response temporarily suspends his preoccupation with being assaulted – but only momentarily. The Counterpane dream brings back his terrified wish. While he masks his passive expectation of sexual assault as a giddy chumminess, his suppressed fear of the man who holds him fast has turned into desire, which in turn strangely evokes a feeling of having been possessed by power, stripped of its gender or any human facade.

Wishing to be bound to a man much stronger than himself, yet pursuing 'that story of Narcissus, . . . the key to it all,' Ishmael goes to sea to escape and find the self writ large as Ahab: an uncontrollable fusion of aggressive and suicidal impulses. Ishmael presents his hypos as the norm. All around the city, he says, 'stand thousands upon thousands of mortal men fixed in ocean reveries.' Why? Because they 'are all landsmen; of week days pent up in lath and plaster – tied to counters, nailed to benches, clinched to desks.' Such men, slaves to an anonymous urban marketplace, gaze at the water like Narcissus, Ishmael says. Seeking and fleeing the phantom of himself, Ishmael affixes himself to Ahab's quest to avenge his manhood. If Ishmael is a manhood junkie, Ahab will be a manhood pusher.

. . . Ahab's monomania focuses a general male sense of helplessness. He claims to be empowered with a representative, redemptive mission to avenge all those who have been unmanned and who therefore feel simultaneously enslaved and murderous. For the first two-thirds of his story Ahab has been manhood at the cutting edge – what D.H. Lawrence, another such man, called 'the last phallic being of the white men.'[14] Everything with him has been manly rage and rivalry. Ahab's passion for dominance is the obsession of nineteenth-century American men, the complement to female hysteria, which has so much to do with women's feelings of powerlessness.

. . . Monomania, a label that came into usage in the 1820s, hitched its own wagonload of male anxieties to the star of entrepreneurial competition. . . . In Ahab's case, he feels possessed by overmastering evil and talks about it as if he were a cosmic prisoner. But his voice bristles with competitive fire. 'I'd strike the sun if it insulted me,' Ahab says to the crew in 'The Quarter-Deck.' All greatness, he insists, is built on the 'fair play' of rivals in combat, 'jealousy presiding over all creations.' Ahab's confusion of jealous rivalry with greatness anticipates Harold Bloom's equally American sense of strong creativity by 120 years. Not even fair play is Ahab's master, he says. 'Who's over me? Truth has no confines.' His wild, exultant, metaphysical claims bring Starbuck to 'enchanted, tacit acquiescence'(144).[15] 'Who's over me?' is Ahab's fundamental question, just as 'Who aint a slave?' (15) is Ishmael's.

Ahab's monomania inflates the emerging middle-class ideology of manhood. His fair play of masterless, jealous rivals is entrepreneurial capitalism on a cosmic scale, reflecting at least two entrepreneurial modes of power: a will to exploit fluid resources and a will to dominate weaker men. Disdaining the actual marketplace, Ahab voices the metaphysics of manhood and humiliation under the pasteboard mask of profits. In his monomania he becomes an exaggerated prototype for the male behaviour pattern that helped ensure the worldwide dominance of American industry. He not only inherits Miltonic and Byronic patterns of pride but anticipates what has come to be known in America as the type A personality: the hard-driving, finger-drumming, aggressive, and insensitive executive, whose life so frequently ends its heartlessness in a heart attack. If we take literally Ishmael's blood-and-thunder imagery for his captain's body, Ahab's life seems to be one continuous heart attack, as he strives to 'burst his hot heart's shell' upon Moby Dick (160). He could represent every workaholic whose anger explodes at home. Birthing the narcissistic phantoms that consume him, with no life except in his quest for mastery, he thinks of his body as he thinks of any subordinate – at best a 'craven mate' (458).

. . . [It is the] renewed threat of symbolic castration [that] takes Ahab first toward a manic self-criticism, then to a paranoid disowning of himself, and finally to a fantasy of self-dissolution that denies any aggressiveness of his own. These confusions set the stage for Ahab's discovery of his 'queenly personality.' In 'The Candles,' Ahab's growing sense of himself as less and less alive, more and more a victim, veers from the language of paranoid monomania to the language of hysterical desire.

The change from manly rage to the pose of female hysteria comes when Ahab realizes for the first time that he is about to be beaten. The discovery transforms rage to desire. In 'The Candles,' his rhetorical fireworks function in at least three contradictory ways: to flaunt his masochistic craving, to intensify his domination of the crew, and to expose the absence of self binding Ahab to the power he defies. Paradoxically, as readers precipitously detach themselves from his demonic delirium, his wild and whirling words coerce the crew's mesmerized submission. Still more paradoxically, his words implicitly acknowledge that he will lose, that he is driven, and that he is already dead inside.

'The Candles' takes place in a storm so intense that the lightning rods at the ends of the masts start to burn with an eerie, mesmerizing flame. The crew stands stupefied. Up in the rigging some men 'hung pendulous, like a knot of numbed wasps from a drooping, orchard twig.' Meanwhile, their captain reaches out his left hand and grabs hold of the links to the lightning rods. It seems a demonic parody of Benjamin Franklin's kite experiment.

Then, as if to parody American race relations as well, Ahab plants one imperial foot on the tawny back of the Parsee who kneels in front of him. He sticks up his right arm, fixes his 'upward eye' on the 'lofty tri-pointed trinity of flames,' and announces that he is a woman. 'In the midst of the personified impersonal, a personality stands here . . . the queenly personality lives in me, and feels her royal rights' (416–417).

It's a startling line, especially when it stands by itself. At this point in the story I've become impatient with Ahab's majestic uproar of metaphysical brag and flailing desperation. Yet almost nothing prepares me for the gender change. Moreover, his announcement is strangely ambiguous. It's not *his* personality, but '*a* personality,' a queen that 'lives in me,' as if Ahab's brain were her castle. He now equates his 'me' with the outer shell, the 'personified impersonal,' within which some queenly stranger 'stands . . . and feels her royal rights.' What these rights are, he doesn't say. Nor is it clear how he/she can 'feel' a 'right.' All we can say with certainty is that he now thinks of his defiance as female. While his rigid manly stance seems to be petrifying into a mask for the personified impersonal, a woman takes command of his feelings. More seems to be at stake here than simply proving he's not a coward.

Ahab's queenly personality lives in him only for a moment. Then it vanishes from his self-consciousness, with no reappearance. Critics have never known quite what to make of it. It stands like a lighthouse on a nonexistent island. Faced with such an unnerving self-dislocation, Melville scholars tend to let the line rush by as an odd, quirky gust in the midst of a basically theological storm. But God, Lucifer, and Gnostic heresy are more pretext than text. The 'queenly personality' line seems so memorable, and so anomalous, because it brings to the surface the gender inversion latent in the story's beating fantasy.

What are the queen's royal rights? Astonishingly, it appears, to wed and bed the king, her hateful husband, in slavish desire and helpless defiance. 'I now know thee, thou clear spirit,' Ahab declaims to the fire, 'and I now know thy right worship is defiance. . . . I own thy speechless, placeless power; but to the last gasp of my earthquake life will dispute its unconditional, unintegral mastery in me' (416–417). Ahab simultaneously 'owns,' or acknowledges, the fire's power over him ('Who's over me?') and 'owns,' or possesses, that power within him. Fire and queen are both inside him, yet alien and mutually hostile. The rest of Ahab's wild speech tries to couple them. With an extravagantly artificial blending of gothic melodrama and Elizabethan soliloquy, his queenly defiance becomes the first step in a hysterical dance of seduction. First his manhood, then his queenliness yield to his desire to be ravished by the power he hates and hallucinates.

. . . Like a classic hysteric, Ahab has presented himself rhetorically as a flaming queen and a passive victim whose desires have been scripted. More and more he thinks of himself as the latter, an errand boy for some alien, demonic force that drives him on. His voice becomes a babble of poses, a gothic Lear on the outside, 'indifferent' at the core. While Ishmael disowns his body's submissiveness by floating off into the vapors of philosophical indeterminacy, where he covertly deconstructs the reader's expectations for a consistent voice and a continuous plot, Ahab both worships and defies the experience of being beaten that he discovers again and again under his rage for dominance.

. . . Ahab's madness gains allegiance and credibility, or at least awed submission, not because he makes sense but because he shouts the stresses of manhood with a shaman's intensity. In granting psychological authenticity to his woe, however, we accept his metaphysical aggrandizement of manhood, which for Ahab means dominating or being dominated, as the only interpretive frame for subjective experience. If 'self' becomes the inscription of a sadomasochistic boss-slave intercourse, then Ishmael's decentered fluidity of voice becomes the only alternative for the survival of the mind.

We also accept Ishmael's appropriation of mothering to nurture his self-deconstruction, while Ahab appropriates a queenly personality to voice his defiant desire to be beaten. Ishmael's appropriation is much more seductive and long-lasting. The buoyancy of an orphan dependent on faceless maternal care becomes the survivor's alternative to Ahab's tyrannical quest. Especially toward the end of *Moby Dick*, Ishmael mutes his attacks on 'the step-mother world' (443) and celebrates maternal love in a variety of ways: not just in the exuberant sexuality and regressiveness of 'The Grand Armada' but in many quiet images of nurturance at the margins of Ahab's quest, such as the contrast between the lone bulls and the loving concern of female whales (330), the account in 'The Life-Buoy' of seal dams who have lost their cubs (429), or 'the devious-cruising Rachel' that picks up orphaned Ishmael in the epilogue (470). These mothers, like Ishmael, are victims.

A perhaps more feminist reading would argue . . . that Ishmael moves from Ahab's male consciousness of power as dominance to a perception of relational female powers in the ocean, the whale, the self, and language. Female powers give birth to a womb-like, fluid creativity that regenerates rather than destroys. This model of non-competitive power has been popular in recent feminist theories as a celebration of patriarchal subversion and free play. . . .

In my reading, Ishmael's images of loving maternity constitute a powerfully seductive erasure of conflicted feelings. His recurrent fantasy of bereft mothers solacing bereft children indulges a narcissistic self-pity that veils his narcissistic rage.

. . . The structuring fantasy in *Moby Dick* is to watch a man being beaten. It has two sources: Melville's personal narcissistic trauma, which recasts helpless resentment as a raging desire to be punished by a godlike, yet malevolent father-mother, and Melville's depth of intuition about the code of entrepreneurial manhood, which made men like his father so fear humiliation. Unlike Allan Melvill, Ahab rejects the market out of hand. But Ahab participates wholeheartedly in the underlying dynamic of the new capitalist class: the one-against-the-universe struggle for dominance. He *has* been possessed, by a drive that turns him against himself.

. . . What makes *Moby Dick* so exhilarating is its extravagant plunge into the manly American mind: its zest for exploration, its awe at pain, its rapture at the hunt for whales and ideas, its craving for dominance and fluidity all at once. Toward the end, however, the narrative starts to expose both the pain and the scripted conventionality of manhood. A stark passivity belies Ahab's rhetorical posturings, while the narrative's tightening vortex of dominance and humiliation, malevolence and helplessness, circles inexorably toward the final beating. There the bad self exists as hapless victim.

In Ahab's last act of aggression, the king-turned-spear-carrier gives up the spear. He throws his harpoon; the harpoon hits Moby Dick. But the rope runs foul. 'Ahab stooped to clear it; he did clear it; but the flying turn caught him round the neck, and voicelessly as

Turkish mutes bowstring their victim, he was shot out of the boat, ere the crew knew he was gone' (468).

Ahab's quest for manhood ends in the passive voice: 'he was shot out of the boat.' The tyrannical shouter dies as he inwardly lived, incapable of speech. Here is hysteria's most classic symptom, what Amariah Brigham called 'a feeling of stiffness and suffocation about the throat.'[16] His life ends in a choking seizure. At that moment, carried away by his bond to power, Ahab may have sensed what it felt like to be voiceless and terrified, an emotionally battered child-bride of the nineteenth century.

Or is it Melville's last devious twist to compel our own trancelike bond with the bully as victim?

It's not enough to subside into Ishmael's whalelike view of things, and regard both possibilities 'with equal eye' (314). That's evasive, frustrating, mocking, even maddening. Yet it's where his narration comes to rest. To go further, we have to look through the text to the social origins of feelings about power and powerlessness. Where power is felt as narcissistic compensation, there can never be enough. What remains in the ripples of powerlessness is Ishmael, afloat on the mystery of himself, telling a story of men pursuing a demon beyond themselves. That demon, I have been arguing is manhood. As the most searing exploration of manhood in the American Renaissance, *Moby Dick* bears full witness to the aspirations and terrors of American men at mid-century, and bears partial witness to Melville's personal pain.[17] □

Whereas the previous essays in this chapter focused on specific topics in *Moby-Dick* to illustrate its exemplary place within American ideology, the next two extracts read *Moby-Dick* more generally, as a text that throws light upon the culture of Melville's America as a whole. These are two of the most important critical examinations of *Moby-Dick* ever to have been written. Both attend to the political underpinnings of Melville's novel. And in so doing, both mark crucial new ways of reading the book. David S. Reynolds – whose essay closes this chapter – sees the novel as the first truly American literary masterpiece, the realisation of America's democratic promise because of its reliance upon American popular culture. Leo Bersani's essay – from which the following extract is taken – is, itself, a masterpiece of critical writing. Answering *Moby-Dick* in its own beautifully written and measured cadences, Bersani's essay argues that *Moby-Dick* dramatises the impossibility of the very idea of democracy in America. Democracy, like *Moby-Dick*'s own self-deflating rhetoric, maintains Bersani, presents us with an 'oxymoronic impasse'. For Bersani, therefore, if *Moby-Dick*'s blankness of whiteness means anything, then that meaning is precisely its refusal to mean anything to the culture which it, nevertheless, 'still manages to define'.[18] In this paradoxical sense, then, Bersani's reading of *Moby-Dick* witnesses its transformation into the radical text that it had always seemed to be.

■ In his essay 'Hawthorne and His Mosses,' Melville argues that American originality will write a glorious new chapter in the history of world literature only if it rejects its place in that history. Is it possible to write *like* nobody – without, however, eliminating the possibility of writing *better* than anyone else or being favorably compared with those to whom one owes nothing?

Moby-Dick, in extraordinary ways, accepts and struggles with the pressure of these contradictions. It is clear that Melville has no intention of waiting for those men just being born on the banks of the Ohio to prove their genius. *Moby-Dick* is the great original American book invoked in 'Hawthorne and His Mosses'; or, at the very least, it squarely meets the challenge of that essay. Melville will take an American subject – even a provincial American subject: the industry of whaling – and show that the greatest literature can be made from that subject. It is not a question of proving that a lot can be made out of a little, but rather of showing that what may seem to be a little is already a lot. . . . There is a cultural encyclopedism in *Moby-Dick* as well as a cetological encyclopedism. It is not that the entries exhaustively treat any subject, but the encyclopedic intention . . . is obvious with respect to foreign cultures as well as to whaling. It is as if the great American novel had constantly to be measuring itself against the highest achievements of other cultures, and in *Moby-Dick* this means testing the American book's capacity to appropriate a vast field of cultural reference. Melville's splendidly arrogant claim is that almost everything in world culture might be made to serve his subject. . . . It is not merely that *Moby-Dick* is worthy of being compared to either *King Lear* or *Oedipus Rex*. Instead it must be compared to both at the same time; only an encyclopedic range of cultural reference can do justice to Melville's mighty theme. . . . *Moby-Dick* is therefore not only as great as any one of these references; in needing them all to explain itself, it also proposes to surpass them all. Cetological erudition in *Moby-Dick* is only the first step in an enterprise of cannibalistic encyclopedism. Like its monster-hero, Melville's novel opens its jaws to devour all other representations from Lear's Fool to Vishnoo the Hindu god.

. . . The cultural appropriations meant to authenticate *Moby-Dick*'s claim to greatness are exposed as both laughingly inappropriate to the book's subject and even somewhat ridiculous in themselves. Not only that: in spite of what might seem like a heavy dose of cetology for a work of fiction, Ishmael actually encourages us to be distrustful of his research and presumed knowledge about the whale. The book's cetological erudition – based on remarkably partial sources – is often nothing more than a parody of the erudition of others, and the 'proofs' offered of the whale's extraordinary powers most frequently consist (as in 'The Affidavit' chapter) of hearsay and assertion. More is at stake here than Ishmael's resistance to Ahab's monomania, more than a presumably viable humanistic alternative to interpretive madness. It is as if the writing of Moby-Dick became for Melville the eerie process of dismissing the very ambitions that the novel also seeks so strenuously to realize, as if a kind of levelling indifference had taken over or – most interestingly – as if the notion of American literary greatness were dropped in order to be reinvented, but reinvented as something lost, indefensible, abandoned.

What is it, in Moby-Dick's primary project, that might explain Melville's apparent indifference toward it, even his subversion of it? In Moby-Dick the political implication of the contradictions hinted at in 'Hawthorne and His Mosses' becomes inescapable. More exactly, the notion of American literary greatness is politically represented in Moby-Dick, and this means trying to give some coherence or plausibility to the idea of democratic greatness. . . . In Moby-Dick the rhetoric of democracy has become oxymoronic: in a democracy equality founds and legitimates inequality.

. . . Far from being a democratic rejection of emperors and kings, Moby-Dick proposes a unique expansion of the monarchic principle. Ahab will earn his right to be called King Ahab, to have his meals with his three mates compared to 'the Coronation banquet at Frankfort, where the German Emperor profoundly dines with the seven Imperial Electors.' Ahab embodies and realizes the ambition of the novel itself: to have a royal preeminence over European literature without borrowing anything from European models of literary greatness.

And yet the very condition of this success is of course a massive borrowing from those models. . . . Moby-Dick's greatness is unlike that of any other book, and Ahab's royal nature is not to be thought of as comparable to that of other kings and emperors precisely because they can be compared to so many other books and kings. Originality occurs, as it were, after a certain threshold of absorption has been passed, and Moby-Dick's cultural encyclopedism is a peculiarly American attempt to quantify quality, to produce originality through mass. Once again we are forced to recognize the novel's oxymoronic argument: democracy produces the greatest kings, and analogy authenticates originality. Thus Melville wins his argument for Ahab by destroying the very reason for making the argument in the first place: the unassimilable, incomparable uniqueness of the democratic personality.

. . . Against those aristocratic societies where individual personality is largely irrelevant to a hierarchy of power determined by inherited privileges and reinforced by external arts and embellishments, Melville argues for a society (if not a universe) where the individual personality counts, indeed is determinant, in the distribution of power. But it is the very assertion of the rights of self which risks destroying those conditions allowing for it in the first place. In terms of an unrelenting logic enacted by *Moby-Dick*, democracy ultimately promises the unintended and politically tragic consequence of its own extinction. Melville persuasively expresses the thrill of the democratic promise, both for the individual and for literature, but that thrill is perhaps inseparable from the prospect of unlimited power. The excitement *about* Ahab in *Moby-Dick* is provoked by the spectacle of what might be called an earned despotism. The *Pequod* is the social realization of a fantasy of intrinsic kingship. The opportunity for self-expression and self-assertion in a democratic society is, Melville's novel suggests, existentially translated as a will to power; despotism is the social logic within an argument for the rights of personality.

. . . I have argued that, principally through Ahab, *Moby-Dick* dramatizes the oxymoronic impasse of democracy: the great man's despotism realizes the democratic dream of equality. But *Moby-Dick* also reinvents that politically infernal rhetoric as a political promise: it dreams a society owing nothing whatsoever to known social ideas. What this society after social death might actually be, we can say no more than Melville (or Ishmael) himself can. What can be said is only what has already been said, and Ishmael's way of coercing all that used speech into unimagined significances is to withdraw humorously from nearly all his propositions. He can say what he means only by refusing to mean what he says. America's history will take place in the space at once cluttered and blank where all imaginable social bonds have been simultaneously figured and dissolved. Melville's America is a historical meta-oxymoron: it defeats the defeating oxymoron of a democracy ruined by the fulfilment of its own promise by erasing all promises in order to make the wholly unauthorized promise of an absolutely new society.

The representation of Melville's America is thus inseparable from a crisis of meaning. On the one hand, the interpretive faculty is associated with madness. It is not that 'all evil' is personified in Moby Dick, but also that Ahab sees evil omens and portents everywhere. The mass of information given to us about whales and whaling is obviously designed to counteract this madness; here the encyclopedia functions as an antidote to overreading, as a source of reliable facts, as a comfortable and necessary myth of a collection of knowledge unaffected by the collector's passions.

. . . What is interesting, as others have noted, is the interpretive habit itself or, more strangely, the inability to stop reading, even though the object to be read may be unreadable.

. . . *Moby-Dick* is a chaos of interpretive modes. As a drama of interpretation, Melville's novel appears to center on Ahab. But Ahab
represents only one type of interpretive activity, and in a sense it is the
crudest and easiest to discredit. For him, Moby Dick is a symbol of
evil that, in its vicious attacks, fittingly partakes of the nature of what
it symbolizes. Ahab is guilty of a double mistake of logic: he unjustifi-
ably infers an agent or course of evil from the observable phenomenon
of human 'sufferings and exasperations,' and then he identifies a possible manifestation of that evil with its essence. Having done that, he –
and with him now the crew – begins to see all things as signs.
Although symbolic reading is particular to Ahab (nothing indicates
that the crew shares Ahab's philosophically sophisticated madness of
attributing the sum of human woes to the whale they are chasing), a
degraded form of symbolic interpretation manifests itself as the super-
stition of signs. Instead of symbols, we have portents: the darting
away of 'shoals of small harmless fish . . . with what seemed shudder-
ing fins,' the 'tri-painted trinity of flames' when the ship's three masts
are set on fire by lightning during the typhoon, and the seizing of
Ahab's hat from his head by a savage sea hawk. Symbolism is a
vertical mode of interpretation (Moby Dick is transcended by the
metaphysical reality he points to), but the ominous sign can be
thought of as a metonymic slip. It is as if part of a pattern of catastrophe
had been detached from the pattern and moved ahead of its realization
in time. The omen announces the event to which it belongs; it is the
beginning of a catastrophe that has not yet begun.

. . . The consequence of all this is that *Moby-Dick* becomes a novel
unavailable to the culture it still manages to define (while making the
generous, even utopian assumption that such readings as the one I am
proposing *are* available to that culture). Melville's novel is the literary
equivalent of that 'dumb blankness full of meaning' which is what
Ishmael finds so awesome in that whale's whiteness. We may continue to speak of *Moby-Dick* (as the novel itself demonstrates, criticism
is unstoppable), but we can at least hope for an appropriately impoverished reading, one that principally describes how the narrative
anticipates, entertains, and withdraws its assent from all our interpretive moves. The chapter on 'The Whiteness of the Whale' analyzes the
symptoms of a mind afflicted with an oxymoronic perception of the
universe. Reality is an infinitely meaningful absence of meaning, and
Moby-Dick – a novel of metaphysical realism – repeats that textuality in
its own apparently unlimited capacity to entertain unauthorized interpretations. But this type of textuality – in which unreadability is
identical to a limitless availability to interpretation – may be the
condition of the novel's originality. American literature can be great
not by being as good as or even better than European literature; it

must be, in the full force of the term, incomparable. Thus Ishmael will not only destroy the terms of comparison; he will also invalidate the very process of comparison – the unrelenting analogical habit – to which he appeals in order to validate his project of writing a 'mighty book'. *Moby-Dick* outdoes the cultural references it appropriates by dismissing itself; the simultaneous proposal and erasure of sense produces a book bloated with unaccepted sense. The extraordinary originality of Melville's work is that it somehow subsists – materially – as a book orphaned by its content.

The only surviving analogy of this shipwreck of sense is the analogy with America itself. . . . It suggests that the originality of America cannot consist in a chimerical absolute break with its European past, but rather in what might be called an encyclopedic nonendorsement of that past. In America, as in Melville's novel, the massive borrowing from other cultures is identical to a self-distancing from other cultures. Sense is borrowed without being subscribed to, and the very indiscriminacy of the borrowing should produce a society without debts, one that never holds what it nonetheless greedily takes. *Moby-Dick* is at once politically, aesthetically, and economically utopian in that it invites America *to dissipate its capital*. This is not, I believe, merely another capitalistic or liberal mystification: far from merely offering the illusion of a break with established orders (an illusion so comforting that it would actually weaken our resistance to those same orders), *Moby-Dick* proposes no object of loyalty or of desire except the continuously repeated gesture of not receiving the wealth it appropriates.

The encyclopedism of *Moby-Dick* is, then, in no way redemptive. Never using either its cetological erudition or its cultural borrowings to monumentalize the truly raw materials of the American life, Melville's novel takes the same risks as the country it finally honors, not by taking the lead in world literature but by repeating its impoverished beginning, its utopian negations. *Moby-Dick* is indeed our mighty book, not because it makes a whole of the fragments of America but rather because, in its sheer massiveness, it never stops demonstrating (as if to inspire courage) the sustaining, self-renewing powers of historical and cultural orphanhood.[19] □

In the final essay of this chapter David S. Reynolds develops and extends the discussion of *Moby-Dick*'s relationship to American popular culture that he initiated in his book *Beneath the American Renaissance* (1988). Reynolds' model of 'reconstructive criticism', which was discussed earlier, draws here on his extensive scholarly researches into the popular writing and culture of antebellum America. In this sense it epitomises what Brian Higgins and Hershel Parker describe, in their introduction to the book from which this essay is taken, as the 'beginning of a new era in Melville scholarship', wherein critical insight and literary scholarship are brought together to reinvigorate our understanding of Melville's great masterpiece.[20] Reynolds' essay is thus a fitting conclusion to this chapter, asking us, as it does, to reconceive our relationship to *Moby-Dick* and to America.

■ It was precisely Melville's *openness* to images from various contemporary cultural arenas – not, as is commonly thought, his *alienation* from his culture – that accounts for the special complexity of *Moby-Dick*. Melville's narrative art was one of wide-ranging assimilation and literary transformation. It reflected his statement in 'Hawthorne and His Mosses' that the American writer was 'bound to carry republican progressiveness into Literature as well as into Life.' A principal misconception about Moby-Dick is that its ambiguities stood in opposition to a popular culture that was uniformly tame and moralistic. Actually, antebellum popular culture was full of contradictions and paradoxes that became textually inscribed in Melville's most capacious novel.

The main types of popular writing Melville drew from in *Moby-Dick* were Romantic Adventure fiction, dark reform literature, [and] radical-democrat fiction. . . . Melville had learned key images and stereotypes from each of these modes by immersing himself in American popular culture as a writer for the mass market earlier in his career. Melville knew that his first two novels were, as he wrote his publisher about *Omoo*, 'calculated for popular reading.'[21] . . . As dismissive as Melville was about some of this early fiction, he learned much from his forays into popular culture. Taken together, Melville's early works show him to have been a daring experimenter with popular images. The breadth of his experimentation placed him in an ideal position to produce a novel of full cultural representativeness. When Melville is studied in terms of his popular cultural backgrounds, we see the validity of a contemporary reviewer's remark that in *Moby-Dick* he seemed 'resolved to combine all his popular characteristics.'[22]

. . . To find cultural roots for the mythic, richly ambiguous quality of *Moby-Dick* we must look not to Romantic Adventure fiction, which [is] generally nonsymbolic and merely adventurous, but to other areas of antebellum popular culture, particularly dark-reform literature and radical-democrat fiction. A principle distinction between *Moby-Dick* and other adventure fiction was Melville's assimilation of a full range of zestful, paradoxical images from such dark popular literature.

The capacity for a richly imagistic work such as *Moby-Dick* had been inherent in American popular culture since the early 1830s, when vehement reformers began coining larger-than-life, mythic metaphors for the social vices they fiercely denounced. Virtually every reform movement of the day – temperance, antislavery, antiprostitution, naval reform, utopian socialism – became notably sensationalized in the hands of popular reformers competing for the attention of an American public increasingly taken with Dark Adventure novels and crime-filled penny newspapers. The 'dark' or 'immoral' reformers, as I call them, righteously proclaimed that they were wallowing in foul moral sewers only to scour them clean; but their seamy writings prove that they were more powerfully drawn to wallowing than cleaning. . . .

The dark reformers introduced a fierce new rhetoric that featured veil-lifting imagery, mythic metaphors, and post-Calvinist gloom. In popular reform newspapers and pamphlets, vice was regularly described as a 'monster' stalking over mountains and rivers, or a 'whirlpool' sucking helpless victims to destruction, or an 'ocean' threatening to engulf the world, or an all-controlling 'fate.' . . .

By the time he wrote *Moby-Dick* Melville had gained full exposure to popular reforms, for he had experimented broadly with reform themes and images in his first five novels. In *Typee* and *Omoo* he had assumed a standard reform stance in his exposure of hypocrisy among white Christians on South Sea islands; other reforms he utilized were antiprostitution, temperance, peace reform, and utopian socialism, all of which had been widely debated in the popular press. In *Mardi* such reforms as temperance, socialism, and antislavery provide a backdrop to Melville's pondering of moral paradoxes and social conflict. The popular-oriented *Redburn* is filled with dark-temperance and city-mysteries images of the crassest variety, such as the picture of frivolous rich people and huge dens of sin in the modern city or a sailor's horrid suicide after heavy drinking or the sensational account of another sailor burned alive in flames produced by spontaneous combustion produced by cheap liquor he has drunk. In *White-Jacket* Melville used naval reform as a vehicle for diving into the mire of nineteenth-century social vices and for probing deep ironies in human nature and society. . . .

Since *Moby-Dick* can be viewed as the culmination of Melville's early permutations of the dark-reform mode, it is understandable that the novel has far more direct references to popular reform movements than even the most reform-minded of his previous novels. Temperance, antislavery, socialism, anti-Catholicism, antiwar – these and other popular reforms provide a wealth of images to Melville in *Moby-Dick*. Ironically, however, the novel does not seem reformist at all. This is because reform imagery has eventually become for Melville a colorful shell, largely devoid of political or didactic content, that can be arranged at will in the overall mosaic of a subversive novel.

This stylization of reform runs throughout the novel. It is visible, for example, in Melville's creative adaptation of dark-temperance imagery. Such imagery abounds in the early scene in which Ishmael witnesses the *Grampus* crew, just home from a three years' voyage, rushing straight into the Spouter-Inn's bar (the entrance to which is a huge whale jaw) and getting drunk on drinks poured by the bartender Jonah, while the temperate Bulkington watches aloof and then disappears. Just as popular reformers had regularly described alcohol as an all-devouring 'whale' or all-consuming 'poison,' so Melville described the *Grampus* crew entering through 'jaws of swift destruction' to be served 'deliriums and death' by a prophetically named bartender (14).[23] Just as reformers had emphasized the illusoriness of alcohol's pleasures, so Melville writes: 'Abominable are the tumblers into which he pours his poison. Though true cylinders without – within, the green goggling glasses deceitfully tapered downward to a cheating bottom' (14). The Spouter-Inn barroom scene shows Melville typically adopting a popular mode as a preparatory literary exercise: just as the bartender pours poisonous drinks to rambunctious sailors who are inside symbolic whale's jaws, so in a sense the dark-temperance mode 'pours' *Moby-Dick* by providing Melville with various subversive images.

Melville is now so sensitively attuned to all possible permutations of the dark-temperance mode that he can shift with ease between antitemperance and protemperance stances, giving full moral credence to no single viewpoint and always seeking the rhetorical potentialities of whatever stance he assumes. He sounds antitemperance when he has the comical mate Stubb, a boisterous advocate of grog, snicker at Dough-Boy for giving someone ginger-water . . . On the other hand, Melville sounds protemperance in his portrait of the wretched Perth, the blacksmith who had been driven to sea after alcohol had shattered his family and who is now the lonely forger of harpoons for Ahab. . . .

It would be easy enough to run through the entire novel and suggest specific reform influences for other scenes as well. The city-mysteries mode (as popularized in antebellum novels that portrayed crime and desolation in American cities) enhances the gloom of Ishmael's opening entrance into New Bedford, as he stumbles over an ashbox and asks, '[A]re these ashes from that destroyed city, Gomorrah?' (9). Ishmael's ironic query 'Who aint a slave?' (6) would seem to owe much to the fiery New York radical Mike Walsh, who in the late 1840s famously universalized the notion of slavery by stressing that *both* Northern wage slaves and Southern chattel slaves were equally oppressed. . . .

Such individual sources, however, are less important than the overall dark-reform *écriture* that governs the novel. Scholars have long sought historical prototypes for several scenes and characters, but the results have often proven contradictory. Ahab, for instance, has been variously associated with the radical abolitionist Garrison, with Garrison's arch-opponent Calhoun, and with the moderate politician Daniel Wester! Such historical source-study can be constricting, for in fact *Moby-Dick* moves beyond slavery or antislavery, protemperance or antitemperance, to a literary realm in which subversive reform energy and rhetoric, rather than reform message, become the literary artist's central concern. The many explicit reform devices in *Moby-Dick* are pushed toward literariness by Melville's devotion to the subversive images that formed a rhetorical sub-basis of *all* dark-reform writings. Ultimately, Melville in *Moby-Dick* is a gigantic dark-reformer towering above all reform programs but driven by his age's powerful reform impulse. . . .

If reform literature supplied Melville with potent, often disturbing images, the allied mode of radical-democrat fiction contributed various paradoxical character types. The group of popular writers I am calling *radical democrats* – most notably George Lippard, A. J. H. Duganne, George G. Foster, and George Thompson – in the 1840s carried both social protest and literary irrationalism to new extremes. Alarmed by widening class divisions and all forms of social oppression, the radical democrats used every degree of literary invective to expose what they regarded as the prevailing depravity of America's ruling class. They translated into nightmarish fiction the prevailing metaphors of dark reform. America in their eyes was no more than a whited sepulchre with rottenness within, a place of appalling 'city mysteries.' . . . Best-selling novels such as Lippard's *The Quaker City* (1844–45), Duganne's *The Knights of the Seal* (1845), Thompson's *New York Life* (1849), and Ned Buntline's *The G'hals of New York* (1850) depicted a topsy-turvy world in which justified outcasts and likable criminals actually seemed more worthy than conventionally virtuous characters, whose probity was held suspect because it reflected an inherently unjust social system. The great conflict in radical-democrat fiction was between the smirking justified criminal and what may be called the oxymoronic oppressor: the outwardly respectable but inwardly corrupt social leader who variously appeared as the church-going capitalist, the religious slaveholder, the unctuous reverend rake, and so on. The hero of this fiction was a mixed figure known as the 'b'hoy' (street slang for 'boy'), the crude yet acute, wicked yet thoroughly likable city youth who had arisen in the street gangs of the Eastern cities and then was mythologized in pamphlet novels and melodramas. These radical-democrat stereotypes reflected deep working-class aggressions and fantasies in the turbulent decade following the crushing economic panic of 1837.

In time, however, radical-democrat literature became notably vulgarized when it was taken up by opportunistic authors who exaggerated gross sensationalism but left behind serious political goals. In the late 1840s, a sudden explosion of cheap pamphlet novels, stimulated mainly by mass publishers' adoption of the new cylinder press, brought about a cheapening of the radical-democrat mode. . . .

By the time he wrote *Moby-Dick* Melville's imagination was bristling with the polarities of American radical democracy. . . . He could proclaim himself simultaneously the greatest democrat and the greatest misanthrope. He had arrived at the very core of the popular paradox that fused criminality and goodness, iconoclasm and patriotism.

Melville's transformation of popular strategies in *Moby-Dick* is revealed in his willed *fusion* of the justified criminal and the oxymoronic oppressor. True, sometimes he is quite close to the popular radical democrats, as in his satirical portrait of the oxymoronic Captain Bildad, the querulous Quaker and penny-pinching Christian. Because he had immersed himself so completely in the inverted value system of radical democracy, he could now deal convincingly only with paradoxical characters. Throughout *Moby-Dick*, conventionally virtuous figures (the 'pious, good man' Starbuck (79), the noble Bulkington, Aunt Charity, Dough-Boy) are doomed to impotency, while richly paradoxical figures (the 'swearing good man' Ahab (79), the likable outcast Ishmael, the humane cannibal Queequeg, the whole rollicking *Pequod* crew) control the narrative. . . .

If Ahab represents a humanized version of the oxymoronic oppressor and the justified criminal, Ishmael is the transformed version of another radical-democrat stereotype: the b'hoy. A figure of both reality and legend, the b'hoy had been an appropriate hero of radical-democrat fiction, since he was a mixture of bad qualities (rebelliousness, egotism, indolence) and good ones (native intelligence, confidence, an inclination to adopt the manners of the upper-class). By 1850, widespread vulgarization of the b'hoy figure in the popular press made this figure seem a great ideal that had gone sour. . . .

In his portrait of Ishmael, Melville borrows from the b'hoy stereotype. In the opening pages of the novel Ishmael is established as the indigent, loafing, acute, brash, genial New Yorker who plays pranks, hates respectable jobs, and aches for adventure. Melville's contemporary readers surely saw signs of the b'hoy in an unconventional narrator who boasts that he travels not with commodores and who abominates 'all honorable respectable toils, trials, and tribulations of every kind whatsoever' (5). Like the typical sensation-loving b'hoy, Ishmael feels an 'everlasting itch for things remote' and is attracted by 'the wild and distant seas' with their 'undeliverable, nameless perils' (7). The images that surround him in the early chapters – images of suicide, funerals, coffins, cannibalism, the gallows, tombstones – place him in the blackly humorous domain familiar to the popular b'hoy. His entire voyage becomes a kind of popular culture text when he imagines 'WHALING VOYAGE BY ONE ISHMAEL' squeezed as on a theater poster between sensational headlines about a hotly contested election and a bloody battle in Afghanistan (7).

But in the process of adopting the b'hoy Melville reconstructs him. Ishmael was not the first b'hoy narrator in American fiction, but he was the first pressed in the direction of the humane and the broadly tolerant. He is the b'hoy reconceived by a writer who recognized the universal, fully human potentialities of his own culture's popular images. Ishmael is not merely the 'Mose' or 'Sikesy' of melodramas and pamphlet novels, the two-fisted b'hoy who mocks aristocrats and gets involved in comical pranks. He is also the flexible, loving youth who stirs our deepest democratic sympathies when he embraces Queequeg, a man he had previously feared as a bloodthirsty cannibal.

Through the developing Ishmael–Queequeg relationship, Melville enriches not only the b'hoy but another stereotype who had figured largely in radical-democrat fiction: the savage non-white. Radical democrats had regularly depicted even the most fierce oppressed peoples and minority groups as more noble than secretly corrupt social leaders.

. . . Melville is able to lift Queequeg out of the mire of sensationalism because he has him embraced by an enriched version of that flexible radical-democrat hero, the b'hoy. The 'marriage' of Ishmael and Queequeg is Melville's rhetorical intermerging of two popular characters – the b'hoy and the oppressed non-white – on the ground of common humanity. Melville burrows through the cheapened radical democracy of popular culture to a genuine radical democracy signalled by the deep affection between two good-hearted human beings of different races. . . .

Surveying the popular images and devices in *Moby-Dick* – from Romantic Adventure, reform literature, radical-democrat fiction . . . – it is safe to call the novel the most broadly absorptive fiction of the antebellum period. . . .

Melville's overriding technique in *Moby-Dick* is to allow all the centrifugal, disorienting forces within the American popular mind to be fully released momentarily through structural 'escape valves,' usually a chapter or a small cluster of chapters, and then, having released some of the subversive steam, disperse its remaining energy through counterbalancing factual chapters or through the powerfully centripetal plot line, main characters, and symbols. Melville could incorporate all his culture's images, from the religious to the sensational, and yet rescue them from their native directionlessness by introducing a centripetal action (the quest for the white whale) with a centripetal object (the whale itself) through a centripetal agent (Ahab, and then the whole crew) – all driven by hope for a centripetal reward, the doubloon fixed to the mast.

Even in fashioning these centripetal images, Melville borrowed from popular culture. For instance, his use of the Biblical names Ishmael and Ahab lend depth and grandeur to common figures such as the b'hoy and the tyrannical captain; and this very fusion of sacrosanct Biblical archetypes with modern-day figures was made possible by a widespread secularization of popular religious culture in nineteenth-century America, a phenomenon also visible in Father Mapple's anecdotal sermon and in Ishmael's homely fantasy of 'rows of angels in paradise, each with his hands in a jar of spermaceti' (416). This secularized reapplication of the religious imagery contributed as well to the supernatural overtones of Fedallah, often associated with the devil, and of the white whale itself, a magnificent combination of God and Satan. Another popular phenomenon that greatly aided Melville was pseudosciences such as mesmerism (mind control through what was seen as electrical, magnetic energy) and phrenology and physiognomy (the interpretation of character through the reading of physical characteristics). In the fluid atmosphere of antebellum popular culture, these pseudosciences were handled with unprecedented flexibility and creativity. The popular mesmerists' belief in mind control through electrical fluid was inventively reapplied by Melville to enhance the centripetal quality of his main plot and characters. Ahab is not merely a charismatic sea captain. In antebellum terms, he was one of very few individuals gifted with enough 'odic force,' or magnetic energy, to govern the wills of others. . . .

Melville's broad-scale assimilation of popular images greatly complicates the longstanding issue of 'meaning' in *Moby-Dick*. The issue becomes even more complex when we keep in mind not only Melville's reapplications of popular cultural phenomena but also his omnivorous gatherings from elite sources. Ahab is, as we have seen, a combination of many popular types; but he is also drawn, as various critics have suggested, from the wicked Ahab of 1 Kings, Prometheus, Faust, Lear, Milton's Satan, . . . and other figures of fact and legend. Ishmael, likewise, is not merely a refashioned b'hoy but also derives from the old Testament outcast beloved of God, just as Pip resembles Lear's Fool, and so on. The white whale is an especially ambiguous repository of popular and archetypal images.

But in all these cases, precise meaning matters less than the dazzling ability of Melville's characters and symbols to radiate meanings.

Melville's comprehensive pillaging of classic religious and literary sources reveals his overarching interest in adding resonance and suggestiveness to popular cultural chronotopes that were formless, neutral, or contradictory in their native state. The *Pequod*'s quest for the whale is ultimately self-destructive and the book's truth remains tantalizingly elusive; but this does not place *Moby-Dick* at odds with American culture, as is commonly believed. What distinguishes this novel from its many popular prototypes is that it absorbs numerous American images and treats them not frivolously or haphazardly, as did the popular texts, but instead takes them seriously, salvages them from the anarchically directionless and gives them new intensity and mythic reference. Melville's quest is dangerous, but it is also exhilarating and finally joyful. Upon completing the novel Melville could express his paradoxical feeling of danger and peace by writing to Hawthorne: 'I have written a wicked book, and feel spotless as the lamb. Ineffable socialities are in me' (*Letters*, 142). Having written a novel that fully absorbed the subversive forces of his culture, Melville could nonetheless feel warmly calm because he had produced a lasting testament to the creative spirit.[24] □

CHAPTER SEVEN

Deconstructive Reading, 'Post-humanist' Critiques and 'New Americanists'

W E TURN, in this final chapter, from the 'reconstructive criticism' of the previous chapter to readings of *Moby-Dick* that might, broadly, be seen as 'deconstructive'. The following three critical pieces all share a postmodern concern with language and ideology as a system of power, one that can be unpicked through an examination of *Moby-Dick*. The sort of deconstructive critical practice that operates, to a greater or lesser degree, in these essays is perhaps best summed up by Jonathan Culler in his book *On Deconstruction* (1983). Culler writes that

■ to deconstruct a discourse is to show how it undermines the philosophy it asserts, or the hierarchical oppositions on which it relies, by identifying in the text the rhetorical operations that produce the supposed ground of argument, the key concept or premise.[1] □

This closing chapter, then, provides a sampling of the ways in which *Moby-Dick* is being read by yet another new generation of critics. Whilst charting the impact of postmodern thought on the process by which both *Moby-Dick* and contemporary America can be read critically, it also points to some of the pitfalls and excesses of this critical practice. This is most especially the case in the final – but brief – extract of this chapter, which is taken from William V. Spanos' book *The Errant Art of Moby-Dick* (1995). In this book Spanos puts forward what he terms a 'post-humanist' critique of American culture and ideology. His deconstruction of *Moby-Dick* sees it, somewhat perversely, as a text that foreshadows American intervention in Vietnam. *Moby-Dick*, he maintains, speaks to the crisis in liberal humanist ideology that, after the Cold War, 'postmodern' America is now experiencing. This way of reading *Moby-Dick* is

DECONSTRUCTION, 'POST-HUMANISM', 'NEW AMERICANISTS'

both exciting and intensely frustrating. Though Spanos challenges responsive readers of *Moby-Dick* to re-think their political and ideological position, ultimately, once the dust of his seemingly new and difficult terminology has settled, his reading of *Moby-Dick* (and the novel's critical reception) as a text that demonstrates 'a struggle to appropriate it for present ideological purposes'[2] says little more than what has been apparent throughout this whole Critical Guide. As a short epilogue to this book, then, Spanos' piece demonstrates that *Moby-Dick* continually resurfaces from its wreckage at the hands of its critics to tell a tale of the struggles for power, dominance and orphaned survival upon which American ideology is grounded.

The two main essays in this chapter, as with the essays in the previous chapter, attempt to return *Moby-Dick* to its cultural setting by seeing it as a product of antebellum America. But what they do with this setting is very different from how it is treated by Royster, Leverenz, Bersani and Reynolds. Both Donald Pease and Wai-chee Dimock stress *Moby-Dick*'s enormous cultural power and influence. For them, its importance is not just because it so clearly reflects the state of American culture in the mid-nineteenth century. *Moby-Dick*, they argue, has been used by each succeeding generation of critics to portray an image of America that is particularly conducive to that specific generation of readers. If *Moby-Dick* has come to be read as an archetypal American text, they argue, then this is because the tensions and struggles within antebellum America have come to be seen as epitomising American identity and culture generally. Both of these essays may therefore be described as 'New Americanist' because they seek to deconstruct the key concepts and premises upon which traditional readings of American literature and culture are grounded.

In the first extract that follows, Donald Pease argues that *Moby-Dick*'s cultural setting, and hence its prominent place within the American literary canon and its persuasive cultural power, is not simply nineteenth-century America, but the *version* of nineteenth-century America that is proposed in 1941 by Matthiessen's critical model of an 'American Renaissance'. Wai-chee Dimock's essay also challenges such ideas about American culture of the last century. She argues, from a 'post-colonial' perspective, that critical models such as an American Renaissance, through which *Moby-Dick* and other texts have traditionally been read, promote an agenda of white cultural superiority. What her essay points out, through its close examination of Melville's rhetorical strategies, is that *Moby-Dick* discloses the underlying faultlines in an American culture of imperialist expansionism. What is interesting in both these essays is the degree to which they return, perhaps somewhat perversely, to some of the concerns and ways of thinking about the text that were prevalent in its criticism before Matthiessen. Therefore, whilst their methods are postmodern and deconstructive, their focus is upon Ahab and the structures of power that his rhetoric engages, rather than upon the pluralist humanism that Ishmael seems to endorse. Dimock's reading of Ahab sees him as a 'victim' of nineteenth-century American culture. He is, according to her, both imprisoned by, and representative of, his nation's claims to a 'Manifest Destiny'. Ahab's fate then, claims Dimock, is analogous to the fate of the Native American Indian at the time. And for Pease, Ahab is also a victim, but a victim who is imprisoned by the persuasive powers of two cultures. Pease's essay deconstructs the ways in which Ahab is read as a representative figure for the pressures of mid-nineteenth *and* mid-twentieth-century American cultures. For Pease, Ahab is the embodiment, in his mad wilfulness, of Emersonian self-reliance. He is also, though, argues Pease, used by Matthiessen to represent the forces threatening American democracy in 1941. Both these 'scenes of cultural persuasion', as Pease calls them, highlight Ahab's victimhood. Ahab's fate is both that of tragic hero who over-reaches himself, and that of monomaniac dictator who precipitates the cultural and political stalemate of the Cold War.

The essays that make up this chapter, then, are concerned to explore and to deconstruct those points in *Moby-Dick* that seem to expose forces at work in American ideology which its cultural apparatuses struggle to conceal. The essays also share the realisation that *Moby-Dick*'s critical history is, itself, one of the most powerful of those cultural apparatuses. This exposing of the *interestedness* with which *Moby-Dick* has been read since its publication is the starting point for Pease's essay, which follows shortly. And the marking of such critical interestedness also sounds an appropriate note for this concluding chapter in a critical guide to Melville's masterpiece.

The book of essays from which Pease's essay is taken (*The American Renaissance Reconsidered*, first published in 1985) is the first significant publication employing revisionist and deconstructive ways of reading the 'American Renaissance'. It is the starting point, therefore, for 'New Americanist' criticism, a way of thinking about America and its culture(s) that has had a profound effect on American Studies. Such New Americanist reconsiderations of America and its meaning have recently led, in publications such as the journal *boundary* 2 and the 'New Americanists' series for Duke University Press edited by Donald Pease, to a serious questioning of the applicability of the very notion of nationality to a country as culturally diverse as the United States of America. Predictably, *Moby-Dick* remains a central text in such re-evaluations. Pease's essay, '*Moby Dick* and the Cold War', from which the following extract is taken, is therefore crucially important in the history both of *Moby-Dick* criticism, and of critical thinking about America.

■ The broad topic of this discussion will be the scene of cultural persuasion at the time of the publication of *Moby Dick*. Although the encyclopedic range of that narrative as well as the crucial place it occupies in the cultural context that F. O. Matthiessen called the American Renaissance might provide sufficient grounds for this rather broad context, my motive entails a much more narrow concern: a personal failure to remain persuaded by a reading of *Moby Dick* that has become canonical – the one in which Ishmael proves his freedom by opposing Ahab's totalitarian will. What is at issue here, however, is not my ability to convert this failure into the power to prove the superiority of one reading over another, but the power of a cultural context to designate, in what I am calling a scene of persuasion, the terms in which a text *must be read* in order to maintain cultural power.

By locating what I mean by a scene of cultural persuasion in a context that may seem foreign to any responsible discussion of *Moby Dick* I shall argue that it is crucial to the ongoing reception of that narrative within what Matthiessen called the American Renaissance and we call the American canon: namely, the arena for cultural discussion provided by the Cold War. Unlike other paradigms in the public sphere, the Cold War does not adjudicate or mediate discussions. Instead it derives all its force by simply being persuasive. As *the explanation*, it appears persuasive without having undergone the work of persuasion.

. . . We might best ascertain this compelling persuasive force by attempting to locate any cultural arena external to the Cold War frame. In totalizing the globe into a super opposition between the two superpowers the United States and the Soviet Union, the Cold War economizes on any opposition to it by relocating all options within its frame. So inclusive is this frame and so persuasive is its control of world events that there appear to be no alternatives to it.

. . . For those who feel 'wasted' by the sheer accumulation of unassimilable details, connotations, cultural time lags in modern life, the Cold War turns into a massive debriefing ceremony, the location for a dramatic turning point in a scene where all the complications, doubts, and conflicts of modern existence get resolved in a single opposition that then clears up the whole mess and puts everybody back to work: 'Us against them.'

In this . . . scene accompanying everyday life, all the doubts, confusions, conflicts, and contradictions constitutive of the lived experience of everyday existence can be reexperienced as participation in a decisive opposition, a last judgement in which the sides are no sooner drawn up than victory is declared. Informed by personal doubts and indecisions, the Cold War only appears the more compelling out of its capacity to convert indeterminacy into this overdetermined scene.

. . . Put somewhat differently, in the Cold War as drama, the Cold War paradigm *pre*occupies all the positions – and all the oppositions as well. Consequently, all the oppositions – whether of the Battista regime against Cuban rebels, Ishmael against Ahab, or, as was reported in a recent psychoanalytical case study, the mind against the body – can be read in terms of 'our' freedom versus 'their' totalitarianism. Since the Cold War paradigm confines totalizing operations to the work of the other superpower, the Cold War drama is free to expose even its own totalization of the globe as the work of the other superpower. Consequently, 'I' cannot but choose this paradigm, even though it confines choice to the 'human right' to choose this paradigm and limits 'freedom' either to the 'choice' of the correct position within it, or, given the sense that the paradigm has already 'performed' all the difficult choices, to the 'freedom from' the need to choose. That is to say, the Cold War paradigm relocates public persuasion not in the sphere of discussion but in a scene: one in which all the arguments have been premediated if not quite settled, with the only work left that of becoming the 'national character' through whom the paradigm can speak.

I began with a broad topic, the scene of cultural persuasion at the time of the publication of *Moby Dick*. . . . The reading to which I was not persuaded (in which Ishmael's freedom is opposed to Ahab's totalitarianism) effectively turned *Moby Dick* into a Cold War text. But the scene of cultural persuasion at the time of the publication of *Moby Dick* enabled me to imagine a scene sufficiently alienated from the Cold War to make *Moby Dick* unfit for that *pre*occupied opposition. Now the distinction between these two scenes of persuasion permits me to restate my purpose. I do not quite wish to recover the scene of cultural persuasion at the time of the publication of *Moby Dick* but to recover from the scene of persuasion, the Cold War drama, that has appropriated it.

Stated so starkly, this struggle tends toward a melodrama of its own, with the sides no sooner drawn up than victory is declared. To come to terms with a failure to be persuaded by a canonical reading of *Moby Dick* should lead only indirectly to that time when *Moby Dick*, if recognized at all, was acknowledged chiefly as a sign of the author's madness. The more direct confrontation involves us less with the reception of *Moby Dick* in Melville's time than with the man whose work received *Moby Dick* as part of the American canon. Should we persist in the convention of locating persons and works in scenes, we shall find F. O. Matthiessen writing at a time – 1941 – as distant from the present as was the Second World War, destined to eventuate in the Cold War. Matthiessen wrote a work he hoped would establish American literature as a discipline and America as a culture at a time

America needed consciousness of the great tradition threatened by a totalitarian power different from the present one. Matthiessen's work reminded Americans of the global duties of Renaissance men, with loyalty to America as a nation.

Acting as a means of consensus-formation as well as canon-definition, Matthiessen's *American Renaissance* displaced the need to acknowledge dissenting opinions· onto the power to discover unrecognized masterworks. Among the dissenting opinions that American Renaissance silenced was Matthiessen's own, for in returning to the time of Whitman and Emerson, his politics seemed already to have been achieved in the past. But with the return, after World War II, of his political opinions to his literary works, the progenitor of the American Renaissance became, in the tragedy of his suicide, the sign of the cultural power of another consensus-formation. If we read Matthiessen's dissenting opinions as the discourse of the enemy within, the Cold War paradigm turned him into one of its first casualties.

. . . the *American Renaissance* (as a consensus formed at the expense of Matthiessen's own dissenting position) strategically promotes Whitman's and Emerson's rhetoric, in which national self-consciousness becomes indistinguishable from personal self-consciousness, into a cultural asset. Moreover, this act of promotion constitutes the historical power of consensus-formation in 1941. For in order to sanction America's national right to a free culture at a time when that right was threatened less by national than international politics, *American Renaissance* locates a cultural past so united that even the political issues surrounding the Civil War seem petty. . . . Seeming, then, to distinguish Emerson and Whitman from the politicians, *American Renaissance* in fact locates in their writings an organicist aesthetic justification for the rhetoric of national individualism at precisely the moment when the politicians seem to be losing the divine justification for that rhetoric. . . . [This] bracketing out of politics through a turn to aesthetic questions in fact served Matthiessen's 'higher' political purpose – to devise a national consensus.

. . . When conceived in terms of this 'higher' purpose, however, Emerson and Whitman lose their purely aesthetic characters and reveal the explicitly rhetorical use to which *American Renaissance* put them. Nowhere does Emerson lose this character and Matthiessen lose control of the working of his consensus-formation more definitively than in the midst of an analysis of the tyranny of Captain Ahab in the quarterdeck scene in *Moby Dick*. Curiously, Matthiessen presents this analysis in what we could call a scene of critical persuasion. When considering Ahab's compelling domination of the men in the quarterdeck scene, Matthiessen pays no attention to specific lines but reads the compulsion in Ahab's language as a 'sign' of Shakespeare's 'power over' Melville. . . . Having first *posited* Shakespeare's language as the rhetorical power informing Ahab's exchanges, Matthiessen then redis-covers this power Shakespeare wields *through* Ahab at work in the spell Shakespeare cast *over* Melville's prose. This dramatic conflict ends only after Melville 'masters' the power Shakespeare's rhetoric wields over him by discovering the secret of this own dramatic power.

Of course all the power in this drama inheres less in Melville's dis-covery than in the dramatic use to which Matthiessen puts it. When Matthiessen's drama, which should have concluded with an example of Melville's triumphant 'mastery' of Shakespeare, comes to its close, Melville's 'mastery' of Shakespeare neither reveals itself through one of Melville's own characters nor represents one of Melville's own themes. Instead, Melville's 'vital rhetoric' is said to 'build up a defence of one of the chief doctrines of the age, the splendor of the single personality.' In other words, Melville's recovery from Shakespeare's rhetoric becomes a means for Emerson to defend his doctrine of self-reliance.

. . . The compelling logic of this dramatic sequence is clear. Matthiessen wants to see the doctrine of self-reliance at work, but when Matthiessen 'hears' this doctrine enunciated by Ahab, he loses all the benefits accrued by the rest of his drama. . . . If Ahab served as the dummy figure through whom Matthiessen could reveal Melville's act of 'working through' his possession by Shakespeare's rhetoric, does he not, once Matthiessen hears him speaking Emerson's rhetoric of self-reliance, disclose Matthiessen's unstated fear that compulsion might be at work in the doctrine of self-reliance? In short, does not the quarterdeck scene become Matthiessen's awareness not of the need to defend but of the need to defend himself against Emerson's ideology of self-reliance, which informs the consensus-formation he called the American Renaissance?

. . . In his analysis of the quarterdeck scene . . . Matthiessen displays a contradictory relation, a conflicting attitude unresolvable by the ideal opposition between Ahab and Ishmael. In his analysis, Matthiessen identifies Ahab as both totalitarian will and the freedom a self-reliant man must use to oppose it. Put another way, through the figure of Ahab Matthiessen reads the feared *compulsion* at work in what he formerly regarded as the sovereign freedom of the self-reliant man.

. . . This ambivalence in Ahab never puts him at odds with Ishmael, but it does, as Matthiessen points up, put him at odds with Starbuck, the one member of the crew who, in talking back to Ahab, voices [a] dissenting opinion . . . Unlike the rest of the crew, Starbuck refused to hunt Moby Dick for gold. And Starbuck's refusal seems both rational and Christian. Although he could work to bring whale oil to the Nantucket market, for Ahab to 'wreak vengeance' against a 'dumb thing' like Moby Dick seems to Starbuck blasphemy.

Whichever tradition of consensus-formation we place him in, however, an analysis of what happens when Ahab responds to a dissenting opinion should disclose something about the dynamics of consensus-formation. In taking Starbuck 'down a little lower layer,' Ahab first makes Starbuck experience the limits of his rational Christianity. He begins with an implicit either/or: Either all visible objects are pasteboard masks informed by some deeper purpose, or else 'there's nought beyond.' This alternative stops Starbuck short. For if he kills whales for oil, they do not reveal God's glory. Instead these 'dumb things' only represent Starbuck's need for capital, and Ahab's vengeance, in informing the whale with at least a human purpose, turns Starbuck into the blasphemer. For he prefers his capital to God's purposes. More importantly, Ahab brings Starbuck up against this recognition with such intensity that Starbuck displays malice toward Ahab. That is to say, Ahab, in his response, has put Starbuck in precisely the position Starbuck claims he cannot occupy. For more than anything else, Starbuck now feels all the rage he needs to kill Ahab. When Starbuck feels this, Ahab has him precisely where he wants him, in a state of mind enabling him to identify Ahab's rage with an impulse in his own inner life. Then, in a remarkable move, Ahab, after provoking Starbuck to 'anger-glow,' separates him from an anger *Ahab agrees to embody alone.* In other words, Ahab provokes his own reaction to the universe, a defiance grown out of rage, in Starbuck; then he recovers Starbuck's defiance as *his trial* and not the burden of a Christian man.

. . . That Ahab says all this in cadences borrowed from Shakespeare only underscores the 'scenic' character of his separation from the crew. If he talks to the men at all, he talks to the men in a language that immediately encloses him in a theatrical scene: a theatrical frame, moreover, claiming all the 'unapproachable' cultural power that Melville, in his review of Hawthorne, claimed Shakespeare wielded over the mob. Thus Ahab not only 'acts out' and 'ideally resolves' the principle of rebellion he invokes in all of the men, but he does so in a language so invested with cultural power that they can only be inspired by the cultural heights to which Ahab elevates their will to rebel. In short, Ahab embodies not only the crew's inner life but also the best means of articulating it.

Here the contrast between Melville's use of Shakespeare in the quarterdeck scene and Matthiessen's in his quarterdeck scene is illuminating. . . . Matthiessen not only acknowledges the political power of Shakespeare's language. (Shakespeare, in the politics of canon formation, had, after all, functioned as Matthiessen's means of securing

English Renaissance validity for American Renaissance figures.) But he also reenacts Starbuck's scenario. For Ahab performs for Matthiessen the same function he performed for Starbuck: in embodying compulsion as his inner life alone, he releases Matthiessen from the need to find compulsion in the doctrine of self-reliance informing the body of his work.

But Ahab's very power to silence dissent also causes him to re-experience his sense of loss. . . . Ahab cannot depend on Divine Writ to sanction his words. Consequently, a dual recognition accompanies each act of persuasion: the terrible doubt that it may be without foundation, and the 'experience' of his separation from another. Both recognitions remind him of the loss of his leg. It is Ahab's need to justify this sense of loss – to make it his, rather than God's or Fate's – that leads him to turn his will, which in each act of persuasion repeats that separation of his body from his leg, into the ground for his existence.

Indeed, all of Ahab's actions – his dependence on omens, black magic, thaumaturgy – work as regressions to a more fundamental power of the human will. They constitute his efforts to provide a basis *in* the human will for a rhetoric that has lost all other sanction. Ahab, in short, attempts to turn the coercion at work in his rhetoric into Fate, a principle of order in a universe without it. But since this will is grounded in the sense of loss, it is fated to perfect that loss in an act of total destruction.

That final cataclysmic image of total destruction motivated Matthiessen and forty years of Cold War critics to turn to Ishmael, who in surviving *must*, the logic would have it, have survived as the principle of America's freedom and who hands over to us our surviving heritage. When juxtaposed to Ahab, Ishmael is said to recover freedom in the midst of fixation; a sense of the present in a world in which Ahab's revenge makes the future indistinguishable from the past; and the free play of indeterminate possibility in a world forced to reflect Ahab's fixed meanings.

. . . Like Emerson, Ishmael uncouples the actions that occur from the motives giving rise to them, thereby turning virtually all the events in the narrative into an opportunity to display the powers of eloquence capable of taking possession of them. Indeed, nothing and no one resist Ishmael's power to convert the world that he sees into the forms of rhetoric that he wants. The question remains, however, whether Ishmael, in his need to convert all the facts in his world and all the events in his life into a persuasive power capable of re-coining them as the money of his mind, is possessed of a will any less totalitarian than Ahab's. . . .

. . . Ishmael occupies three different spaces in his narrative. As the victim of Ahab's narrative, he exists as a third person; as the narrator of his own tale, as a first person; and as the subject of such urgent addresses as 'Call me Ishmael,' a second person. But since, as a first-person narrator, he turns Ahab into the figure who has victimized Ishmael, Ishmael does not have to be perceived as taking anyone else in. Ishmael turns Ahab into both the *definitive third-person* victim and the perfect *first-person* victimizer. In perfecting both roles, Ahab becomes Ishmael's means of exempting his narrative in advance of the charge of trying to victimize anyone.

. . . We can begin to understand all of this better when we turn to the crucial distinctions that critics during the Cold War draw between Ishmael and Ahab. In their view, Ishmael, in his rhetoric, frees us from Ahab's fixation by returning all things to their status as pure possibilities. What we now must add is that Ishmael has also invested all the rest of the world of fact with possibility, then invests possibility with the voice of conviction. When all the world turns out to be invested with the indeterminate interplay of possibility, it does not seem free but replicates what Ishmael called the hypos and what we call boredom: the need for intense action without any action to perform that motivated the Ishmael who felt the 'drizzly November in his soul' to feel attracted to Ahab in the first place. . . . In short, Ishmael's form of freedom does not oppose Ahab but compels him to need Ahab – not only as the purification of his style, but as the cure of his boredom. . . . Put more simply, Ahab's compulsion to decide *compels* Ishmael *not* to decide.

. . . In terms of the foregoing discussion of *Moby Dick*, we can by way of summary say that Melville does not exercise so much as he exposes the compulsion at work in the scene of cultural persuasion in his own time. He does so, moreover, by disrupting the cultural apparatuses meant to conceal this compulsion.

. . . During Melville's time, in which Ahab was a recognizable compilation of features from such familiar orators as Daniel Webster, Andrew Jackson, and Ralph Waldo Emerson, Ishmael did not arise as a figure of freedom. The constant tendency of Ishmael's rhetoric, located in a space filled with an inconsequentiality the reverse of Ahab's fatal consequence, led the majority of critics to conceive of what Melville called a 'wicked book' as the work of madness. Either they had to conceive him as mad, or they had to reconceive the terms that permitted them to remain convinced of the power of their culture. It would take another scene of persuasion, with a quite different allocation of the relationship between will and action, to appropriate Ahab and Ishmael as means of corroborating its fundamental lesson. We might say that, having failed to be persuaded by the scene of persuasion in its time, *Moby Dick* reappeared in 1941 to persuade the world of the cultural power of the opposition between the free world and a totalitarian power.

. . . As we have seen, Ishmael's freedom does not oppose Ahab's will, however totalitarian that may appear. Instead Ishmael's expansive rhetoric depends on the groundlessness of Ahab's exercise for its legitimacy. In *Moby Dick*, Melville does not alienate opposition by positioning all opinions within this conflict; instead he 'works through' the vicious circularities informing the conflicted will at work in Ahab and Ishmael. Instead of letting Ishmael appear *opposed* to Ahab he reveals the ways in which Ishmael's obsession depends on Ahab's compulsion. If the Cold War consensus would turn *Moby Dick* into a figure through whom it would speak its own totalizing logic, Melville, as it were, speaks back through the same figure, to alienate the obsessive-compulsive character capable of putting a totalizing logic to work. Should we begin to hear the voice that can speak when such totalizing opposition has been 'worked through,' that voice will not speak through either Ahab or Ishmael, but will speak words that neither their rhetoric nor the Cold War logic can acknowledge: 'I prefer not.'[3] □

A similar sense of the possibility of reading *Moby-Dick* as a radical (though clearly politically troubled) text is apparent in the following extract from Wai-chee Dimock's 1991 essay 'Ahab's Manifest Destiny'. Dimock argues that *Moby-Dick* undermines the controlling ideology of antebellum America, namely individualism, by disclosing the tautological and circular argument upon which such individualism is founded. This is demonstrated, she maintains, by the way in which *Moby-Dick* exposes to ridicule the logic which says that Ahab must suffer punishment because Ahab is to be punished: 'He is both doomed and free: free, that is to choose his doom.' Such logic, Dimock further argues, also operates in the language with which nineteenth-century America described what it took to be the predestined fate of the Native American Indian. Dimock's essay, then, marks a shift of emphasis in *Moby-Dick* criticism. But such a shift marks, perhaps, a realisation of what has been apparent throughout the history of *Moby-Dick* criticism. As Dimock implies, *Moby-Dick*'s crucial importance in American culture lies in the fact that its aesthetic concerns cannot be divorced from its ideological concerns. By suggesting that *Moby-Dick* has resonance and importance to readers who do not share its white, male, Anglo-American cultural background, Dimock's essay demonstrates *Moby-Dick*'s peculiar power to fascinate, to baffle and to address the concerns of many subsequent generations of readers and critics of America and its cultures.

■ Ahab's sins . . . have been abundantly documented. My focus in this essay, however, will not be on those sins, but on the punitive logic his author administers. To dispatch Ahab, to disarm him, to make him die not only inevitably but also deservedly, Melville needs an executory instrument, a logic that explains and justifies the fate of this character. That logic is all too easy to come by, for it is already a provision in individualism. What we might expect to find in Ahab, then, is an individualism that afflicts its bearer, one that apprehends and incriminates, one that disciplines the self in its very freedom. And that, in fact, is what we do find.

Being a product of individualism, Ahab is by definition a free agent. But, since his individualism happens to be the negative variety, he is, also by definition, an overdetermined character. He is both doomed and free: free, that is to choose his doom. This is a strange logic, to say the least, but within the terms of negative individualism, nothing is more reasonable, or more necessary, for such a logic – a logic that inscribes discipline in freedom – is just what makes the autonomous self governable as such. Embracing this logic, *Moby-Dick* will find itself in intimate communion with antebellum America, for both the text and the nation agree about what it means to be 'doomed' – about the cause, character, and trajectory of that unfortunate condition.

The narrative of doom in *Moby-Dick* comes into play even before Ahab appears. His ship is introduced with the accompanying information that *'Pequod*, you will no doubt remember, was the name of a celebrated tribe of Massachusetts Indians, now extinct as the ancient Medes' (67).[4] The crucial words here are 'now extinct' – and it is crucial, too, that the word should be 'extinct,' rather than 'exterminated.' 'Extermination' betrays the work of an exterminator; 'extinction,' on the other hand, suggests a natural process, as if time alone were responsible for this fated course of events. Melville is not alone in favoring the word. Andrew Jackson, in his Second Annual Message (1830), had used the same word to defend his Indian policy. 'To follow to the tomb that last of his race and to tread on the graves of extinct nations excite melancholy reflections,' Jackson admitted, but quickly added that 'true philanthropy reconciles the mind . . . to the extinction of one generation to make room for another.'[5]

. . . 'Extinction' is what happens in an autotelic universe: it naturalizes the category of the 'doomed,' not only by recuperating it as an evolutionary category but, most crucially, by locating the cause for extinction within the extinct organism itself. If Indians die out it is their own fault. Their extinction is a function of their . . . benighted refusal to quit their savage ways. This is the logic of blaming the victim; within the terms of our discussion, we might also call it the logic of negative individualism. The strategy here is to equate phenomenon with locus, to collapse cause and casualty into an identical unit, to make the Indian seem at once the scene and agent of his own destruction. No less than the whale, the Indian too is a self-contained figure. He is both necessary and sufficient for his own condition: his impending doom refers to nothing other than his own savage self.

The Indian, as he is described by antebellum ethnographers and politicians, is therefore always the subject of a predestined narrative, in which he is responsible for, guilty of, and committed to a fated course of action, in which he appears not only as both victim and culprit, but also as a legible sign of his own inexorable end. Negative individualism could have found no better exponent. Ahab's kinship with the Indian is, under the circumstances, only to be expected. A single narrative works for both, for like the doomed savage, Ahab too is a product of negative individualism. He too is a victim of his own fault, and an instrument of his own fate. *Moby-Dick*, then, is not just a story of doom, but the story of a particular kind of doom, self-chosen and self-inflicted.

. . . The constellations of terms that seal Ahab's fate are therefore exactly those that sealed the fate of the Indians. Yet, seeing Ahab as an allegory of the Indian would be wrong, for the representational relation here is not so much one between the two as one encompassing both of them. Both are encompassed, that is, by a punitive representation of the self, what I have called negative individualism. Thus filiated in their genesis, Ahab and the Indians logically share a common end. We might speak of this punitive representation as broadly allegorical, for it operates through a set of signifying attributes, out of which it produces both 'persons' and 'destinies.' Indeed, if we are right to detect in *Moby-Dick* a 'hideous and intolerable allegory' (177) (whose existence Melville denies), that allegory works, I believe, primarily as an economy of ascription, as the production of narrative through the assignment of attributes. Ahab and the Indians are both bearers of attributes. They happen to inhabit two (apparently) disparate realms, one literary and the other social, but that fact finally matters less than the attributes they share. Those attributes make them analogous characters, produce them as analogous signs, and inflict on them analogous narratives – narratives of extinction.

. . . *Moby-Dick* . . . is a meditation on yengeance: on the deflection of it and the deterrence of it. Melville is fascinated . . . by the savage energy of the undeflected and the undeterred. . . . Ahab believes in vengeance. He refuses to locate it, moreover, in a circuit of identity, in the reflexive self-punishment of the victimizer. For him, the dismembered and the dismemberer are mutually engendering but by no means identical. His 'vengeance' is a question of relation, not to oneself but to someone else; it is also a question of action, inflicted on another and perhaps returned in kind by that other. Such a model entails not the spatial containment of victim in victimizer, but the temporal reversal of positions between the two. In short, Ahab's syntax of vengeance invokes the agency of time not only to preserve both victim and victimizer but, more crucially, to constitute one as the potential of the other. The two will trade places in time. Change is possible, indeed logical, as far as Ahab is concerned. It will not be absolute change, of course – his world will always have two positions, victims and victimizers – but one can at least move from one position to the other.

. . . Ahab's . . . syntax of vengeance – 'to dismember my dismemberer' – turns out to be anything but circular. It activates, on the contrary, a temporal process, a process of reversals at once inevitable and interminable. Against and around this temporal menace, Melville would have to erect other spatial forms of defense. The most effective form, he discovers, turns out once again to be the form of the tautology, for nothing works better as a vehicle of containment, and nothing keeps Ahab's vengeance under tighter control. And tautologies are easy enough to come by. All Melville needs is five short words: 'Ahab is for ever Ahab' (459). Those are Ahab's own words, defiantly spoken; ironically they are also the words that condemn him. From our standpoint, these words must stand as the very epigraph of negative individualism, the punitive logic centered on the autonomous self. That punitive logic, we can now see, is tautological almost by necessity: it begins and ends with the self, a self constituted here not only as the seat of agency but also as the circuit of discipline. The version Melville comes up with – 'Ahab is for ever Ahab' – therefore operates as two related tautologies, both of which begin and end with Ahab, and condemn him in just that circularity. Both are vehicles of containment, mobilized to contain Ahab's syntax of vengeance, and we might speak of them, accordingly, as the syntax of fate and the syntax of self.

Fate begins, in Ahab's case, with the name itself. Such a name is clearly 'not without meaning,' as Melville might say, and it is just this meaning that dooms its unlucky bearer. Ishmael and Peleg allude to that meaning even before Ahab appears. In response to Peleg's remark that 'Ahab of old, thou knowest, was a crowned king!' Ishmael replies, 'And a very vile one. When that wicked king was slain, the dogs, did they not lick his blood?' (77). No nineteenth-century reader would have missed the meaning of such a name, and few of them would have been surprised by what happens to Ahab at the end. Ahab can only mean what his name says he means: he is characterized by that name, summarized by it, and doomed by it. As a bearer of meaning, at once unmistakable and immutable, Ahab is less a living thing,

perhaps, than a legible sign. He is a personified name, a human recep-
tacle invested with a signifying function. That signifying function is
quite literally his fate: he lives in it and dies in it, since his whole life
is really nothing more than a recapitulation of what his name has
made abundantly clear at the outset. To be called Ahab is to inhabit a
narrative tautology, in which the end is already immanent in the
beginning, and in which all temporal development merely reenacts
what is in place from the very first.

Ahab, of course, has hoped for change. He has hoped that time will
help him. He should have known better, for his own name ought to
have taught him the futility of his hope. Personifying that name, Ahab
can have only one narrative, not a narrative of vengeance, but a narrative of doom.[6] His story is therefore (as Elijah says) 'all fixed and
arranged a'ready' (87), already inscribed in the fate of his Biblical
namesake. Ahab is right, then, to say, 'This whole act's immutably
decreed. 'Twas rehearsed by thee and me a billion years before this
ocean rolled' (459). The passage of time ('a billion years') brings no
change, no prospect of vengeance, for time turns out to be completely
unavailing here. Its status is summed up in the five words, 'Ahab is
for ever Ahab,' a tautology that, quite literally, puts time in its place,
in the spatial confines of the personified name. Ahab's story can only
be a story of fate, because personification is, in effect, a vehicle of pre-
destination. Under its dictates, time counts only as duration, not as
potentiality. The circuit of identity between 'Ahab' and 'Ahab' marks
the circuit from immanence to permanence, and affirms a timeless
design, the design of 'for ever.'

. . . The familiar strategy for antebellum expansionists was to
invoke some version of 'Providence,' whose plans for the future happened to coincide exactly with America's territorial ambitions.
American expansion in space and providential design in time turned
out to be one and the same. In the famous words of John L.
O'Sullivan, it was America's 'manifest destiny to overspread the continent allotted by Providence for the free development of our yearly
multiplying millions.'[7] This manifest destiny had no spatial limits, for
as another expansionist enthusiastically put it, America was bounded
'on the West by the Day of Judgement.'[8] For this hopeful soul, and for
many others, spatialized time legitimized and empowered. Yet the
same mechanism could just as easily victimize and destroy. For
Indians, too, happened to be the subjects of spatialized time. As much
as America, they were 'destined' – destined, that is, 'to melt and
vanish'. . . . Within the spatialized time of providential design, the fate
of the doomed savage became legible as a text.

Spatialized time is also what *Moby-Dick* invokes to make Ahab's
fate legible. Reading that fate, Melville's prophets turn Ahab, too, into

a doomed figure, spatializing his temporal endeavor into a timeless script. Melville's 'imperial folio,' then, logically shares the same temporal economy with its imperial environment, for a structure of dominion is inseparable from a structure of time. . . . Fate in *Moby-Dick* and Manifest Destiny in antebellum America are kindred constructs. Ahab and America, bearers both of a timeless destiny, mirror each other in familial likeness.

. . . Ahab . . . is not only named Ahab but also called 'immutable.' Indeed, in an uncanny parallel, he seems to have been fashioned out of just those attributes that antebellum Americans bestowed on the Indian. . . . He commands an 'iron soul' (438) and an 'iron voice' (439); his face is 'set like a flint' (369). To [Francis] Parkman, the Indian seemed 'hewn out of a rock'; to Melville, Ahab's very coat appears 'stone carved' (438).[9]

. . . The tautology 'Ahab is for ever Ahab' functions here, not as the syntax of fate, then, but as something altogether analogous to it, what we might call the syntax of self. At once subject and predicate, instrument and embodiment of his own misfortune, Ahab stands convicted the moment he is ascribed with a self, the moment he is bound, himself to himself, by 'is for ever.' The verb here can only be 'is,' only the present tense, for the syntax of self, like the syntax of fate, invokes a timeless regime, a circuit of identity. Following Lacan, we might say that such an identity is itself the mark of alienation, that it 'symbolizes the mental permanence of the I, at the same time as it prefigures its alienating destination.'[10] That unhappy fate is what afflicts Ahab, and what afflicted the Indians. 'Identity,' in both cases, would thus seem to be as much a sociopolitical category as a psychoanalytic one. Certainly it has its sociopolitical uses. Negative individualism, the punitive logic based on the autonomous self, cannot operate outside its province.

For the punitive logic must reside in the very identity of selfhood. As a self-contained unit, the self is the seat of agency, we have said, but, as we can also see, such a unit is no less the seat of penalty. Within its circuit of identity, as Ahab and the Indians embody it, the self encapsulates both cause and consequence, both injury and blame. Even as it generates a circuit of closure, the attribution of identity would seem also to generate, in the same process, a circuit of discipline, one that regiments the self, fashions it into the seat of 'self-government.' This it accomplishes not just by enclosure but equally by exclusion: by marking the self's boundary against a companion domain, that of the 'extraneous,' posited as outside the self. As we shall see, it is in tandem with this companion category, paradoxically, that the self bodies forth its most powerful punitive logic.

Starbuck gives voice to that logic when he advises Ahab, 'let Ahab beware of Ahab; beware of thyself, old man' (394). In a sense, this is merely another way of saying what Ahab has already said about himself – 'Ahab is for ever Ahab' – for Starbuck's injunction, too, centers on 'Ahab,' the all-encompassing, all-responsible individual self. What is striking about Starbuck's formulation, however, is what it manages to exclude, and, in the process of exclusion, where it manages to locate blame. According to Starbuck, Ahab must beware of himself, presumably because he is his own worst enemy. There is no mention here of Moby-Dick, no mention of what has been done to Ahab, no mention, in short, of either adversary or antecedent. Relation and temporality alike are excluded in Starbuck's formula for selfhood. Portrayed as such, Ahab indeed has no one to fear but himself, and no one to blame but himself.

. . . What we are witnessing is that most pervasive and persistent of phenomena: the phenomenon of blaming the victim. Starbuck dramatizes the connection between that phenomenon and the institution of 'selfhood.' It is no accident that the spokesman for 'Nantucket market' should be a champion of the autonomous self, no accident that such a self should be exhorted as the seat of agency, and no accident, either, that the same self should be invoked as the grounds for damnation. Starbuck only advises Ahab, 'beware of thyself,' but he might also have said, 'help thyself.' The two mottoes go hand in hand. If the latter ushers in the self-reliant entrepreneur, the former dispatches the self-victimizing savage. There is no contradiction here: for self-reliance and self-victimization, too, are kindred, the freedom of the one making up the fate of the other, the penalty for one being the other's reward. To make the self the seat of agency is to invoke the agency of both.

Even in *Moby-Dick*, we see not just the spectacle of self-victimization but also the spectacle of self-reliance. We see it, quite graphically, in the whale, the proud owner of 'thick walls' and 'interior spaciousness,' who lives 'in the world without being of it' (261). We see it, less graphically, in the book named after the whale – or rather, we see it in Melville's image of the book. The image remains ideal, however, for Melville, his dream of freedom notwithstanding, is haunted always by its obverse. Ahab's death is, for that reason, not quite the last word in *Moby-Dick*, and certainly not the last word as Melville goes on to reconsider it in *Pierre*. In that book the doomed savage returns, in logic if not in person, but vengeful as ever.[11] □

The final extract is offered as a sort of short epilogue to this Critical Guide. It comes from William Spanos' book *The Errant Art of Moby-Dick: The Canon, the Cold War, and the Struggle for American Studies* (1995), the most recently published full-scale examination of Melville's novel. As is clear from its title, Spanos' book places *Moby-Dick* centrally in its critique of American culture since World War Two. We may accept or reject its major premise that *Moby-Dick* prefigures American involvement in, and understanding of, the war in Vietnam. But what Spanos' book clearly underscores is the fact that warfare provides the most appropriate metaphor (and in some cases, reality) in the reading and understanding of *Moby-Dick*. Indeed, as we have seen repeatedly throughout this Critical Guide, *Moby-Dick* is a product of conflict. Written in antebellum America, its sense of tension and struggle has engaged readers deeply during two world wars, it has been read as a text of the Cold War, of Vietnam, of America's imperialist obliteration of its native peoples, and of the metaphysical struggle between good and evil. For Spanos *Moby-Dick* articulates a struggle between humanism and 'post-humanism'. In this respect, he reinvents Melville's masterpiece as a text that speaks to the condition of America at the approach of the next millennium.

■ It has become a commonplace of canonical Melville criticism that *Moby-Dick* is, in the 'richness of its human vision,' capable of accommodating as many interpretations as the Ecuadorean doubloon Ahab nailed to the mast does for the crew of the *Pequod*. This cliché of traditional Americanist criticism is, of course, a manifestation of its humanist 'pluralism': its tolerance of different points of view. But it is also symptomatic of a pluralism that, in its 'benign' disinterestedness – its calculated disdain for 'ideological' reading – conceals a complexly effective ideological agenda. For a pluralism that allows for a multiplicity of 'incommensurable' readings of *Moby-Dick* is grounded in the assumption that all the positions informing these differential readings, in so far as they are adequately argued, are equal and thus negotiable. This pluralism, in which power is represented as equally distributed, that is, takes place *nowhere*: in a free-floating zone beyond the reach of history. As Melville is at great pains to show in *Moby-Dick* and his later novels, however, power relations in history are not equal; they are characterized by injustice, conflict, and contestation: by the uneven struggle for power. In thus transforming worldly conflict to the value-free arena of debate, the dominant pluralist tradition has produced an identical *Moby-Dick*, despite the apparent diversity of its interpretations of Melville's novel. This criticism, in other words, is informed by an undeviating commitment to the monumentality of a novel that, like the fiction that followed, was dedicated to the subversion of the American will to monumentalize 'America.' To be more specific, this criticism is informed by a commitment to permanentize the status of *Moby-Dick* as a memorial to a pluralist American value system against an Old World authoritarianism and/or its ideological criticism that reflects, confirms, and enhances the hegemony of its pluralist ideology: its authoritarianism by deception.

. . . As I suggested in the 'final' comments of my 'interpretation' of *Moby-Dick*, my 'study' is not intended to be History: a retrospective reading from the point of view of the present which would put Melville's novel in its *proper* place in the inclusive table of American literary and cultural history. My de-structive reading, rather, has been intended as genealogy. It is meant, that is, to be a contribution to the 'history of the present' place of *Moby-Dick* in the discourse of the American Cultural Memory, a history written from the perspective of the countermemory precipitated by the retrieval of the multiply situated relay of differences that 'American History' has repressed in the process of constructing *Moby-Dick* as a monument to America's exceptionalist destiny: a monument that not only memorializes the 'Revolutionary' past, but prophesies the end of the post-Cold War and the advent of the 'New World Order.'

The recent history of Melville criticism, in other words, has been shown to be a history reflecting, not, as it is assumed, impartial debate over the aesthetic greatness of Melville's fiction, but a struggle to appropriate it for present ideological purposes.

. . . The reading of *Moby-Dick* sponsored by the founders of American literary studies in the late 1940s would go far not only to legitimize the massive amnesiac project of the American Cultural Memory to forget Vietnam, to 'heal the wound' opened up in the collective American psyche by the brutal American intervention (and defeat) in Vietnam (an amnesiac initiative the most recent moment of which is the rehabilitation of Richard Nixon at the time of his death in May 1994). It would also lend itself to the legitimation of the present representation of the recent global events in Central and Eastern Europe and the former Soviet Union as the dialectical 'triumph' of (the principles of) liberal American democracy and the 'fall' of communism, that is, as the advent of the 'New World Order' or, as one highly visible exponent of this representation puts it, 'the end of history,' presided over by the United States.[12]

Whatever its blindnesses . . . *Moby-Dick* speaks resonantly across the great divide of time not to (American) Man but to the present historical occasion. It is not, to extend a resonant motif in Michel Foucault, simply a genealogy, a 'history of [Melville's] present': it is also a history of the American future, of the present historical occasion that we precariously inhabit.[13] □

Moby-Dick's power, it seems, is one of survival into a precarious future. As testimony to such powers of survival, the history of *Moby-Dick*'s critical reception is proof of its eloquent ability continuously to reinvent both itself and the culture which gave birth to it. This pattern of survival seems set by Ishmael's final words, the *Epilogue* of *Moby-Dick*, where we see him as an orphan floating clear of *Pequod*'s wreckage. But even earlier, in chapter 22, 'The Doubloon,' the survival of *Moby-Dick* in the hands of its readers and critics seems eerily anticipated by Stubb:

■ 'There's another rendering now; but still one text.' □

BIBLIOGRAPHY

Editions of *Moby-Dick*

References to *Moby-Dick* throughout the editorial narrative are to Herman Melville, *Moby-Dick, or The Whale*, ed. Harrison Hayford, Hershel Parker and G. Thomas Tanselle (Evanston and Chicago: Northwestern University Press and The Newberry Library, 1988). This is the 'standard' critical edition of the novel (and comprises Volume Six of the *Northwestern–Newberry Edition of The Writings of Herman Melville*).

There are many different editions of *Moby-Dick* available, and some are very inexpensive. It is always, though, worthwhile checking to see that you have a full and unabridged version. A good general rule of thumb for checking this is to see if an edition starts with the 'Etymology' and 'Extracts' sections, and ends with the *Epilogue* (and the narrative itself should run to 135 chapters).

Personally, I like the Penguin edition by Harold Beaver: Herman Melville, *Moby-Dick; or, The Whale*, ed. Harold Beaver (1972; rpt. Harmondsworth: Penguin Books, 1985). This has substantial notes that are full of fascinating and quirky information. Another important edition, which includes a sampling of early criticism is: Herman Melville, *Moby-Dick: An Authoritative Text, Reviews and Letters by Melville, Analogues and Sources, Criticism*, eds Harrison Hayford and Hershel Parker (New York: W.W. Norton & Co., 1967).

Works Cited

Catherine Belsey, *Critical Practice* (London and New York: Methuen, 1980).

Leo Bersani, *The Culture of Redemption* (Cambridge, Mass.: Harvard University Press, 1990).

Walter E. Bezanson, '*Moby-Dick:* Work of Art', in *Moby-Dick Centennial Essays*, ed. Tyrus Hillway and Luther S. Mansfield (Dallas: Southern Methodist University Press, 1953), pp. 30–58.

Watson G. Branch, ed., *Melville: The Critical Heritage* (London and Boston: Routledge and Kegan Paul, 1974).

Amariah Brigham, *An Inquiry concerning the Diseases and Functions of the Brain, the Spinal Cord, and the Nerves* (New York: Arno Press, 1973; 1st pub. New York, 1840).

Richard H. Brodhead, ed. *New Essays on Moby-Dick* (Cambridge and New York: Cambridge University Press, 1986), pp. 1–21.

Lawrence Buell, '*Moby-Dick* as Sacred Text', in *New Essays on Moby-Dick*, ed. Richard H. Brodhead (Cambridge and New York: Cambridge University Press, 1986), pp. 53–69.

Richard Chase, *Herman Melville: A Critical Study* (New York: Macmillan, 1949).

Jonathan Culler, *On Deconstruction: Theory and Criticism after Structuralism* (London: Routledge & Kegan Paul, 1983; Ithaca: Cornell University Press, 1983).

Alexis de Tocqueville, *Democracy in America*, ed. J. P. Mayer, trans. George Lawrence (Garden City, N.Y.: Doubleday, 1969; London: Fontana Press, 1994).

Wai-chee Dimock, 'Ahab's Manifest Destiny', in *Macropolitics of Nineteenth Century Literature: Nationalism, Exoticism, Imperialism*, ed. Jonathan Arac and Harriet Ritvo (Philadelphia: University of Pennsylvania Press, 1991), pp. 184–212.

Ralph Waldo Emerson, 'Self-Reliance', in *Emerson's Essays*, ed. Sherman Paul (New York: Dutton, 1969; London: Dent, 1980 pp.   29–56.

Charles Fiedelson, Jr., *Symbolism and American Literature* (Chicago: University of Chicago Press, 1953).

E.M. Forster, *Aspects of the Novel* (New York: Harcourt, Brace, 1927).

Northrop Frye, *Anatomy of Criticism* (Princeton: Princeton University Press, 1957).

Francis Fukuyama, *The End of History and the Last Man* (New York: Free Press, 1992).

Michael T. Gilmore, *American Romanticism and the Marketplace* (Chicago: University of Chicago Press, 1985).

Kevin J. Hayes, ed., *The Critical Response to Herman Melville's Moby-Dick* (Westport, Connecticut: Greenwood Press, 1994).

Harrison Hayford and Hershel Parker, eds, *Moby-Dick as Doubloon: Essays and Extracts* (New York: W.W. Norton & Co., 1970).

Hugh Hetherington, *Melville's Reviewers* (Chapel Hill: University of North Carolina Press, 1961).

Brian Higgins and Hershel Parker, eds, *Critical Essays on Herman Melville's Moby-Dick* (New York: G.K. Hall & Co., 1992).

Leon Howard, *Herman Melville: A Biography* (Berkeley and Los Angeles: University of California Press, 1967).

Myra Jehlen, ed., *Herman Melville: A Collection of Critical Essays* (Englewood Cliffs, NJ: Prentice Hall, 1994).

Jacques Lacan, *Ecrits*, trans. Alan Sheridan (New York: Norton, 1977).

D.H. Lawrence, *Studies in Classic American Literature* (New York: Thomas Seltzer, 1923).

Anika Lemaire, *Jacques Lacan*, trans. David Macey (London and Boston: Routledge and Kegan Paul, 1977).

David Leverenz, *Manhood and the American Renaissance* (Ithaca and London: Cornell University Press, 1989).

Harry Levin, *The Power of Blackness: Hawthorne, Melville, Poe* (New York: Alfred A. Knopf, 1976).

R.W.B. Lewis, *The American Adam: Innocence, Tragedy and Tradition in the Nineteenth Century* (Chicago and London: The University of Chicago Press, 1955).

F.O. Matthiessen, *American Renaissance: Art and Expression in the Age of Emerson and Whitman* (London and New York: Oxford University Press, 1941).

Herman Melville, The Letters of Herman Melville, ed. Merrell R. Davis and William H. Gilman (New Haven: Yale University Press, 1960).

———, *The Piazza Tales and Other Prose Pieces 1839–1860*, ed. Harrison Hayford, Alma A. MacDougal and G. Thomas Tanselle (Evanston and Chicago: Northwestern University Press and The Newberry Library, 1987).

———, *Correspondence*, ed. Lynn Horth (Evanston and Chicago: Northwestern University Press and The Newberry Library, 1993), Volume 14 of *The Writings of Herman Melville*.

Lewis Mumford, *Herman Melville* (London: Jonathan Cape, 1929; New York: Harcourt & Brace, 1963).

Henry A. Murray, 'In Nomine Diaboli', *New England Quarterly* 24 (December 1951), pp.435–52.

Charles Olson, *Call Me Ishmael: A Study of Melville* (San Francisco: City Light Books, 1947; rpt. London: Jonathan Cape, 1967).

Hershel Parker, 'Five Reviews not in *Moby-Dick as Doubloon*', *English Language Notes*, 9 (1972), pp.182–5.

————, *Herman Melville; A Biography, Volume I, 1819–1851* (Baltimore and London: The Johns Hopkins University Press, 1996).

Francis Parkman, *The Conspiracy of Pontiac*, 2 vols. (1851; rpt. Boston: Little Brown, 1909).

Donald E. Pease, 'Moby Dick and the Cold War', in *The American Renaissance Reconsidered*, ed. Walter Benn Michaels and Donald E. Pease (Baltimore and London: The Johns Hopkins University Press, 1985), pp. 113–55.

David S. Reynolds, *Beneath the American Renaissance: The Subversive Imagination in the Age of Emerson and Melville* (Cambridge, Mass. and London: Harvard University Press, 1988).

————, '"Its wood could only be American!": *Moby-Dick* and Antebellum Popular Culture', in *Critical Essays on Herman Melville's Moby-Dick*, ed. Brian Higgins and Hershel Parker (New York: G.K. Hall & Co., 1992), pp. 523–44.

Robert D. Richardson, *Myth and Literature in the American Renaissance* (Bloomington: Indiana University Press, 1978).

Paul Royster, 'Melville's Economy of Language', in *Ideology and Classic American Literature*, ed. Sacvan Bercovitch and Myra Jehlen (Cambridge: Cambridge University Press, 1986), pp. 313–24.

John Seelye, *Melville: The Ironic Diagram* (Evanston: Northwestern University Press, 1970).

Rowland A. Sherrill, *The Prophetic Melville* (Athens: University of Georgia Press, 1979).

Henry Nash Smith, 'Can "American Studies" Develop a Method?' in *Studies in American Culture: Dominant Ideas and Images*, ed. Joseph J. Kwiat and Mary C. Turpie (Minneapolis: University of Minnesota Press, 1960).

William V. Spanos, *The Errant Art of Moby-Dick: The Canon, The Cold War, and the Struggle for American Studies* (Durham and London: Duke University Press, 1995).

Cecil F. Tate, *The Search for a Method in American Studies* (Minneapolis: University of Minnesota Press, 1973).

Carl Van Doren, 'Contemporaries of Cooper', *The Cambridge History of American Literature*, ed. W.P. Trent *et al.*, Vol. 1 (New York: G.P. Putnam's Sons, 1917), pp. 322–3.

Further Reading

The standard biography of Melville is Leon Howard, *Herman Melville: A Biography* (Berkeley and Los Angeles: University of California Press, 1967). This is certain to be superseded by the recently published Hershel Parker, *Herman Melville; A Biography, Volume I, 1819–1851* (Baltimore and London: The Johns Hopkins University Press, 1996). A vital research tool is Jay Leyda's *The Melville Log* (New York: Gordian Press, 1969), and its various re-incarnations.

The following is a brief list of some of the more useful critical or background works that are not cited above.

Harold Bloom, ed., *Ahab, Major Literary Characters Series* (New York: Chelsea House, 1991).

Richard Chase, ed., *Melville: A Collection of Critical Essays* (Englewood Cliffs: Prentice-Hall, 1962).

Marvin Fisher, *Going Under: Melville's Short Fiction and the American 1850s* (Baton

Rouge: Louisiana State University Press, 1977).

Stuart M. Frank, *Herman Melville's Picture Gallery: Sources and types of the 'pictorial' chapters of Moby-Dick* (Fairhaven, Mass.: Edward J. Lefkowicz, 1986).

John Irwin, *American Hieroglyphics* (Baltimore: Johns Hopkins University Press, 1980).

A. Robert Lee, ed., *Herman Melville: Reassessments* (London: Vision/Barnes & Noble, 1984; Totowa, N.J.: Barnes & Noble, 1984).

Leo Marx, *The Machine in the Garden: Technology and the Pastoral Ideal in America* (New York: Oxford University Press, 1964).

John P. McWilliams, *Hawthorne, Melville and the American Character: A looking-glass business* (Cambridge and New York: Cambridge University Press, 1984).

Donald Pease, ed., *Revisionary Interventions into the Americanist Canon* (Durham and London: Duke University Press, 1994).

David S. Reynolds, *Walt Whitman's America: A Cultural Biography* (New York: Alfred A. Knopf, 1995).

Michael Paul Rogin, *Subversive Genealogy: The Politics and Art of Herman Melville* (New York: Alfred A. Knopf 1983).

Edward Rosenberry, *Melville* (London and Boston: Routledge & Kegan Paul, 1979).

Pamela Schirmeister, *The Consolations of Space: The Place of Romance in Hawthorne, Melville and James* (Stanford: Stanford University Press, 1990).

David Simpson, 'Herman Melville: Chasing the Whale', in *Fetishism and Imagination: Dickens, Melville, Conrad* (Baltimore and London: The Johns Hopkins University Press, 1982), pp. 69–90.

Milton Stern, *The Fine Hammered Steel of Herman Melville* (Urbana: University of Illinois Press, 1957).

Tony Tanner, *Scenes of Nature, Signs of Man* (Cambridge and New York: Cambridge University Press, 1987, 1988).

Herbert Walker, *Moby-Dick and Calvinism: a World Dismantled* (New Brunswick: Rutgers University Press, 1977).

Larzer Ziff, *Declaring Independence: The Declaration of Cultural Independence in America* (New York: Viking Press, 1981).

Three films have been made that are based on *Moby-Dick*, all of them by Warner Brothers: *The Sea Beast* (1925) a silent movie starring John Barrymore, its remake *Moby-Dick or The White Whale* (1930), also starring Barrymore, and – most famously – *Moby-Dick* (1956) with script by Ray Bradbury, directed by John Huston and starring Gregory Peck and Orson Welles.

There are also a number of Melville websites. Try browsing at
http://www.melville.org
http://www.keele.ac.uk/depts/as/Literature/Moby-Dick/amlit.whale-pages.html

And, finally, ISHMAIL is an on-line discussion group of 'the life, works, contemporaries and impact of Herman Melville'. To subscribe to ISHMAIL send the following E-mail message to
MAILSERV@VAXC.HOFSTRA.EDU:
subscribe ishmail-l [your name]

NOTES

INTRODUCTION

1 Alexis de Tocqueville, *Democracy in America*, ed. J.P. Meyer, trans. George Lawrence (London: Fontana Press, 1994), p.471.

2 Alexis de Tocqueville, p.474.

3 Herman Melville, 'Hawthorne and His Mosses', first published anonymously in the New York *Literary World*, VII, no. 185 (August 17, 1850), pp.125–7, and no. 186 (August 24, 1850), pp.145–7. Extracted here from Herman Melville, *The Piazza Tales and Other Prose Pieces 1839–1860*, ed. Harrison Hayford, Alma A. MacDougal and G. Thomas Tanselle (Evanston and Chicago: Northwestern University Press and The Newberry Library, 1987), pp.239–53. This comprises Volume 9 of *The Writings of Herman Melville*. The extracts given are from pp.242–4.

4 Herman Melville, 'Hawthorne and His Mosses', p.244.

5 Herman Melville, *Moby-Dick, or The Whale*, ed. Harrison Hayford, Hershel Parker and G. Thomas Tanselle (Evanston and Chicago: Northwestern University Press and The Newberry Library, 1988), p.164. All subsequent references in the editorial narrative are to this edition.

6 Herman Melville, 'Hawthorne and His Mosses', pp.246–8.

CHAPTER ONE

1 Letter to Nathaniel Hawthorne, 17(?) November 1851, in Herman Melville, *Correspondence*, ed. Lynn Horth (Evanston and Chicago: Northwestern University Press and The Newberry Library, 1993), Volume 14 of *The Writings of Herman Melville*, pp.210–14.

2 Herman Melville, *Correspondence*, p.213.

3 See Herman Melville, *Correspondence*, p.140. See also Leon Howard, *Herman Melville: A Biography* (Berkeley and Los Angeles: University of California Press, 1967), p.151, and Hershel Parker, *Herman Melville; A Biography, Volume I, 1819–1851* (Baltimore and London: The Johns Hopkins University Press, 1996), p.725.

4 Letter to Richard Henry Dana, Jr., 1 May 1850, in Herman Melville, *Correspondence*, p.162.

5 Herman Melville, *Correspondence*, p.160.

6 Herman Melville, *Correspondence*, p.160.

7 See David S. Reynolds, *Beneath the American Renaissance: The Subversive Imagination in the Age of Emerson and Melville* (Cambridge, Mass. and London: Harvard University Press, 1988), esp. chapter six: 'The Sensational Press and the Rise of Subversive Literature,' pp.169–210. The unprecedented growth of publishing and of a highly literate public is documented by Michael T. Gilmore in the 'Introduction' to his *American Romanticism and the Marketplace* (Chicago and London: The University of Chicago Press, 1985), pp.1–17.

8 See Harold Beaver's note in Herman Melville, *Moby-Dick; or, The Whale*, ed. Harold Beaver (1972; rpt. Harmondsworth: Penguin Books, 1985), p.835.

9 Ralph Waldo Emerson, 'Self-Reliance,' in *Emerson's Essays*, ed. Sherman Paul (London: Dent, 1980) p.31.

10 Letter to Nathaniel Hawthorne, 29 June 1851, in Herman Melville, *Correspondence*, p.196.

11 'Review of *Moby-Dick*,' *Harper's New Monthly Magazine*, 4 (December 1851), p.137. This anonymous review was attributed to George Ripley by Hugh Hetherington, '*Moby-Dick*', in *Melville's Reviewers* (Chapel Hill: University of North Carolina Press, 1961), pp.212–13. The early reviews included in this chapter are reprinted in (at least one of) the following collections: *Herman Melville, Moby-Dick: An Authoritative Text, Reviews and Letters by Melville, Analogues and Sources, Criticism*, eds Harrison Hayford and Hershel Parker (New York: W.W. Norton & Co., 1967), pp.613 ff.; Harrison Hayford and Hershel Parker, eds, *Moby-Dick as Doubloon: Essays and Extracts* (New York: W.W. Norton & Co., 1970); Watson G. Branch, ed., *Melville: The Critical Heritage* (London and Boston: Routledge and Kegan Paul, 1974); Brian Higgins and Hershel Parker, eds, *Critical Essays on Herman Melville's Moby-Dick* (New York: G.K. Hall & Co., 1992); and Kevin J. Hayes, ed., *The Critical Response to Herman*

Melville's Moby-Dick (Westport, Connecticut: Greenwood Press, 1994).

12 Ripley, p.137.

13 London *Spectator*, 24 (25 October 1851), pp.1026–7.

14 See Hayes, ed., p.xv; and Hayford, Parker and Tanselle, eds, *Moby-Dick*, p.771.

15 London *Spectator*, 24 (25 October 1851), as above.

16 London *Athenaeum*, No. 1252 (25 October 1851), pp.1112–13.

17 From the New York *Literary World*, No. 251 (22 November 1851), pp.403–4.

18 New York *Albion*, New Series 10 (22 November 1851), p.561.

19 *Bell's New Weekly Messenger*, 23 (2 November 1851), p.6. The same review appeared simultaneously in the London *News of the World*. See Hershel Parker, 'Five Reviews not in *Moby-Dick as Doubloon*', *English Language Notes*, 9 (1972), pp.182–5; and Hayes, ed., p.5.

20 *The Southern Quarterly Review*, 5 (January 1852), p.262.

21 London *New Monthly Magazine*, 98 (July 1853), 307–8. This review was attributed to William Harrison Ainsworth by Hetherington (1961), p.202.

22 Washington *National Intelligencer* (16 December 1851). This review was attributed to William A. Butler by Hetherington (1961), p.214.

23 London *Bentley's Miscellany* (January 1852).

24 Henry S. Salt, 'Herman Melville,' *Scottish Art Review* [London], 2 (November 1889), pp.188–9.

25 Henry S. Salt, 'Marquesan Melville,' *Gentleman's Magazine* [London], 272 (March 1892), pp.252–4.

CHAPTER TWO

1 See Brian Higgins and Hershel Parker, eds, *Critical Essays on Herman Melville's Moby-Dick* (New York: G.K. Hall & Co., 1992), pp.9–15; and Kevin J. Hayes, ed., *The Critical Response to Herman Melville's Moby-Dick* (Westport, Connecticut: Greenwood Press, 1994), pp.xviii–xx.

2 Joseph Conrad, Letter to Sir Humphrey Milord, 15 January 1907, from Harrison Hayford and Hershel Parker, eds, *Moby-*

Dick as Doubloon: Essays and Extracts (New York: W.W. Norton & Co., 1970), p.123.

3 Carl Van Doren, 'Contemporaries of Cooper', *The Cambridge History of American Literature*, ed. W.P. Trent *et al.*, vol. 1 (New York: G.P. Putnam's Sons, 1917), pp.322–3.

4 Van Doren, pp.322–3.

5 D.H. Lawrence, *Studies in Classic American Literature* (New York: Thomas Seltzer, 1923), p.11.

6 Richard Henry Dana, Jr., author of *Two Years Before the Mast* (1840).

7 Futurism: *c.* 1912–15, an artistic movement dedicated to promoting anarchic aesthetics based on the energy, power and beauty of the machine. It was a precursor of modernism.

8 Lawrence mistakes the name of Queequeg's idol, Yojo. This could be due to the particular edition of the book which he was reading. It is clear from later in the essay, where he clearly believes Ishmael to have drowned along with the rest of the crew of the *Pequod*, that he was reading an edition based on the original English edition of *The Whale* which omitted the 'Epilogue'.

9 D.H. Lawrence, *Studies in Classic American Literature* (New York: Thomas Seltzer, 1923), pp.156–61.

10 Woodrow Wilson, American President, chaired the peace conference at Versailles following the First World War.

11 'It is finished' (Latin), the final words of Jesus on the cross.

12 D.H. Lawrence, *Studies in Classic American Literature* (New York: Thomas Seltzer, 1923), pp.161–74.

13 E.M. Forster, *Aspects of the Novel* (New York: Harcourt, Brace, 1927), p.129.

14 Forster refers here to a scene from Dostoevsky's *The Brothers Karamazov* from which he quotes earlier in this lecture.

15 E.M. Forster, *Aspects of the Novel* (New York: Harcourt, Brace, 1927), pp.199–203.

16 Lewis Mumford, *Herman Melville* (London: Jonathan Cape, 1929), pp.158–95.

CHAPTER THREE

1 F.O. Matthiessen, *American Renaissance: Art and Expression in the Age of Emerson and*

Whitman (London and New York: Oxford University Press, 1941), p.vii.

2 F.O. Matthiessen, *American Renaissance: Art and Expression in the Age of Emerson and Whitman* (London and New York: Oxford University Press, 1941), p.ix.

3 F.O. Matthiessen, *American Renaissance: Art and Expression in the Age of Emerson and Whitman* (London and New York: Oxford University Press, 1941), p.xiii.

4 F.O. Matthiessen, *American Renaissance: Art and Expression in the Age of Emerson and Whitman* (London and New York: Oxford University Press, 1941), pp.423–30.

5 Letter to Evert A. Duyckinck, Saturday 3 March 1849. See Herman Melville, *Correspondence*, ed. Lynn Horth (Evanston and Chicago: Northwestern University Press and The Newberry Library, 1993), Volume 14 of *The Writings of Herman Melville*, p.121.

6 F.O. Matthiessen, *American Renaissance: Art and Expression in the Age of Emerson and Whitman* (London and New York: Oxford University Press, 1941), pp.435–66.

7 Francis Parkman, author of *The Conspiracy of Pontiac* (1851).

8 Whitman's collection of poems, *Leaves of Grass*, in which he attempted to 'sing' America, was first published in 1855. Whitman added to and altered this book throughout his lifetime.

9 i.e. novices.

10 *King Lear*, Act III, scene vii.

11 *King Lear*, Act IV, scene ii.

12 i.e 'no good'.

13 See Melville's Letter to Evert A. Duyckinck, Saturday 3 March 1849. Melville writes: 'I would to God Shakespeare had lived later, & promenaded in Broadway. Not that I might have had the pleasure of leaving my card for him at the Astor, or made merry with him over a bowl of the fine Duyckinck punch; but that the muzzle which all men wore on their souls in the Elizebethan [sic] day, might not have intercepted Shakespeare's full articulations. For I hold it a verity, that even Shakespeare, was not a frank man to the uttermost. And, indeed, who in this intolerant Universe is, or can be? But the Declaration of Independence makes a

difference.' In Melville, *Correspondence*, p.122.

14 Charles Olson, *Call Me Ishmael: A Study of Melville* (1947; rpt. London: Jonathan Cape, 1967), pp.15–70.

15 Richard Chase, *Herman Melville: A Critical Study* (New York: Macmillan, 1949), pp.43–102.

CHAPTER FOUR

1 Henry Nash Smith, 'Can "American Studies" Develop a Method?' in *Studies in American Culture: Dominant Ideas and Images*, ed. Joseph J. Kwiat and Mary C. Turpie (Minneapolis: University of Minnesota Press, 1960), pp.3–15. This essay was originally published in *American Quarterly*, 9 (Summer 1957), pp.197–208.

2 Henry Nash Smith, p.5 and p.15.

3 See Cecil F. Tate, *The Search for a Method in American Sudies* (Minneapolis: University of Minnesota Press, 1973), esp. the chapter 'Myth and Holism in American Studies', pp.9–24.

4 See Brian Higgins and Hershel Parker, eds, *Critical Essays on Herman Melville's Moby-Dick* (New York: G.K. Hall & Co., 1992), p.408.

5 Melville's experiences living amongst the Polynesian people are detailed in his first book, *Typee*.

6 Henry A. Murray, 'In Nomine Diaboli', *New England Quarterly* 24 (December 1951), pp.435–52.

7 For an excellent synopsis of 'New Criticism' see Catherine Belsey, *Critical Practice* (London: Methuen, 1980), pp.15–20.

8 Charles Fiedelson, Jr., *Symbolism and American Literature* (Chicago: University of Chicago Press, 1953), pp.3–4.

9 Charles Fiedelson, Jr., *Symbolism and American Literature* (Chicago: University of Chicago Press, 1953), pp.29–34.

10 R.W.B. Lewis, *The American Adam: Innocence, Tragedy and Tradition in the Nineteenth Century* (Chicago and London: University of Chicago Press, 1955), p.138.

11 R.W.B. Lewis, *The American Adam: Innocence, Tragedy and Tradition in the Nineteenth Century* (Chicago and London: University of Chicago Press, 1955), pp.138–46.

CHAPTER FIVE

1 Northrop Frye, *Anatomy of Criticism* (Princeton: Princeton University Press, 1957), p.119. See also Catherine Belsey, *Critical Practice* (London: Methuen, 1980), pp.21–9, for a discussion of Northrop Frye and formalism.

2 Richard H. Brodhead, 'Trying All Things: An Introduction to *Moby-Dick*', in *New Essays on Moby-Dick*, ed. Richard H. Brodhead (Cambridge: Cambridge University Press, 1986), pp.4–8.

3 Bezanson's essay was first given as a paper at Oberlin College on 13 November 1951. See Brian Higgins and Hershel Parker, eds, *Critical Essays on Herman Melville's Moby-Dick* (New York: G.K. Hall & Co., 1992), p.421.

4 Walter E. Bezanson, '*Moby-Dick:* Work of Art', in *Moby-Dick Centennial Essays*, ed. Tyrus Hillway and Luther S. Mansfield (Dallas: Southern Methodist University Press, 1953), pp.30–58.

5 John Seelye, *Melville: The Ironic Diagram* (Evanston: Northwestern University Press, 1970), p.2.

6 John Seelye, *Melville: The Ironic Diagram* (Evanston: Northwestern University Press, 1970), pp.3–4.

7 Seelye refers to *Moby-Dick: or, The Whale*, ed. Luther S. Mansfield and Howard P. Vincent (New York: Hendricks House, 1952).

8 John Seelye, *Melville: The Ironic Diagram* (Evanston: Northwestern University Press, 1970), pp.63–73.

9 Harry Levin, *The Power of Blackness: Hawthorne, Melville, Poe* (New York: Alfred A. Knopf, 1976), p.224.

10 [Buell's note] Rowland A. Sherrill, *The Prophetic Melville* (Athens: University of Georgia Press, 1979), p.100.

11 Buell refers here to Robert D. Richardson, *Myth and Literature in the American Renaissance* (Bloomington: Indiana University Press, 1978), pp.212–13.

12 Lawrence Buell, '*Moby-Dick* as Sacred Text', in *New Essays on Moby-Dick*, ed. Richard H. Brodhead (Cambridge: Cambridge University Press, 1986), pp.53–69.

CHAPTER SIX

1 David S. Reynolds, *Beneath the American Renaissance: The Subversive Imagination in the Age of Emerson and Melville* (Cambridge, Mass. and London: Harvard University Press, 1988), pp.561–2.

2 David S. Reynolds, *Beneath the American Renaissance*, p.563.

3 David S. Reynolds, *Beneath the American Renaissance*, p.563.

4 Michael T. Gilmore, *American Romanticism and the Marketplace* (Chicago: University of Chicago Press, 1985), pp.114 and 118.

5 [Royster's note] Herman Melville, *Moby-Dick* (New York: The Library of America, 1983), p.1021. [Subsequent references throughout Royster's essay are to this edition.]

6 Paul Royster, 'Melville's Economy of Language', in *Ideology and Classic American Literature*, ed. Sacvan Bercovitch and Myra Jehlen (Cambridge: Cambridge University Press, 1986), pp.313–24.

7 See Jacques Lacan, 'The Mirror Stage', in *Ecrits*, trans. Alan Sheridan (New York: Norton, 1977), p.2. See also Anika Lemaire, *Jacques Lacan*, trans. David Macey (London: Routledge and Kegan Paul, 1977), p.64; and Catherine Belsey, *Critical Practice* (London: Methuen, 1980), pp.30–1 and 64–5.

8 David Leverenz, *Manhood and the American Renaissance* (Ithaca and London: Cornell University Press, 1989), p.280.

9 Leverenz, p.280.

10 See Leverenz, pp.279–81.

11 Leverenz, p.281.

12 Leverenz, p.281.

13 Leverenz, p.281.

14 See Lawrence's essay on *Moby-Dick*, above. Leverenz makes two mistakes here. Firstly he misquotes slightly, replacing Lawrence's 'white man' by his 'white men'. And secondly, for Lawrence it is Moby Dick who is this 'last phallic being', not Ahab, as Leverenz implies.

15 Page numbers given by Leverenz refer to *Moby-Dick*, ed. Harrison Hayford and Hershel Parker (1851; rpt. New York: Norton, 1967).

16 Leverenz here quotes Amariah

Brigham, *An Inquiry concerning the Diseases and Functions of the Brain, the Spinal Cord, and the Nerves* (New York: Arno Press, 1973; 1st pub. New York, 1840), p.240.

17 Leverenz, pp.283–306.

18 See Myra Jehlen 'Introduction', in *Herman Melville: A Collection of Critical Essays*, ed. Myra Jehlen (Englewood Cliffs, NJ: Prentice Hall, 1994), pp.9–10.

19 Leo Bersani, 'Incomparable America', in *The Culture of Redemption* (Cambridge, MA.: Harvard University Press, 1990), pp.136–54.

20 See Brian Higgins and Hershel Parker, 'Introduction', in *Critical Essays on Herman Melville's Moby-Dick*, ed. Brian Higgins and Hershel Parker (New York: G.K. Hall & Co., 1992), p.29.

21 [Reynolds' note] Melville to John Murray, 29 January 1847, *The Letters of Herman Melville*, ed. Merrell R. Davis and William H. Gilman (New Haven: Yale University Press, 1960), p.53.

22 [Reynolds' note] New York *Home Journal*, 29 November 1851, reprinted in *MOBY-DICK as Doubloon: Essays and Extracts (1851–1970)*, ed. Hershel Parker and Harrison Hayford (New York: Norton, 1970), p.56.

23 Parenthetical page numbers given by Reynolds refer to *Moby-Dick; or, The Whale*, ed. Harrison Hayford, Hershel Parker, and G. Thomas Tanselle (Evanston and Chicago: Northwestern University Press and The Newberry Library, 1988).

24 David S. Reynolds, '"Its wood could only be American!": *Moby-Dick* and Antebellum Popular Culture', in *Critical Essays on Herman Melville's Moby-Dick*, ed. Brian Higgins and Hershel Parker (New York: G.K. Hall & Co., 1992), pp.523–44.

CHAPTER SEVEN

1 Jonathan Culler, *On Deconstruction: Theory and Criticism after Structuralism* (London: Routledge & Kegan Paul, 1983), p.86.

2 William V. Spanos, *The Errant Art of Moby-Dick: The Canon, the Cold War, and the Struggle for American Studies* (Durham and London: Duke University Press, 1995), p.251.

3 Donald E. Pease, '*Moby Dick* and the Cold War', in *The American Renaissance Reconsidered*, ed. Walter Benn Michaels and

Donald E. Pease (Baltimore and London: The Johns Hopkins University Press, 1985), pp.113–55. In this final sentence, Pease refers to Melville's short story 'Bartleby, the Scrivener' (1853). Bartleby's unwillingness to perform the tasks of his job increasingly exasperates and infuriates his employer, the story's narrator, a New York lawyer, to the point of resigned incomprehension. Bartleby signals this unwillingness in his repeated phrase of dissent 'I would prefer not to', to which the narrator has no adequate reply.

4 [Dimock's note] The citations are from *Moby-Dick*, ed. Harrison Hayford and Hershel Parker (1851; rpt. New York: Norton, 1967).

5 [Dimock's note] Andrew Jackson, Second Annual Message, 6 December 1830, in *The State of the Union Messages of the Presidents, 1790–1966*, 3 vols. (New York: Chelsea House, 1967), I: p.335.

6 [Dimock's note] It is no accident, surely, that – even though he is really a victim – Ahab is nevertheless given the name of a biblical aggressor doomed by his deeds of aggression.

7 [Dimock's note] The statement here, marking the first time the phrase 'manifest destiny' was used, appeared in the July 1845 issue of the *United States Magazine and Democratic Review*. The anonymous article was attributed to John L. O'Sullivan.

8 [Dimock's note] *A Treasury of American Folklore*, ed. B.A. Botkin (New York: Crown Publishers, 1944), p.276.

9 Here, Dimock quotes Francis Parkman, *The Conspiracy of Pontiac*, 2 vols. (1851; rpt. Boston: Little Brown, 1909), I: p.48.

10 [Dimock's note] Jacques Lacan, 'The Mirror Stage', in *Ecrits*, trans. Alan Sheridan (New York: Norton, 1977), p.2.

11 Wai-chee Dimock, 'Ahab's Manifest Destiny', in *Macropolitics of Nineteenth Century Literature: Nationalism, Exoticism, Imperialism*, ed. Jonathan Arac and Harriet Ritvo (Philadelphia: University of Pennsylvania Press, 1991), pp.184–212.

12 [Spanos' note] Francis Fukuyama, *The End of History and the Last Man* (New York: Free Press, 1992).

13 William V. Spanos, pp.247–76.

ACKNOWLEDGEMENTS

The editor and publisher wish to thank the following for their permission to reprint copyright material: Jonathan Cape (for material from *Herman Melville* and *Call Me Ishmael*); Laurence Pollinger Ltd. (for material from *Studies in Classic American Literature*); Macmillan (for material from *Herman Melville: A Critical Study*); University of Chicago Press (for material from *Symbolism & American Literature* and *The American Adam*); G.K. Hall & Co. (for material from *Critical Essays On Herman Melville's Moby-Dick*); Northwestern University Press (for material from *Melville: The Ironic Diagram*); Southern Methodist University Press (for material from *Moby-Dick Centennial Essays*); Cambridge University Press (for material from *New Essays on Moby-Dick* and *Ideology and Classic American Literature*); Cornell University Press (for material from *Manhood and the American Renaissance*); Harvard University Press (for material from *The Culture of Redemption*); Johns Hopkins University Press (for material from *The American Renaissance Reconsidered*).

Every effort has been made to contact the holders of any copyrights applying to the material quoted in this book. The publishers would be grateful if any such copyright holders whom they have not been able to contact, would write to them.

Nick Selby is Lecturer in American Studies at the University of Wales, Swansea. He has published on Walt Whitman, Allen Ginsberg and the Beats, sexuality and 1950s American culture, as well as on Ezra Pound and modernism. He is currently writing a book on American poetics and culture that examines (among others) the work of Ezra Pound, Gary Snyder and Jorie Graham.

INDEX

Adam and *Moby-Dick* 90–3
aesthetics, myth and symbolism 84
aggression 81
Ahab 27–8
    against Ishmael 104, 105–6
    cf American Indian, 148, 158
    anger 92–3
    and capitalism 74
    and chance 109
    Chase on 70–2
    as Christ 71
    Cold War paradigm 149–51, 155
    death of 72
    domination by 60–1
    Fiedelson on 88–9
    gender change 129
    hatred and revenge personified 32
    Lawrence on 38
    madness 60–1, 123, 129–30
    and manhood 127–9
    Matthiessen on 53–63
    meaning of name 159–60
    Mumford on 48
    Olson on 65
    oppressor 142
    Prometheus 71–2, 82
    punishment 156–7
    rebellion 153
    as Satan 80–1
    Seelye on 105–9
    and Starbuck 10–11, 152–3
    symbolic American hero 62
    vengeance of 158–9
    victim of culture 148
'Ahab's Manifest Destiny', essay 156
Ainsworth, William H., reviewer 30
Albion, review 29
allegory, *Moby-Dick* as 17, 23, 74, 112, 158
ambiguity in *Moby-Dick* 22, 23
America
    cultural independence 51–75
    as a democracy 94
    and European literature 92
    image in 1950s 77, 78
    see also American Studies
American
    culture and *Moby-Dick* 114, 117, 132, 147, 149–51

economy 118
    literature before 1940s 51
    nationality, question of 148
    Studies 76–93, 94
    writing 7–8, 32
American Adam, the 90
American Renaissance 116, 117
    see also Matthiessen, F.O.
American Renaissance Considered, The 148
American Romanticism and the Marketplace 118
anger in *Moby-Dick* 90
art and *Moby-Dick* 103
Aspects of the Novel 41
atheism 57
Athenaeum review of *The Whale* 25

Barnum, *Moby-Dick* compared with 73
Beethoven, *Moby-Dick* and 78
Beneath the American Renaissance 116
Bersani, Leo, reviewer 132–7
Bezanson, Walter, reviewer 96–103
biblical archetypes 144–5
Billy Budd, Sailor 15
Brodhead, Richard, reviewer 95–6
Brontë, Emily, compared with Melville 42
Buell, Lawrence, reviewer 111–14
Butler, William, reviewer 30

Calvinism 82
capitalism, *Moby-Dick* 21, 22
    Chase 74
    Olson 70
    Royster 123, 125
Captain Ahab *see* Ahab
Chase, Richard, reviewer 70–5
Christ, Ahab as 71
Christianity *see* divinity of man; religion
    see also Satan, Ahab as
coin *see* doubloon
Cold War paradigm 149–51, 155
conflict in *Moby-Dick* 163–4
Conrad, Joseph on *Moby-Dick* 34
critical reviews
    most important 132
    see also reviewers *and individual names*
Culler, J. on deconstruction 146
cultural materialism 115–45

culture *see under* American
cynicism 22

Dana, Richard Henry, jr. 18
    Lawrence's reference to 36
    Melville's bond with 19–20
dark-reform literature *see* reform
    literature
dark temperance imagery 140
deconstruction defined 146
democracy 94, 134–5
devil *see* Satan, Ahab as
Dimock, Wai-chee, reviewer 147, 156–62
divinity of man 59–60
Doren, Carl Van, reviewer 34
doubleness of *Moby-Dick* 19, 23, 112
    doubloon 121–2
    Leverenz on 126
doubloon, 107–8, 121–3, 125
Dostoevski compared with Melville 42
dream quality of *Moby-Dick* 101–2
duality: Melville and Dana 19
dynamic of *Moby-Dick* 98–100, 102

Emerson, R.W.
    Buell on 111
    Matthiessen on 54
    Pease on 151
epilogue, missing 24
Errant Art of Moby-Dick, The 162
European literature and America 92
evil in *Moby-Dick* 47, 62
    whale as symbol of 56–7

feminist view 131
Fiedelson, Charles, reviewer 76–7, 83–9
food, metaphors using 26, 27
formalism
    defined 94–5
    Reynolds 116
Forster, E.M., reviewer 41, 42–3
Freud and *Moby-Dick* 81, 126

gender change, Ahab 129
genius of Melville 30, 31
Gilmore, Michael, reviewer 118
God *see* divinity of man; religion
    see also Satan, Ahab as

hatred and rage of Ahab 32
Hawthorne and His Mosses 8–13, 133, 134

Hawthorne, Nathaniel 8–10, 11–13
    compared with Melville 55–6
    letter from Melville 22–3
Herman Melville 44
Herman Melville: a Critical Study 70
heterogeneity of *Moby-Dick* 95, 97
humanism
    Bezanson, extract from 96–103
    defined 94–5
humanity and suffering 59

identity of Ahab 161
Ideology and Classic American Literature 119
Indian, extinction 157–8, 160
Intentional Fallacy 83
interpretive modes 136
ironic diagram 104, 106
irony 22
Ishmael 7, 28
    against Ahab 104, 105–6
    as b'hoy narrator 142–3
    as the dynamic figure 99–100
    Fiedelson on 84, 85–7
    ideology of labour 124
    as key figure 96
    and manhood 127, 131
    Matthiessen on 56–8
    as Melville 86–7, 100
    and Queequeg 37, 58
    search for symbolism 119–21
    survival of 87

Job, story of and *Moby-Dick* 113

King Lear and *Moby-Dick* 68

labour
    Ishmael's ideology of 124
    as part of nature 121
language, *Moby-Dick* 54–5, 95–6
    Gilmore on 118
    see also rhetoric
Lawrence, D.H.
    compared to Melville 42
    review 35–41
Leverenz, David, reviewer 125–32
Levin, Harry, reviewer 110
Lewis, R.W.B. 77, 89–93
light and shadow imagery 104

madness, *Moby-Dick* 17–18, 25, 30